Storycraft

Chicago Guides
to *Writing*, **Editing**,
and Publishing

Storycraft

The Complete Guide to Writing

Narrative Nonfiction Jack Hart

Second Edition

THE UNIVERSITY OF CHICAGO PRESS CHICAGO AND LONDON

The University of Chicago Press, Chicago 60637
The University of Chicago Press, Ltd., London
© 2011, 2021 by Jack Hart
Published 2021
Printed in the United States of America

30 29 28 27 26 25 24 23   2 3 4 5

ISBN-13: 978-0-226-73692-1 (paper)
ISBN-13: 978-0-226-73708-9 (e-book)
DOI: https://doi.org/10.7208/chicago/9780226737089.001.0001

Library of Congress Cataloging-in-Publication Data

Names: Hart, Jack, 1946– author.
Title: Storycraft : the complete guide to writing narrative nonfiction /
    Jack Hart.
Other titles: Chicago guides to writing, editing, and publishing.
Description: Second edition. | Chicago : University of Chicago Press,
    2021. | Series: Chicago guides to writing, editing, and publishing |
    Includes bibliographical references and index.
Identifiers: LCCN 2020037073 | ISBN 9780226736921 (paperback) |
    ISBN 9780226737089 (ebook)
Subjects: LCSH: Creative nonfiction—Authorship. | Reportage
    literature—Authorship. | Authorship.
Classification: LCC PN3377.5.R45 H37 2021 | DDC 808.02—dc23
LC record available at https://lccn.loc.gov/2020037073

♾ This paper meets the requirements of ANSI/NISO Z39.48-1992
(Permanence of Paper).

To the extraordinary writers

who worked with me to discover

the craft of narrative.

Contents

Preface to the Second Edition

Nearly forty years ago a police reporter walked into my *Northwest Magazine* office and pitched a story. A drunk driver had killed a young mother, and the reporter had dutifully written a routine news brief. But the woman's death haunted him. What tricks of fate had led her to the improbable place and time of her death? What kind of life had she left behind? And what of the man who killed her? Was he just another drunk, or did unsuspected humanity lurk behind the stereotype? Surely, the story went beyond the two column inches our newspaper had buried on page B6, plugging the space above an ad for dental insurance.

So Tom Hallman came to the *Oregonian*'s Sunday magazine, where I was the newly minted editor, and sold me on a true *story*. The version we'd publish would have a beginning, a middle, and an end. Strong internal structure would regulate pace and create dramatic tension. Instead of sources, it would have characters. Instead of topics, it would have scenes. It would be scrupulously accurate, but it would reveal truths beyond the reach of an ordinary news report.

"Collision Course," the five-thousand-word narrative that resulted, was unlike any journalism Tom or I had ever produced. The way readers responded to it was new to us, too. They called or wrote to tell us how riveting the story had been. They had been lost in it, instructed by it, moved by it. And they wanted more.

That story launched a lifelong love affair with narrative nonfiction.

The timing was perfect. Our experiment with true-life storytelling caught a wave of rising interest in stories drawn from reality. Book-length works of reported nonfiction such as John McPhee's *Coming into the Country* and Tracy Kidder's *The Soul of a New Machine* made regular appearances on the best-seller lists. Tony Lukas's *Common Ground*, a meticulously reported account of forced racial integration in Boston, was about to win a Pulitzer Prize. The trend reached way beyond books. Over the next few years, nonfiction storytelling would explode in major American newspapers and magazines, narrative nonfiction would acquire star status on radio, and the documentary would assume new prominence in film. Eventually, the internet would change the way nonfiction writers worked and push the form in exciting directions. The podcast would marry the newest medium, the internet, with one of the oldest, radio, and find an enthusiastic new audience.

We rode the narrative nonfiction wave through my years at *Northwest*, using the form to explore topics ranging from logging to heart transplants to genetic engineering. The magazine's readership soared, making it one of the best-read parts of the Sunday paper. So when I became the *Oregonian*'s writing coach, I used the skills I'd developed during a dozen years as a full-time university professor to teach narrative theory to the rest of the *Oregonian*'s writers and editors.

They were stunningly successful at putting theory into practice. *Oregonian* narratives won national awards for stories on religion, business, music, crime, sports, and just about any other subject you can imagine. Rich Read worked with me on an international business story that won a Pulitzer Prize for explanatory journalism. Tom Hallman and I joined forces again on a story that won a Pulitzer for feature writing. Michelle Roberts worked with me on a narrative submitted as part of the package that won the Pulitzer for breaking news. Rich Read and Julie Sullivan, another writer who worked with me one-on-one for years, served as part of an Amanda Bennett team that won the 2001 Pulitzer Gold Medal,[1] the highest honor in American journalism.

I remained the writing coach even after I became a managing editor. As the logical spokesman for the paper's writing program, I appeared at national conventions for everybody from newspaper editors and journalism professors to food writers, investigative reporters, travel writers, wine writers, and garden writers. I wrote a column for *Editor & Publisher* magazine and produced a monthly instructional newsletter that circulated nationwide. I continued to teach occasional university classes on writing, and each year my focus shifted more toward nonfiction narrative. Every speech, workshop, class, and article forced me to think more deeply about what attracted readers to true stories about real people.

But my most valuable education came from working with scores of writers on hundreds of stories. Producing for publication, often on tight deadline, gave me a practical grounding in story that the world's best graduate school couldn't possibly match. When I finally retired, I figured it was time to pass along the most useful lessons I'd learned.

My first effort produced *A Writer's Coach*, a survey of the techniques that the best writers I worked with used to make their words powerful, evocative, lyrical, and—most of all—effective. Random House published that book, but over time it grew dated and lost visibility inside the publisher's enormous list. A few years later, I published the first edition of *Storycraft*, which covers the kind of storytelling that had dominated my later career, with the University of Chicago Press.

When the opportunity arose to bring *A Writer's Coach* to UCP, I jumped at the chance. The move allowed me to update the examples and shift the emphasis to audiences beyond newspaper writers. It also made it possible to resurrect my original attempt to make the book the first half of a package that included *Storycraft*. And it allowed me to restore my original title for the book, which reflected that intent. Now *Wordcraft* is paired with *Storycraft* under the UCP imprint, and both books contain cross-references that help them work as the instructional pair I'd originally hoped to create.

I heard from hundreds of writers who benefited from *A Writer's Coach*, as well as from teachers who found that it connected well with students. In part, that connection resulted from the practical emphasis I tried to include on every page. The tips and suggestions I made were, after all, gleaned from working with accomplished professionals, often under tight deadlines. What worked for them usually worked for students and other writers struggling with one of the most complex and difficult crafts human beings have devised. I made every effort to maintain and expand that practical emphasis in the update that turned *A Writer's Coach* into *Wordcraft*.

I've carried the same emphasis on practicality into the second edition of *Storycraft*. The first edition also produced a heartwarming outpouring of feedback from readers. And the emails, calls, and letters that I found most rewarding credited *Storycraft* with helping them overcome tough challenges—finding a structure that fit unusual material, untangling knotty organizational problems, and clearing up questions on point of view, chronology, and level of detail.

As I'd hoped, many of the writers who contacted me also singled out *Storycraft* for its practical value. I kept take-it-to-the-keyboard usefulness high on my list of priorities as I chose examples taken from my work with writers who wanted help, not literary hairsplitting. Help with their reporting, help with their selection of scenes, help with their descriptions of characters, and help with their choices about what to include and what to leave out.

They also wanted to know their options. The classic narrative arc you learn in college fiction classes is only the tip of the tale. And you won't find a particularly full menu of narrative nonfiction forms in the existing technique books, which tend to focus on one variety or another. So I've included guides to a smorgasbord of reported nonfiction types, including explanatory narratives, vignettes, narrative essays, and podcasts.

I approached the second edition with the same priorities, but I expanded them to embrace the changes that have made narrative nonfiction even more important and widespread over the past decade. Podcasting, for example, has exploded as a vehicle for sometimes stunningly good narrative, a development that even the Pulitzer Prize Board has recognized with a rare new annual prize for "audio reporting." The second edition contains an all-new section on podcasting, detailing the ways it differs—and doesn't—from more traditional print and documentary film versions of the form. The text dives into podcasting elsewhere as well, expanding existing theory whenever necessary to accommodate audio storytelling.

Another significant development since the first edition of Storycraft is the explosion of research on storytelling's origins in the structure of the human brain. The first edition certainly recognized that we are biologically designed as storytelling animals, but ten years ago the fMRI was just beginning to make a mark. The research provoked by the new techniques also inspired anthropologists and others to launch scientific research illuminating the central role of storytelling in cultures worldwide. Hundreds of research papers later, we have added understanding that can make all of us more effective storytellers.

The second edition also includes dozens of new examples, which I hope make the point that narrative nonfiction is a vital, growing form, one that's thriving outside of newspaper newsrooms and making a mark in every mass medium.

Some truths remain immutable, however. Mastering a wide variety of narrative forms is still one key to success. Another is learning enough about story theory to avoid the fatal error of forcing narrative onto inappropriate material. Obviously, I'm a huge fan of classic storytelling. But experience has taught me that most subjects are best suited to simple informational writing that makes the key point quickly. Sportswriters start game stories by telling us the final score for a reason. And if your neighbors want to know if their school won't survive the current round of budget cuts, you'd be foolish to begin a report on the critical school board meeting with a long narrative windup. Ditto with the short reports that fill internet news feeds such as those from Google and Apple.

In keeping with the emphasis on practical application, virtually all of my Storycraft examples are from published work, and many of them are from stories I had a hand in bringing to publication. Every work cited is listed in the bibliography, along with some exemplary works of narrative nonfiction not cited. Unpublished material and citations requiring explanation are listed, by chapter, in the notes included at the end of the book.

Storycraft also includes the editor's perspective. Most books on narrative technique ignore editors, and nonfiction narrative editing is included in only a very few educational programs. But storytelling—whether in newspapers, magazines, books, podcasts, or online—thrives only when writers team up with strong narrative editors. Harold Ross and William Shawn built the ongoing nonfiction narrative tradition at the *New Yorker*, and Harold Hayes laid the foundation for much of modern narrative nonfiction during his years editing *Esquire*. In the introduction to *The Hot Zone*, Richard Preston says Sharon DeLano, the Random House editor who handled the book, helped him see the critical role story structure plays in crafting compelling book-length narrative. More recently, Ira Glass has demonstrated the key role of a visionary producer and editor through his role of maestro for public radio's *This American Life* and host Sarah Koenig's hugely successful podcast, *Serial*.

One of the other things I discovered during a quarter century of working with nonfiction storytellers is that successful popular storytelling demands neither blinding talent nor decades in a writer's garret. If you're interested in exploring the art of true-life storytelling, don't let lack of experience intimidate you. Time and again I've seen writers with absolutely no narrative experience grasp a few core principles, find appropriate story structures, and draft dramatic tales that moved readers. Some of those virgin ventures into true-life storytelling achieved far more. At the *Oregonian* David Stabler, the classical music critic, plunged into his first narrative, a series on a musical prodigy, and made the finals for a Pulitzer Prize. Rich Read's first narrative *won* a Pulitzer Prize.

Like me, those writers came of age in newspaper newsrooms, a fertile incubator for great narrative over the past thirty years. But today's newspapers struggle with the fragmentation of their audience and a shift to the digital delivery of news. Long-form narrative can be expensive, and pinched newspaper newsrooms produce far less of it than they did two decades ago. It's safe to assume that the next generation of nonfiction storytellers will travel paths different from the writers who worked with me. Writers tackling narrative in other media may have to find new routes to their audiences, too. The entire media marketplace is in upheaval, and young storytellers everywhere will face unprecedented challenges. The most entrepreneurial will adapt to changing technology, finding new ways to use print, audio, and video in a digital environment. But the most successful will also carry with them the unchanging, universal principles that apply to all stories, regardless of the technology used to deliver them.

Those principles are what Storycraft is all about.

Although fewer writers will discover nonfiction storytelling in traditional newspaper newsrooms, it's reassuring to note that plenty of other doors lead to careers in narrative. Tracy Kidder studied creative writing at Harvard and at the Iowa Writers' Workshop, and narrative nonfiction is a staple in the creative-writing programs that have blossomed in universities all across the country. Ted Conover focused on anthropology at Amherst College and came to nonfiction storytelling through ethnography. Before he became one of the best American magazine writers, William Langewiesche was a professional pilot. Ira Glass has spent most of his professional life in public radio. The only real requirement for great nonfiction narrative is determination to master the craft.

In keeping with the broad reach of today's narrative nonfiction, most of the examples I've used in Storycraft come from sources other than newspapers. But I've used a sizeable number of newspaper examples, too, mainly because I was intimately involved in them as a writing coach and editor. I wanted this book to reflect the depth of my own experience, and one of my principal aims was to share what I learned in the trenches. Good narrative comes from specific real-world decisions made by writers and editors who not only understand the abstract principles of story, but also know how to apply them in the real world. I have to believe that writers working to master narrative learn best from someone who's been there, someone who knows both theory and practice. For me, that means drawing on my newspaper background, and—more recently—conversations with nonfiction narrative writers in workshops and coaching a number of nonfiction narrative books from inception to publication.

Ultimately, I don't think the source of a great true-life story matters much. When it comes to learning by example, where a story appeared is far less important than how well it was told. Skilled, passionate storytellers will excel at their craft in whatever medium allows them to reach an audience. The theory and craft of good storytelling even transcend the mass media. As Ted Conover demonstrated, both ethnography and nonfiction narrative share immersion reporting as a core technique. Lawyers attend workshops on constructing narratives that will persuade juries. Psychologists use storytelling in therapy. I hope Storycraft offers insights valuable across the spectrum of narrative possibilities.

Storytelling has such wide application because, at its root, it serves universal human needs. Story makes sense out of a confusing universe by showing us how one action leads to another. It teaches us how to live by discovering how our fellow human beings overcome the challenges in their lives. And it helps us discover the universals that bind us to everything around us.

Ultimately, the common ingredient in all great storytelling is the love of story itself. If you share that with me, let me tell you what I've learned.

1

Story

Story is about eternal, universal forms.
—Robert McKee

From the back of a Boston hotel ballroom I watched, intrigued, as Ira Glass cued interviews, modulated music, and led hundreds of writers through the theory that guides his storytelling. I'm a print guy, and Glass is a broadcaster. But at that instant I realized that this dynamo, the creative genius behind National Public Radio's *This American Life*, followed exactly the same principles that I did when I chose and edited nonfiction narratives for my newspaper.[1]

It was one of those aha! moments, a point of insight that suddenly brought together ideas I'd never fully connected. I was experienced at editing nonfiction newspaper and magazine narratives, and I knew that many of the same storytelling principles applied to both. But the insights Ira Glass gave me about storytelling for radio made me realize that similar principles of scene-setting, characterization, and plotting apply no matter where writers tell their stories. The same interesting psychological complication can propel a character through a newspaper series, a radio documentary, a magazine article, a book, a film, a podcast, or an online presentation.

I'm not sure how I'd missed that larger point, but the evidence for it was all around me. I was, for example, perfectly aware of Mark Bowden's experience at the *Philadelphia Inquirer*. Bowden, a police reporter, wrote a multipart newspaper series on the American military incursion in Somalia. The internet version of the series attracted nationwide attention, setting the stage for a successful book. Then Ridley Scott turned *Black Hawk Down* into a major mo-

tion picture. Bowden himself went on to become a national correspondent for
the *Atlantic*.

Once I tumbled to the idea that common principles of storytelling apply
regardless of medium, I noticed examples everywhere. Newspaper writers such
as David Simon, a police reporter at the *Baltimore Sun*, used the material cops
collected on their beats to produce books that shape-shifted into other media.
Simon's *Homicide: A Year on the Killing Streets* morphed into *Homicide: Life on the
Street*, a hit television show. That, in turn, led to a series of realistic TV series,
ranging from *The Wire*, to *Treme*, to *The Deuce*. Best-selling nonfiction books such
as Sebastian Junger's *The Perfect Storm*, Susan Orlean's *The Orchid Thief*, and Laura
Hillenbrand's *Seabiscuit* all became successful Hollywood films and launched
their authors on storytelling careers that rolled out a library bulging with additional books and films.

I'd seen the same thing happen with long-form newspaper narratives
I edited at the *Oregonian*. Barnes Ellis, a young reporter, teamed up with me
on "A Ride through Hell," the story of an Oregon couple kidnapped by two
desperados, and the tale was soon adapted as *Captive*, a made-for-TV movie
starring Joanna Kerns and Barry Bostwick. Tom Hallman wrote an inspiring
story about Bill Porter, a disabled salesman. A version appeared in *Reader's Digest*. ABC picked the story up for 20/20, and then it reappeared as *Door to Door*,
a TV movie starring William H. Macy.

Clearly, story is story. The same underlying principles apply regardless of
where you tell your tale. As Jon Franklin, a two-time Pulitzer winner, says, "All
stories have a common set of attributes that are arranged in a certain specific
way."

Anybody who hopes to reach full potential as a storyteller needs to discover
those universals. Successful nonfiction storytelling requires a basic understanding of fundamental story theory and the story structures the theory suggests. Ignore them, and you'll fight a losing battle with human nature. Master
them, and you're on your way to reaching a large and enthusiastic audience in
just about any medium.

Story theory began with the Greeks, and we've been developing structures
consistent with it for millennia. As Robert McKee, the screenwriting guru, puts
it, "In the twenty-three centuries since Aristotle wrote *The Poetics* the 'secrets' of
story have been as public as the library down the street."

True enough, but that doesn't mean the secrets of story are widely appreciated or universally practiced. I stumbled through half my career before I found
my way to the library and asked for the right books. And over the years I've

talked with scores of would-be storytellers who were just as lost. They wasted uncounted hours chasing after doomed narrative lines and ignoring topics with huge potential because they didn't recognize what was passing, unnoticed, right in front of them.

If you want to write successful narrative, half the battle is knowing what you're looking for. A sharp eye for story comes from understanding that its basic ingredients are universal and learning how to spot them in the real world. If you want to *find* a great story, look for the ingredients I'll be explaining in the rest of this chapter. If you want to *write* a great story, study the techniques I'll describe in the rest of the book.

You'll seldom find every element of story in one slice of reality. But choosing to pursue a narrative isn't a black-or-white, all-or-nothing, kind of proposition. If you find a situation filled with lots of story elements, you may want to go whole hog, tackling a full-fledged story that, long or short, brings a character through a complete narrative arc. If you have a more limited action line that helps explain an interesting process, you may still have what it takes for a good piece of explanatory journalism. Or a personal essay. Or a vignette. Or maybe you'll just have enough to drop an anecdote into a more conventional report or news feature.

Or not. If what your audience really wants is unadorned information, straight facts that cut right to the heart of the matter, that's fine, too. The packaging for a loaf of bread usually carries the baker's name, a list of ingredients, and not much more.

On the other hand, the wrapper for my favorite bread comes with a two-hundred-word narrative revealing that the baker's fifteen years in prison "transformed an ex-con into an honest man who is doing his best to make the world a better place . . . one loaf at a time."

Now, who wouldn't at least try a loaf of bread with that kind of story behind it?

A STORYTELLING SPECIES

Joseph Campbell's *The Hero with a Thousand Faces* (1949) showed us that the same deep-seated archetypes lurk in primal stories created by all kinds of cultures. And respected scientific researchers ranging from Stephen Jay Gould, a paleontologist, to Steven Pinker,[2] a linguist, have argued that storytelling has uniformities that suggest an evolutionary basis. Certain systems of organizing information give us an edge, goes the argument, a way of perceiving the world that has helped us survive.

New techniques for analyzing the brain support the notion that we're hardwired for story. When science writer Stephen Hall created a story in his head during an MRI brain scan, an area the size of a sugar cube lit up in his right frontal lobe. In his report for the *New York Times Magazine*, Hall labeled that thimbleful of brain, located in the inferior frontal gyrus, "the storytelling area." It linked with other brain centers, such as the visual cortex. All told, they formed what Hall described as the brain's "storytelling system."

Hall's example hardly qualified as a rigorous scientific study, but it strongly suggested a biology of story. To me, that made perfect sense. The myriad ways we use story to cope with the world make it hard to imagine that narrative isn't part of our fundamental nature. A legion of brain scientists noticed the same thing. In the twenty years since Stephen Hall slid into that fMRI machine, neurologists, linguists, and other scientists conducted hundreds of studies aimed at exploring how story fits into our nature, what it does for us as a species, and how our biology directs the structure and content of our stories.

Jeremy Hsu recently surveyed that explosion of research and summarized its findings for *Scientific American*. "Storytelling," he reported, "is one of the few human traits that are truly universal across culture and through all of known history. . . . People in societies of all types weave narratives, from oral storytellers in hunter-gatherer tribes to the millions of writers churning out books, television shows, and movies. And when a characteristic behavior shows up in so many different societies, researchers pay attention: its roots may tell us something about our evolutionary past."

The possibility that a biology of story was somehow hardwired into the human brain also would explain research findings that demonstrated that test subjects displayed better grasp of narrative than other forms, that narrative delivered a clearer message to a majority of readers, and that audience members preferred narrative presentations. Research also demonstrated that we remember facts more accurately if we're exposed to them in a story, rather than a list, and that we're more likely to buy the arguments that lawyers make in a trial if they present them as part of a narrative.[3]

Those tantalizing early findings led to an explosion of research activity over the past ten years. (Enter "storytelling brain research" into a Google search and you'll get over a thousand hits, most citing fairly recent studies.) Among other things, that frenzy of activity has revealed that:

- **Story dominates human existence**. "If you start adding up the hours that you spend in imaginary worlds," Jonathan Gottschall writes, "you get to a pretty astonishing figure. We spend four hours a day watching TV, our children make believe, we spend hours and hours, actually about eight hours per day, lost in daydreams. We dream in stories. When you add all this time up, for me it was a startling conclusion, that humans aren't really Earthlings. We're more like citizens of this weird omni-dimensional world called Neverland. We spend most our lives wandering inside imaginary worlds."

· **Human storytelling has ancient roots**. A forty-four-thousand-year-old cave painting discovered on the Indonesian island of Sulawesi in 2017 showed human-animal hybrids hunting. Maxime Aubert, an Australian archaeologist, says, "This is the oldest rock art in the world and all of the key aspects of modern cognition are there." He concluded that ability to imagine characters and shape stories fully formed in Sulawesi suggests it "was probably already present in the early modern humans who left Africa and populated the rest of the world."[4]

   Or, as Lisa Cron puts it, "Opposable thumbs let us hang on; story told us what to hang on to."

· **In hunter-gatherer societies, storytelling has clear survival value**. Daniel Smith, an evolutionary anthropologist at University College, London, led a rigorous study with the Agta, a Filipino hunter-gatherer tribe. He concluded that storytelling promoted social cooperation, mating success, social status, and sharing, all behaviors with obvious evolutionary benefits.

· **The brain is hardwired for story at an extremely deep level**. Even brain-damaged children with IQs ranging between twenty and thirty points can comprehend stories. Daniel Smith says this ability among such children "implies story comprehension is so basic that it survives severe neurological damage." Smith went on to argue that "the human brain is essentially a narrative device. It runs on stories. The knowledge that we store in the brain, our 'theory of the world' is largely in the form of stories."

· **"Mirror neurons" in the brain echo emotions created by story**. In the 1990s Italian researchers discovered that the same areas of monkeys' brains would light up when they grabbed a nut as when they saw another monkey grab a nut. The brain's ability to generate true emotion when merely observing emotion-generating events was, researchers concluded, the product of "mirror neurons," which duplicated the feelings observed in the outside world. the finding unleashed "a flood of mirror neuron research in monkeys and humans." Marco Iacoboni wrote that movies feel authentic "because mirror neurons in our brains re-create the distress we see on the screen."[5]

- **Young children organize their play around storytelling that fits classic narrative forms.** Jonathan Gottschall summarizes the research on kids, play, and storytelling by noting that "story is so central to the lives of young children that it comes close to defining their existence."

- **Character and plot may work together as a story unfolds, but character reigns supreme.** Contrary to widespread belief among nonfiction storytellers, the driving force for most audience members is not "what happens next?" but "how will what happens next affect this character I've come to care about."

- **Story is more important to engaging reader interest than writing quality.** Lisa Cron looked at the research and concluded that "writing poorly can be far less damaging than you think. That is, if you can tell a story." A glance at the best-seller lists, which are filled with books by ham-handed and tin-eared writers who are nonetheless great storytellers, confirms the finding.

  It also confirms an opinion two-time Pulitzer-winner Jon Franklin made more than thirty years ago. Franklin argued that writers and editors who devote huge amounts of time to the polishing work at the word, sentence, and paragraph level are missing the chance to make a much bigger impact on readers by focusing on major story elements at the beginning of the writing process.

- **We construct our own identities out of the stories we tell about ourselves.** We see our own lives as a kind of narrative, too, which may explain why we're so fascinated by the narratives of others. Psychologists have studied the way we picture our own life stories. They've found, according to the New York Times, that each of us has a kind of internal screenplay, and that "the way we visualize each scene not only shapes how we think about ourselves, but also how we behave."[6] Which explains why some psychologists now urge the use of storytelling to reconstruct self-identities in the wake of traumatic brain injuries.[7] The notion that we build our self-identity out of stories we tell ourselves has so grabbed the popular imagination that that Jack Goldsmith used it to condemn the way the FBI tapped and recorded his mob-connected stepfather's phone conversations. As a result of the wiretaps, Goldsmith argued in the Atlantic Monthly, his stepfather was forced to confront the truth of his criminal history, rather than live with the delusions he'd created in his personal stories. The government's illegal wiretaps, Goldsmith said, did "violence against his [stepfather's] intimate spaces and relationships, and the annihilation of the stories he told himself and the world about these spaces and relationships, and thus the power to define and shape his life."

This small selection of recent research findings confirms that storytelling is even more deeply rooted in our biology than we suspected. Understanding that story has deep foundations in our brains and behavior helps explain why successful storytelling contains so many common elements. Sometimes a finding translates into direct application at the keyboard. (It pays the storyteller, for example, to find topics containing lessons in living that suggest ways of solving common problems.) But more often the research merely teases the storyteller without providing much concrete direction. (When you're at the keyboard, what value is there in the fact that forty-four thousand years ago humans told stories on the wall of an Indonesian cave?)

Perhaps the most important finding turned up by the recent flurry of research on the biology of storytelling is that two thousand years of trial and error have given us a staggering range of storytelling techniques consistent with what science now tells us about what works. We can rely on those techniques with renewed confidence, knowing that science has our backs.

STORY'S KEY INGREDIENTS

Lajos Egri, who in 1942 wrote an influential guide for playwrights that's still in print as *The Art of Dramatic Writing*, argued that character was the driving force in story. Human needs and wants, he said, set stories in motion and determine all that follows.

We live in a world of scarce resources, whether they be caviar or companionship. So characters who want something usually have to overcome opposition to get it. Wants, in other words, create conflict. "A story is a war," said Mel McKee. "It is sustained and immediate combat."[8] Others expand the idea of conflict to include the array of problems that keep human beings from achieving their goals, some of them purely internal. They usually refer not to conflict, but to "complications."

So, at its most basic, a story begins with a character who wants something, struggles to overcome barriers that stand in the way of achieving it, and moves through a series of actions—the actual story structure—to overcome them.

As Steven Pinker puts it, "A story is how what happens affects someone who is trying to achieve what turns out to be a difficult goal, and how he or she changes as a result."[9]

That's a succinct expression of what's generally known as the protagonist-complication-resolution model for story. You see it in various forms. Philip Gerard, who writes both novels and book-length narrative nonfiction, says a story follows when "a character we care about acts to fulfill his desires with important consequences." Bruce DeSilva, a former writing coach at the Associated Press who retired to become a successful mystery writer, says, "Every true tale . . . has the same underlying structure. . . . Character has a problem. He struggles with a problem. Most of the piece is about the struggle, and then you get a resolution in the end in which the character overcomes the problem or is defeated by it."

I'm partial to the story definition Jon Franklin included in *Writing for Story*, his groundbreaking text on narrative nonfiction:

> A story consists of a sequence of actions that occur when a sympathetic character encounters a complicating situation that he confronts and solves.

Franklin's definition is simple, yet precise. And it lends itself to more detailed analysis of the key ingredients in story.

A *sequence of actions*. In any story, principal characters do one thing, then another, then another, and the writer's recounting of that sequence creates the narrative. At its simplest level, then, a narrative is just a chronology of events.

Plot, on the other hand, is clearly something different than mere narrative. A plot emerges when a storyteller carefully selects and arranges material so that larger meanings can emerge. A plot, says Janet Burroway, "is a series of events deliberately arranged so as to reveal their dramatic, thematic, and emotional significance." For Eudora Welty, "Plot is the 'Why?'" Or, as the novelist E. M. Forster famously put it, the narrative is that "the king died and then the queen died." The plot is that "the king died and the queen died of grief."[10]

Narrative plus plot, according to this view, equals story.

Plot unfolds as a pattern of cause and effect and winds its way through a series of "plot points," defined by Robert McKee as "any development that sends the story spinning off in a new direction." One of the most valuable things I do when coaching a writer is to list the plot points. That gives us what we need to plan the story's trajectory.

Consider a short breaking-news narrative I once worked on with Stuart Tomlinson, then a police reporter in one of the *Oregonian*'s metropolitan bureaus. He called my office, excited about what he'd learned, and I asked him to walk me through the story.[11]

A police officer had been sitting at an intersection, watching traffic whiz by. No plot point yet. Nothing had happened to change the ordinary direction of events. Then "a pickup blew by, pushing eighty." Now *that's* a plot point. Once a patrolman sees a vehicle roaring through an urban intersection at nearly eighty miles an hour, his day's bound to go spinning off in a new direction. And for this patrolman, Jason McGowan, things were just beginning to get interesting.

The pickup truck smashed into a passenger car, trapping the woman driver in twisted metal (Plot Point No. 2). The pickup driver fled on foot (Plot Point No. 3). McGowan ran him down and asked a couple of bystanders to watch him (Plot Point No. 4) while he dashed back to the passenger car. It burst into flames (Plot Point No. 5), threatening to incinerate the woman inside. Two more patrol cars arrived (Plot Point No. 6). The police officers used fire extinguishers from their patrol cars to suppress the fire (Plot Point No. 7), but it flamed up again (Plot Point No. 8). One of them rushed into a nearby convenience store and grabbed another extinguisher. Same result (Plot Point No. 9). The woman in the wrecked car moved—she was still alive! (Plot Point No. 10). Firefighters arrived with the "jaws of life," a device used to pry wreckage apart (Plot Point No. 11). An ambulance whisked the victim off to the hospital (Plot Point No. 12), where she later met with McGowan and thanked him for saving her life.

Phew! One plot point after another. And once Stu and I had identified them, we had everything we needed to construct a narrative arc for the story. We knew what to include and what to leave out. We knew the possible starting points for the story, the best material for cliff-hangers and other dramatic devices, where we'd have to shift points of view, and the answers to just about all the other questions that come up when you're plotting a story.

A sympathetic character. The character who drives the story forward is the protagonist, and the protagonist is an active player, the one who takes action to achieve a desire, overcome an antagonist, or solve a problem. So when you're looking for a protagonist search for *the person who makes things happen*.

A conventional police reporter covering Stu Tomlinson's story would have focused on the victim, writing a report that put her at the center of a standard who-what-where-why? news report. Stu wisely chose to tell the story via Jason

McGowan, who had the hallmarks of a good protagonist. For one thing, he was accessible. Stu knew him from earlier stories and had rapport with him. So McGowan was available for the kind of extensive interview Stu needed to reconstruct the whole story. McGowan also had been in a position to observe the whole series of events that made up the story. Lots of otherwise ideal protagonists pop in and out of a story line, appearing for short periods of active struggle with a problem before disappearing while someone else steps up. In Stu's story, the other cops who arrived and tried to put out the fire were potential protagonists. So were the firefighters who operated the jaws of life. But none of those witnessed the whole story. True, you can tell a story by shifting point of view through a series of players. But you're usually better off sticking with one.

Note, too, Franklin's emphasis on a *sympathetic* character. Not surprisingly, novices often want to write narratives with bad-guy protagonists, but bad guys seldom work as narrative protagonists. For one thing, they seldom show us the way things *should* be done. For another, readers can't identify with them. And for yet another, readers expect heroic—or at least likable—protagonists, which is why criminal protagonists in Hollywood movies usually come off as loveable rogues. If you give some sociopath protagonist status in a nonfiction story, readers will invest the brute with positive qualities he doesn't deserve.

All of which is consistent with the scientific research indicating that we use story to learn lessons of life, to understand how a character *we can identify with* solves the kind of complication *we might one day face.*

That doesn't mean you can't write about bad guys, of course. You just don't make them your protagonists. Ann Rule, who's made a lucrative career out of true-life crime fiction, focused her 1987 book *Small Sacrifices* on Diane Downs, a pathological narcissist who shot her own children. But Rule chose Fred Hugi, the prosecutor who put Downs in prison, as her protagonist. Not only did Hugi put the monster behind bars, but he and his wife adopted two of the killer's surviving children, one of them partially paralyzed. Now *that's* a sympathetic character.

Jason McGowan wasn't quite that heroic, but he certainly was a sympathetic character. A handsome family man with young children, he worked full-time as a firefighter, one of society's most admired jobs. He did double duty as a reserve police officer, another public-service role that cast him in a positive light as he captured the perp and saved the damsel in distress.

A complication. "In literature," Janet Burroway says, "only trouble is interesting." Your protagonist, in other words, needs a problem. Why pay attention to somebody who's content, who has no reason to act, no challenge to meet, and nothing to teach us about coping with the world? If there is no knotty problem," Jonathan Gottschall says, "there is no story."

Any problem constitutes a complication, but only certain complications justify a story. You're probably not going to read much about a woman who lost her car keys, unless that minor irritant leads to something much more consequential. And, in that case, the keys may set the story in motion, but they won't end up as the complication that drives the story.

Not every complication has to have life or death consequences. We're drawn to exciting, action-filled episodes like Jason McGowan's, but quieter stories are often even more meaningful. "The great dangers in life and in literature are not necessarily the most spectacular," Janet Burroway says. "The profoundest impediments to our desire most often lie close to home, in our own bodies, personalities, friends, lovers, and family. Fewer people have cause to panic at the approach of a stranger with a gun than at the approach of mama with the curling iron."

Another way to think about complications is in terms of human wants. Once somebody realizes he wants something and sets out to get it, he sets a potential story in motion.

The bigger the complication, the bigger the story. Jon Franklin likes complications that are "fundamental to the human condition, involving love, hate, pain, death, and such." Lajos Egri, as you might expect, expresses the same principle in terms of character. A protagonist with great strength of will, he says, who really wants something and will stop at nothing to get it, will produce the kind of intense conflict that can power a story of great literary weight.

But don't start thinking that you need an earthshaking complication to write something compelling. Good little complications make for good little stories. The late Ken Fuson, who was one of the country's best feature writers during his years at the *Des Moines Register*, built a career out of subjects like a boy on his first pheasant hunt or an immigrant woman voting in her first election.

A resolution. Resolution is the ultimate aim of every story. The resolution releases the dramatic tension created as the protagonist struggles with the complication. It contains the lesson that the audience carries away, the insight that the story's readers or viewers or listeners can apply to their own lives.

In simple yarns, resolutions are purely physical. (The firefighters arrive with the jaws of life and pry the victim out of the twisted wreckage.) In more complex and meaningful stories, a deep and permanent psychological change resolves the complication. Tom Hallman's "The Education of Richard Miller" followed a coffeehouse barista who, tired of poverty and his own slacker lifestyle, cut his hair, bought a suit, and took a job in the corporate business world. But life as a hardworking member of the middle class, he soon discovered, demanded far more than he'd ever imagined. Tom tagged along as the former barista learned about competition, ambition, responsibility, and consistency, and he was still there when his protagonist emerged as a new person who could enjoy the rewards of his new life.

You can resolve a complication, in other words, by changing the world or changing yourself.

Not every narrative has a resolution. An explanatory narrative uses an action line to explore a subject, and it requires no resolution to accomplish its purpose. The narrative simply progresses along a flat trajectory, one event after another, with occasional digressions for more abstract discussions of interesting topics that come up along the way. David Grann's fascinating New Yorker piece about an obsessed New Zealander's quest to capture a giant squid typifies the genre. The story was about squid, their history, their mystery, and the current state of scientific knowledge about them. The squid hunter's quest served as a vehicle for exploring the subject. So it really didn't matter that, in the end, he came up empty-handed.

Narrative essays often begin with a short action line that seldom contains a resolution. The point is to bring readers into the writer's thought process as he ponders something that happened to him and reaches some conclusion about the meaning of life. I once wrote an essay that opened as I observed one of my sons standing in the lift line at a ski area. Not much happened during the narrative portion of the essay—my son worked his way to the head of the line and climbed on the chair lift. I wasn't out to resolve an action line, but to make a larger point. We live on after death, I concluded, not only in our genetic legacy to our children, but also in the activities we teach them to enjoy even after we're gone.

You don't need a resolution for a vignette, either—your aim is simply to capture a revealing slice of life. When Native Americans returned to fish at Willamette Falls for the first time in a century, the Oregonian's Bill Monroe went out on their rickety scaffolding with them and described their all-night vigil with the huge dip nets they used to scoop up thirty-pound salmon. The goal of "A Night on the River" wasn't to create and resolve dramatic tension, but to take readers to the falls, where they could experience that extraordinary event for themselves.

Novelists, in contrast, usually want more complete story lines with definitive resolutions. Most Hollywood movies contain clear-cut resolutions, too, although the director of an action film may tease his audience with a series of false endings. The Terminator always dies hard, ratcheting up the dramatic tension as he springs back to life and threatens the protagonist one more time.

Robert McKee calls the typical Hollywood ending "closed" because it results in "absolute, irreversible change that answers all questions and satisfies all audience emotion." Some critics consider Hollywood endings as simple-minded distortions of life's inevitable complexities. They prefer what McKee calls "open" endings, which follow "a climax that leaves a question or two unanswered and some emotion unfulfilled."

Jon Franklin sides with Hollywood, insisting that a real-world complication without a resolution is "worse than useless" to the writer. But accurate, honest nonfiction often lacks the pure protagonist-complication-resolution structure of fiction. That's especially true when a nonfiction writer commits to following his subject in real time, as opposed to reconstructing a narrative backward from a resolution that's already occurred. Ted Conover, a master of the observational narrative, injects himself into some corner of the culture and spends months hanging around watching the action unfold. He started his nonfiction career riding the rails as a hobo (Rolling Nowhere) and later worked as a Sing Sing prison guard (Newjack). "If you're really blessed," he says, "you get resolution. But life doesn't usually work out that way."[12]

You're twice blessed if you find what Franklin calls a "constructive resolution," a more precise term for what the rest of us call a happy ending. For the Greeks such a resolution made for a comedy, whether it was funny or not, in contrast to a tragedy, which ended with a negative resolution. Those polarities are still represented by the sad and happy masks that signify drama acted out on stage.

The Greeks preferred tragedy, and Shakespeare earned immortality with it. But classical tragedy deals with the really big negative resolutions, fundamental human flaws such as hubris, narcissism, and greed. Some sins are so central to human failure that they can support narratives that end not with a victory parade, but with what the Greeks called "the catastrophe," a gloomy send-off in which the protagonist dies and the survivors bemoan their fates.

Journalists, freighted with cynicism and used to reporting on victims, often lean toward tragedy, finding losers who go down in flames more attractive than winners who learn to manage life's challenges. Once I foolishly agreed to coach a narrative about a prisoner who tried to hang himself in his cell, botched the job, and ended up as a brain-damaged vegetable living out his days in a rest home as an expensive ward of the state. Because of the outrageously high cost to taxpayers, the facts made for a decent news story. But as a narrative, they went nowhere and taught us nothing.

So I side with Franklin's preference for winners. As he points out, you can learn something from a negative resolution, but eliminating the things you *shouldn't* do—one by one—is a terribly inefficient way of learning about the world. Far better to focus on winning strategies. Each one, after all, is a keeper.

I share another of Franklin's prejudices on resolutions as well. They, he insists, "absolutely and without exception, must be products of the character's own efforts." We learn something useful from active players who solve their own problems and who create their own destinies. Their stories are what Robert McKee calls "archplots." An action line that displays the protagonist as a mere victim, someone buffeted by forces beyond his control, is, in McKee's terms, an "anti-plot."

One final note on resolutions: A preference for positive endings doesn't mean you should avoid telling the stories of protagonists who at first glance seem to be failures. Gay Talese said he always found the locker rooms of losers more interesting than those of winners.[13] But that's because losing athletes, as well as losers in love, elections, workplace competitions, and the like, must find some constructive way to cope with their disappointments. So the story of a loser can, in fact, be inspiring and positive. We all have to overcome disappointments in life, and we all can learn from the coping mechanisms of others.

THE IMPACT OF STORY

Once you understand the theory of story, you can appreciate the principles of story structure. From there on, a storyteller's education involves practical specifics. You learn how to convey character, action, and scene. You explore point of view, find your own voice, and develop a style. You learn the differences that distinguish narrative forms, and how to report them honestly. Ultimately, you master the craft of story.

For Tom Hallman and me, that long journey began with "Collision Course," the story of the young mother killed by a drunk driver. Study, experimentation, and practice gave us the sense that we'd acquired the basic tools and had a good sense of how to use them, and we moved into two decades of enormously fulfilling work as a writer-editor team. Then, at the turn of the century, a story came along that gave us a chance to put all that we knew about theory, structure, and craft together in one capstone package.

By that time readers were routinely tipping off Tom to stories that fit his distinctive style. One called to tell him about Sam Lightner, a Portland teenager afflicted by a terrible facial deformity. Sam had recently graduated from middle school and faced high school, where appearance, acceptance, and conformity sometimes seem to count for everything. Sam and his family decided to risk life-threatening plastic surgery to correct his condition, Sam almost died in the operating room, and the family abandoned plans for further reconstruction. Sam ultimately rallied, brought new understanding and acceptance to his condition, and got on with his life.

The family welcomed Tom's interest in Sam's story, and he ultimately spent hundreds of hours with the Lightners. He flew across the country with them to Boston, where the surgery took place. He sat in on family meetings, hung out around the house, and was there when Sam registered for high school. The intense reporting produced vivid scenes and a dramatic story arc in a series that unfolded over four days and totaled seventeen thousand words. In 2001 "The Boy behind the Mask" won the Pulitzer Prize for feature writing.[14]

More importantly, the story touched readers. Thousands of letters, emails, and phone calls poured in, a deluge that dwarfed any reader reaction we'd ever experienced. Clearly, "The Boy behind the Mask" was the most successful piece of narrative nonfiction we'd ever produced. Understanding how and why readers reacted to it promised valuable lessons; so I carefully analyzed the written responses. They taught me a lot about what gets through to readers, which in turn suggested a lot about writing and editing to maximize those effects. Those were enormously valuable lessons to me, and I suspect you'll find them useful, too.

The most common responses simply recognized the story's power to hold attention. Hundreds of readers reported that "The Boy behind the Mask" created powerful dramatic tension, locking them into the action line. ("I couldn't put it down," one reader said.) The reaction testified to Tom's skill at showing readers how much was at stake and launching action sequences that put them on the edge of their seats as they wondered what would happen next. Any writer who wants to hold an audience must do the same.

Likewise, a compelling story must immerse readers in another world, carrying them away from their mundane daily cares. ("For as long as it took to read an article," another reader said, "I was oblivious to everything around me.") Writers accomplish that kind of diversion by combining strong action lines with artful scene-setting, reproducing realities where readers can join the story's characters. Recent scientific research emphasizes that "engagement" is a key variable in the power of mirror neurons to cause readers to identify with protagonists and to respond emotionally to their actions. So learning the techniques that create engagement is an important part of the game, too.

Most readers mentioned their emotional response to Sam Lightner's story. ("I wept gallons, turned to mush, and felt like a raw nerve after reading the very first installment.") That testified to Tom's own humanity. As he reported the story, he was in tune with his own emotional responses, targeted the details that produced them, and collected those details so that he could pass them along to readers. They, in turn, experienced events in their hearts as well as their minds. That process also reflects the emotional power of mirror neurons. Tom's self-awareness of his own emotional responses is what allowed him to stimulate the same emotional responses in his audience.

Hundreds of Tom's readers said the feelings the story produced gave them insight that the raw facts would never have generated alone. Others commented on how seeing the world from Sam Lightner's point of view helped them recognize their common humanity, strengthening their sense of solidarity with the rest of society. ("I saw the world through Sam's eyes, and in so doing felt intensely many of the emotions that make us all human.") Still others said that the story put their worries into perspective, making them feel better about their lot in life. ("Next time I sit at a soccer game in knots because my child isn't getting enough playing time, or feel awful because one didn't get asked to a big dance, I will remember Sam.") And some readers said seeing Sam's successes despite much higher hurdles than their own inspired them to work harder at meeting their own challenges. ("Sam's story should be inspiration for many, many who are discouraged or who might need some bit of encouragement to go on with life.")

In the end, what readers seemed most grateful for were the *lessons* that Tom's story offered. ("I've printed out the story, and I'm going to hold onto it for when my eight-year-old daughter readies for high school and the peer pressure that comes with it.") The scientific research reveals that good stories teach, and that essential function must date to the earliest storytellers. Around some primitive campfire, seasoned hunters regaled the young with tales of the chase, passing along understanding of the courage, skill, and tactics it took to bring down prey. Some of those tales ended up painted on cave walls like those in Sulawesi.

Other stories no doubt helped equip new generations with the secrets of child-rearing, the ways of folk medicine, the customs and values that held fragile groups of human beings together in a cold and threatening world. Diversion, emotion, perspective, inspiration, lessons of life—add all those reader benefits together, and you get a pretty good inventory of the goals you can aspire to as a nonfiction writer. But how do you organize your words to do that? What written forms produce those reader reactions, and—more to the point—how do you master them?

The rest of *Storycraft* addresses just those questions. It summarizes what I learned by working with Tom Hallman and dozens of other nonfiction writers over three decades. It's the book I wish I'd had when I started out, the hard-won lessons that cost so much in time and effort. I'm passing them along in the hope that it will save you both.

They may not win you a Pulitzer Prize, but they almost surely will win you an audience.

2

Structure

The art exists purely in the arrangement of words.
—Philip Gerard

In *The Honey Badger*, the novelist Robert Ruark tells the tale of Alec Barr, an aspiring magazine writer who'd been "becoming more and more confused" because he'd been "attempting to adapt the what-where-when technique of newspapers to a different medium." Renowned magazine editor Marc Mantell takes a look at one of Alec's failed pieces and says, "I'm going to show you some tricks with a pencil—carve up your story a bit, after I've drawn you a graph of what a magazine piece is supposed to look like. It has just as much an architectural form as a building or any other precise structure."

Mantell takes pad and pencil in hand and sketches the shape of the era's standard five-thousand-word piece of magazine nonfiction, explaining the function of each part. Alec, wide-eyed, stares through this newly opened window and, for the first time, grasps the importance of structure. Looking at his rejected manuscript, "he could see exactly where form had eluded him and the story had sagged out of shape." Alec grabs a pencil and attacks his article. Mantell skims the marked-up manuscript.

> "You've got it, all right," he says. "I'll guarantee a sale. If not to us, certainly to one of the other slick magazines. Don't ever forget that graph I drew you. It's the signpost to success. And I've got another one for when you tackle fiction. . . ."
>
> "May I have the graph you drew, and will you sign it?" Alec asked as they rose.

"Sure. What are you going to do with it?"

"Frame it," said Alec Barr.

Virtually all the experts on narrative theory, from Aristotle on, stress the importance of structure. Stories tend to certain shapes, and if you stray too far from them, you'll end up with no story at all. "Most important of all is the structure of the incidents," Aristotle wrote, "not of man, but of action and life." Anything that fundamental to storytelling probably has its roots deep in the way our brains are wired. Jonathan Gottschall surveyed recent brain research and concluded that "beneath all of the wild surface variety in all the stories that people tell—no matter where, no matter when—there is a common structure."

He's talking about the protagonist-complication-resolution structure that's the basis of almost all novels and much narrative nonfiction, too. To be sure, many other structures are available to narrative nonfiction writers. But, as Nora Ephron once noted, "If you make the right decision about structure, a huge amount becomes absolutely clear."[1]

Kelley Benham French, a Pulitzer Prize–winning master of nonfiction narrative, explained how structural decisions determine all that follows in a writing project, beginning with the reporting. She joined a team at USA Today as they set to work on "1619: Searching for Answers," a powerful series published on the four hundredth anniversary of slavery's American beginnings. For "The Long Road Home," the team helped Wanda Tucker search for her ancestral roots in Angola, origin of the first Africans sold into slavery in what would become the United States.

"Before we decided to go to Angola," French said, "the story was missing action. We had characters . . . but there wasn't much in the present to chronicle, and they didn't have many family stories we could retell. Once we decided to take Wanda to Angola, we had a clear narrative arc."[2]

Her experience and accomplishment gave French the savvy to know when it was worthwhile to chase halfway across the globe in search of a narrative structure. But the beginning narrative writers I encounter typically have more in common with Alec Barr. Like Robert Ruark's fictional character, they pound away, trying to force the square peg of the standard nonfiction report into the round hole of story structure. When they come to me, I begin by diagramming the new structure they need to contain their material. If they get it, they're on their way to publication.

When we talk about writing, we spend most of our time fussing over word choice, syntax, style, usage, and the myriad concerns that come into play when we're polishing our work. These things are important, of course. But we obsess over them to the exclusion of far more important—and less obvious—elements of success. "Perhaps because polish is so visible," Jon Franklin says, "many people erroneously believe it to be the most important part of writing." But polish, Franklin adds, is merely "the plaster on the walls of structure."

The proof is in the window of the bookstore down the block. The display of current best sellers no doubt contains several titles by tin-eared pop novelists who wouldn't recognize a graceful sentence if it asked them to dance. The likes of Jean Auel, David Baldacci, and Tom Clancy sell books by the millions because they understand story structure, a point that's lost on the critics who savage their syntax.

Richard Rhodes, a Pulitzer-winning nonfiction writer, is a fine stylist who also happens to sell a lot of books. The more important strategies for reaching readers, he says, "have little to do with verbal abilities." Mastering structure, he says, requires more in the way of "pattern ability and administrative abilities." One problem with structure, Rhodes laments, is that "writers don't talk about it much, unfortunately."[3]

Well, let's talk about it.

VISUALIZING STRUCTURE

Structure is more visual than logical, a pattern of parts with its own rules for fitting pieces together, and most experienced writers create some sort of visual guide to the assembly of a story. Like an architect, they express their structural ideas as a kind of blueprint. They must *see* their structure, in graphic terms.

The kind of roman numeral outline that Ms. Grundy taught you in the fourth grade will work fine for a news report, a thesis, or an instructional book like this one. But it won't uncover the patterns at the heart of story. I suspect that topical outlines flow from the verbal part of the brain, the speech center in the left hemisphere. Stephen Hall's little experiment with storytelling during an MRI brain scan strongly suggests that story blueprints emerge from the right brain, and that the neural networks that help us visualize a story's shape are closely linked to the visual cortex.

Marc Mantell, Robert Ruark's magazine editor, showed his acolyte what Mantell called a "graph"—"a series of triangles, squares, rectangles, and thick oblongs, studded with circles and crosses and checkmarks." Tom French, a Pulitzer winner at what is now the *Tampa Bay Times* who moved on to teach at Indiana University, advises writers to "make a diagram, charting the line of the story. I look for the simplest way to let it flow, the most natural path of unfolding. Usually, if I can't diagram it, that means I haven't figured out the structure yet."⁴ Novelist Darin Strauss says, "I find it helpful in the planning stages to draw each line of plot as an arc on a piece of scrap paper. Put an A at one end and a B at the other. A is to be a question; B is its answer. Generally this question should relate to the concrete desire of the protagonist."

John McPhee, the master of the nonfiction explanatory narrative, obsesses on structure, in part because sketching out a simple blueprint helps him find his way through the thickets of information that sprout as he reports a story. When he's ready to write, he looks beyond those thickets to his goal and sketches a route to reaching it. "When I was young," he recalls, "I was so bewildered about how to cope with all that material. Leaning on structural planning is what got me out from under a fifty-ton rock that was lying on my chest."

What McPhee calls "doodles" take various forms. Circles with lines jutting out to indicate different narratives. Lines with loops alongside them to indicate digressions. McPhee shared the blueprint that became one of his best-known works, "Travels in Georgia," with Jennifer Greenstein Altmann for an interview published in Princeton's weekly bulletin. It took the form of a spiral that wound through the story's key scenes. (An expanded version of McPhee's thoughts on structure appears in *Draft No. 4*, a collection of McPhee's *New Yorker* essays on craft.)

"Travels" followed a pair of wildlife biologists whose work took them through the Georgia countryside. McPhee included the more interesting stops on his diagram.

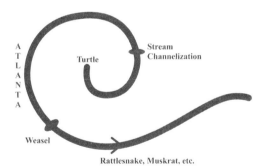

Figure 1. A John McPhee graphic outline

The biologists often stopped to collect fresh roadkills, which they cooked and ate, and McPhee included a muskrat meal on his doodle. They ran across a dredge operator destroying a wetland as part of a stream-channelization project, and that, too, was a key point on the spiraling narrative. During one of the tale's most intense passages, they stopped to examine a critically injured turtle, struck by a passing car, and looked on as a county sheriff clumsily put it out of its misery with his pistol. As the spiral indicates, the narrative builds to the turtle, which McPhee and the biologists ate.

BLUEPRINTS

A general contractor doesn't just start building, deciding day by day whether he'll put a room here or a doorway there, ordering vast quantities of building materials just in case he might need them. He consults his blueprint, ordering what he needs when he needs it as he methodically works his way toward the finished structure depicted in his drawing.

The most confused, anxious, and unproductive narrative writers work like contractors without blueprints. The successful ones eventually figure out that they need a plan. "When I was a beginning writer," Ted Conover told Robert Boynton, "the structure often became apparent to me only after I'd begun writing—sometimes after I'd written a lot. I'd start without a plan and see where my interests took me. But that method wasn't very efficient. I wasted a lot of time on dead ends."

I've long made it a practice to sit down with writers to sketch a blueprint as soon as we had some inkling of a story's direction. If you run into something unexpected, you can always revise the blueprint—contractors do it all the time. In the meantime, you avoid the time and expense of gathering material you ultimately won't need. "I always keep in mind that there is a structure to this," Mary Roach says, "and things are going to have to fit. That saves you from collecting a lot of things you won't use."[5]

A good blueprint eases writing, too. Remember Jon Franklin's warning about placing too much emphasis on polish. He also notes that your first draft should emphasize the structure—getting the right things in the right places—rather than trying to make each sentence perfect. Once you have the whole structure roughed out, you can go back and rewrite for polish. Once again, the building analogy holds. Contractors frame in the entire building before they start worrying about the decorative details in each room. You'll be a lot less anxious, and you'll waste less time polishing material that's ultimately discarded, if you do the same.

THE NARRATIVE ARC

One of my favorite *Seinfeld* episodes began, as they usually did, with an agitated Kramer bursting into Jerry's apartment. Kramer gyrated. Jerry looked impatient. "What's wrong?" he finally asked. "I just realized," Kramer replied, "that I have *no narrative arc*!"

The gag resonated on several levels. A narrative arc is built from the orderly progression of facts through specific story elements. But at the time the *Seinfeld* episode aired, "narrative arc" was in vogue among the New York literati as an almost-meaningless catch phrase. We can assume Kramer was parroting the fad expression and probably wasn't quite sure what he was saying. The irony was that he was absolutely right—his loose-cannon life, devoid of order or consistency, *did* lack a narrative arc. And the bit also tweaked the critics who'd declared *Seinfeld* a show "about nothing," a meander through aimless lives that never seemed to go anywhere.

The tone of the show's humor did indeed obscure any narrative momentum. But, in fact, a typical *Seinfeld* episode incorporated several narrative arcs. Kramer's schemes took off and crashed. Elaine's latest relationship heated up and cooled. George got jobs and lost them. Like all successful storytelling, *Seinfeld* had a structure that gave it shape and kept audiences waiting to see what would happen next.

Analysts have been trying to wrestle that structure to the ground since Aristotle. Most of us have heard his comment that stories have beginnings, middles, and ends. But that doesn't offer much take-it-to-the-keyboard guidance. An aspiring narrative storyteller needs specifics.

Not to worry—specifics abound. Even Aristotle's structural advice goes way beyond beginnings, middles, and endings. And its modern equivalents get quite detailed about the structures most likely to connect with readers. All of them connect the essential elements of the protagonist-complication-resolution model in some kind of visual representation. You can find multiple examples in fiction-writing texts such as Janet Burroway's. Over the years, I've developed my own system for interviewing writers and creating the kind a graphic outline that will help them plan and write stories.

I begin by asking them to outline the key story elements. Then I sketch a narrative arc, which takes the shape of a normal curve skewed to the right. The template looks like figure 2.

I doubt Kramer would have recognized this graphic as a diagram of his missing arc. On the other hand, a lot of experienced nonfiction writers wouldn't either. "In terms of narrative writing, very few writers understand that a story has an arc," says Jim Collins, a former editor of *Yankee* magazine. "Not just a beginning, a middle, and an end, but a sequence of events that will keep a reader moving along. I read a lot of pieces that seem flat. So one thing happens, and then another happens, and another happens, and there's no sense of movement in a piece."[6]

A true narrative arc sweeps forward across time, pushing ahead with con-

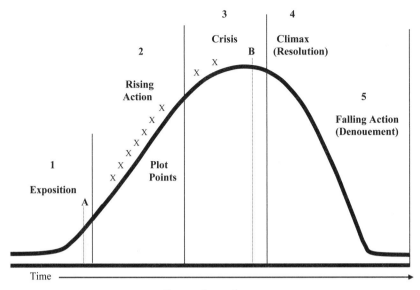

Figure 2. A narrative arc

stant motion. It looks like a wave about to break, a pregnant package of stored energy.

1. EXPOSITION

The arc passes through the five phases that mark any complete story, each indicated by the Arabic numerals hovering above it in figure 2. The first is exposition, the phase that tells readers who protagonists are and gives them just enough information to understand the complications they will face.

Aristotle said the exposition phase of a story was where you define your characters. Lajos Egri, noting that *Webster's* defines exposition as "the act of exposing," asks "Now then, what do we want to expose? The premise? The atmosphere? The character's background? The plot? The scenery? The mood? The answer is, we must expose all these at once."

But not everything. . . . The trick to writing a good expository segment is to tell readers what they *must* understand . . . and no more. The story of Nancy Punches and her drowning foxhounds offers a good case study.

In 2007 a devastating winter storm flooded much of the Pacific Northwest. Mark Larabee, then a hard-news reporter in the *Oregonian*'s Portland newsroom, drove eighty-five miles north, where floodwater had closed the West Coast's main north-south interstate. While he was covering frantic efforts to get the freeway flowing again, Mark heard about a dog breeder who'd lost almost all her animals to the flood, which had almost drowned her as well. He talked to her neighbors and friends and then tracked her down in the hospital for an interview. He had terrific stuff, he said, and he was ready to tackle his first narrative. When he got back to Portland, his editor directed him to me.[7]

We sat down in my office, and—as I always do when I'm coaching a story—I began by asking him about what he'd discovered. The more I asked, the more excited I got. Mark did have great stuff, terrific scenic detail that brought a touching and inspiring story to life: The flood cutting off the isolated house where the woman lived alone. The desperate struggle to save her prize-winning American foxhounds, only to see them drown one by one. The grim hours trapped in the house, the cold water climbing inexorably toward the ceiling. The puppy that survived, the one she named Noah.

Then came the crucial part of the conversation, the kind of thinking that's essential to effective storytelling in any medium. Whether you're planning a newspaper narrative, a magazine feature, a radio documentary, a podcast, or a film, you must understand the underlying essentials of your story before you plunge into the writing.

Mark and I began by talking about the dog breeder's qualities as a protagonist, and the personality traits that saw her through the ordeal. We discussed research on survivors, how this woman resembled them, and what the rest of us could learn from her example. We broke the story down into key parts and plugged plot points onto a narrative arc I sketched on a yellow legal pad. We did a scenic outline.

To actually begin writing the story, Mark had to address exposition. What did readers need to know about his protagonist? Certain basic facts, for sure. (Nancy Punches was seventy-four, lived alone, and raised foxhounds.) And some minimal setting. (Nancy lived alongside the Chehalis, a river flowing through Southwest Washington State.) Aspects of her personality. (Nancy was tough, resourceful, independent.) Some of Nancy's motivation was important, too. (She loved her dogs, a champion bloodline she'd been raising for three decades. And she had a new litter of five-week-old puppies.)

That's about all the exposition Mark's readers needed—it explained Nancy's behavior as she struggled with the complications that would immediately follow.

Novice narrative writers often err by dumping in all the background they've gathered on key characters, delaying the story line that will grab and hold readers. Hence the principle that *exposition is the enemy of narrative*. And this is true regardless of medium. I once consulted with a podcast writer who neglected that maxim by repeatedly swerving off on tangents that had nothing to do with his story's core complication. The resulting podcast frustrated me, as a listener, because I just couldn't see the point to much of his material, and I just *wanted to get on with the story.*

After a conversation about the problem, the writer launched a new, tremendously improved podcast. And—on the strength of that—he landed a full-time job with a major media company in his region.

Good exposition provides just enough backstory to explain how the protagonist happens to be in a particular place, at a particular time, with the wants that will lead to the next phase of the story. Thorough reporting produces overwhelming detail. Good storytellers cut through it to create a clear path leading forward. The need to sift through a vast number of possible background facts to find those absolutely essential to the story may have been what one of my favorite novelists, Cormac McCarthy, had in mind when he said, in *Cities of the Plain,* "Where all is known, no narrative is possible."

Even the little bit that *must* be known will block easy entry to the story if it delays the action line. The secret, Hunter Thompson said, is to "blend, blend, blend." You launch action immediately and then blend the exposition into it, submerging it in modifiers, subordinate clauses, appositives, and the like. When Mark went back to his keyboard and wrote his first paragraph, he came up with something that not only conveyed action, but also provided essential exposition:

> Nancy Punches stared at the turbulent water. Swollen by back-to-back storms, the Chehalis River had filled its channel and fanned out over a wide bench of rain-soaked earth. But, on that soggy Sunday evening, it was still far below the rural road running by her house.

The exposition phase of the story is also the place you tease readers into the action line by foreshadowing the dramatic events that lie just ahead. Mark could have done that crudely: "Nancy never suspected that in a few hours her dogs would be dead and she'd be trapped in her house, fighting for her life." But he wisely chose to be more subtle, writing that:

> In her six years of living thirteen miles west of Chehalis, Nancy had never seen the river flood. Neighbors who'd long lived along that stretch of the Chehalis told her they'd never seen it cover the road, not even in '96, when it flowed over its banks and closed Interstate 5. Surely, this storm was no worse.

Reassured, Nancy turned back home, counting on a restful night's sleep.

Readers know full well that when a writer takes pains to tell them a character doesn't expect the worst, she's about to get it. Notice how Mark Singer began his *New Yorker* tale, "Castaways," about Mexican fishermen who set out on a short trip and ended up lost at sea for more than nine months.

> Very early on the morning of Oct. 28, 2005, in the town of San Blas, on the central Pacific Coast of Mexico, five men boarded a small boat. The day started out looking promising: hurricane season was waning, there were few clouds, and the surface of the broad Bay of Matanchen was calm. . . . Assuming all went well, they'd be at sea for two, maybe three days.

You can find other ways to foreshadow without obvious stage whispers, too. Often it's simply a matter of teasing readers with a pronoun that lacks an antecedent or some other kind of glaring loose end. Joan Didion began one of her best-known pieces of narrative nonfiction by writing, "Imagine Banyan Street first, because Banyan is where it happened." Spencer Heinz, a feature writer for the *Oregonian*, launched another of his stories with "Pat Yost was in bed when she heard the sound."

What happened? What sound? The standard news report reveals all immediately. But little mysteries drive the narrative forward. Bill Blundell, former writing coach at the *Wall Street Journal*, said, "The formula I teach is to tease the folks a little bit in the lead. They don't mind it. You are simply trying to get them interested."

Or, as the Charles Dickens formula for success has it: "Make them laugh. Make them cry. But, most of all, make them wait."[8]

The one thing you can't make them wait for is the exposition they need to let them know what's going on. In a short news narrative like Mark's flood saga, you probably can't blend all the exposition into the action line. But a paragraph or two of unblended backstory won't slow things down too much. Immediately after Mark put Nancy Punches to bed, expecting a peaceful night's sleep, he supplied the rest of the critical backstory in an unblended paragraph of pure exposition:

> An energetic seventy-four-year-old American Kennel Club judge with rosy cheeks and long silver hair, Nancy bred prize-winning American foxhounds, a champion bloodline she'd been perfecting since the mid-1970s. She lived in a double-wide manufactured home set up high on eight acres of pastureland.

The rest of the exposition, such as the fact that Nancy had a five-week-old litter of six puppies, fit neatly into the action line, Hunter Thompson style. With the necessary backstory established, Mark brought the exposition phase of the story to a close with one of the most important parts of any narrative arc. Robert McKee calls it the "inciting incident," and others identify it as "Plot Point A" or "engaging the complication." Whatever you call it, it's the event that sets the whole story in motion, indicated on the narrative-arc diagram by the dotted vertical line with the letter A above it.

Here's Mark's account of the event that launched the Nancy Punches story:

> She rolled out of bed Monday morning and looked out the window. Brown water covered her yard, submerging her Chevy van up to its engine block. Even if she could get the van started, water had reached the road and blocked any possible escape.

With the complication engaged, the exposition phase of the story comes to a close. Then things get interesting.

2. RISING ACTION

The complete narrative arc gives rising action, the second phase of the story, about the same weight as the other phases. Rising action, in fact, contributes most of the bulk to most stories. It's the phase of the story that keeps the audience members in their chairs, and the standard 120-minute Hollywood film might devote more than a hundred of those minutes to it. Rising action creates the dramatic tension that will be released only when the story's climax leads to the resolution.

For Nancy Punches, rising action meant real rising. The water climbed to the front porch of her house, then higher. A whole series of dramatic incidents followed, uncovered by Mark Larabee's careful interviewing. Each contributed a plot point, indicated by the series of X's that follow the narrative arc up through the rising-action curve.

A plot point, as you might remember from the preceding chapter, is any development that spins the story off in a new direction. Plot Point A, the inciting incident, rips the protagonist out of the status quo and initiates a journey toward the new reality that waits at the end of the narrative arc. Novelist Darin Strauss suggests that you "think of your focal character's life before your story begins as a boulder perched unsteadily on a hilltop." The narrative arc begins when a bird comes along and strikes the boulder, starting it down the hill.

The boulder's movement jolts the protagonist, and, at the same time, it jolts the audience, creating tension that grows with each new turn of the plot. Most of those plot points will create new problems for the protagonist. As Ted Conover reminds us, "A narrative is when things go wrong."[9]

Mark Larabee and I went through his story's plot points during our prewriting conversation. The more we listed, the better the story looked. Mark's interviewing had uncovered a sequence of twists and turns, each leading inexorably to the next. That's just as it should be. "There is no moment in a play," Lajos Egri says, "which does not grow from the one before it."

Nancy's saga began when she saw her flooded yard. She struggled to get the puppies, their mother, and five other dogs into the house. Then the water blocked access to the kennels, trapping the remaining ten dogs. In the house, water boiled through the floor and rose to Nancy's knees. Debris blocked the door, trapping her inside. Nancy, soaked and freezing in the icy water but true to her resourceful character, methodically planned one survival move after the next. Two puppies drowned, and she put survivors in a foam shipping container, which floated. Still the water rose. Outside, dogs left in the kennel drowned. Then the adult dogs in the house drowned, one by one.

> Nancy climbed onto the kitchen counter. The water climbed higher, covering her chairs. Over the window ledges. Then up the blinds, one horizontal slat at a time. Furniture tipped and sank.

A bookcase tumbled over and floated. Nancy swam to it and climbed aboard. When the water reached the ceiling, Nancy and the puppies would drown. Or would they?

Each development in skillfully crafted rising action raises a question. Philip Gerard notes that dramatic story structure consists of "a string of mysteries organized in a deliberate order. The mysteries will be large and small, and the writer will make good use of this variation in interest, resolving the mysteries in escalating order, using smaller questions to lead into larger ones, saving the resolution of the biggest mystery for last."

Highlight that last line. I once was appalled, while serving on a Pulitzer Prize jury, by the way one of the entries neglected that principle. The whole story hinged on whether the lead character lived or died. The page designer, oblivious to anything but the look of the package, led off the story with a photo of mourners standing around the protagonist's newly dug grave.

The designer should have read Aristotle: "In the first act set forth the case," he said. "In the second weave together the events, in such wise that until the middle of the third act one may hardly guess the outcome. Always trick expectancy; and hence it may come to pass that something quite far from what is promised may be left to the understanding."

Jonathan Harr's *A Civil Action* became one of the best-selling nonfiction narratives of the twentieth century, in part, because Harr so cleverly piled up one mystery after another. The book follows the true-life story of an obsessed lawyer, Jan Schlichtmann, who pursues corporations that polluted the groundwater in Woburn, just outside Boston. He argues that the toxic chemicals dumped by W. R. Grace Corporation, among others, caused leukemia that killed several children.

In the middle of the trial, the defense puts John Guswa, a groundwater expert, on the stand. He argues that W. R. Grace could not have caused disease and death because groundwater from its plant could not possibly have reached the wells serving Woburn. Jan Schlichtmann's colleague, Harvard professor Charles Nesson, suddenly disappears.

Nesson doesn't return to the courtroom that day. Nor does he show up at the office later that afternoon. Schlichtmann calls Nesson's office at the Harvard Law School, but his secretary hasn't seen him. Then, in rising consternation, he calls Nesson's home in Cambridge. No answer there either. "Where the hell is Charlie?" Schlichtmann yells from his conference room.

Nesson's still missing in the morning. Schlichtmann cross-examines the witness all day, failing to crack his testimony. It looks as though his case will fail on the whole issue of how far the polluted groundwater actually traveled.

Finally, we find out that Nesson has been at the Harvard Law School faculty library, using Darcy's law, a fundamental principle of hydrology, to prove that the defense expert's calculations could not possibly be right. That night, he walks into Schlichtmann's office.

> Schlichtmann jumped up and shouted, "For Christ's sake Charlie, where the hell have you been?"
> Nesson smiled. "I've figured out how to nail Guswa."

The next day, Schlichtmann destroys Guswa on the witness stand, opening up the possibility that he may yet win his landmark case.

Good narrative also follows the rise and fall of hope, another characteristic of effective rising action. Batman wins one. Hope rises. The Joker wins one. Hope falls. Schlichtmann loses a key legal motion, and it looks as though his lawsuit will die. Then he pulls something out of a hat, and he's back in business, his improbable quest renewed.

Similarly, the rise and fall of hope provides much of the drama in Erik Larson's *The Devil in the White City*. Larson's true-life protagonist, Daniel Burnham, sets out to stage the Chicago World's Fair, scheduled to open in 1893. Time is short, the weather's bad, and the odds are long against success. Burnham negotiates one troublesome plot point after another, at times brimming with confidence and at times despairing. A one point, a key player, the renowned landscape architect Frederick Law Olmsted, loses heart. He writes to Burnham.

> "It looks as if the time has come when it is necessary for you to count me out," he wrote. The work in Chicago had begun to look hopeless. "It is very plain that as things are, we are not going to be able to do our duty here."

But, of course, Olmsted rallies, as do the other occasionally demoralized builders of the great fair. And, in the end, the result is one of the high points in American civilization.

This rise and fall, of hope and mystery and suspense, is so ingrained in the rising-action phase of a story, that I sometimes sketch it as a curve writhing its way up another curve, each plot point indicated by an X (see figure 3).

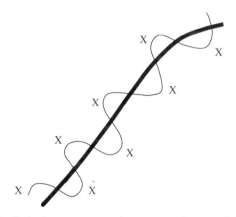

Figure 3. Oscillating hope, mystery, and suspense on the curve of rising action

The final ingredient that's critical to successful rising action is the cliff-hanger. You don't need to create literal cliff-hangers—Indiana Jones dangling from a sapling on a vertical face high above a river—but you do want to close out each little episode with a kicker that leaves your protagonist, and your audience, dangling.

When Jan Schlichtmann closed his daylong cross-examination of John Guswa, he'd run out of ideas to impeach the man's testimony, and he desperately needed help from Charles Nesson. The section closed with a cliff-hanger:

He had no plan for tomorrow. And Nesson was still missing.

Erik Larson described Daniel Burnham inviting several bigwig New York architects to Chicago and pitching them on the fair. If they joined the project, it would win the credibility crucial to its success. But Larson left his readers hanging on the outcome of that key meeting, closing the segment this way:

> He believed he had won them. As the evening ended, he asked, would they join him? There was a pause.

Mark Larabee had some cliff-hangers up his sleeve, too. The rising-action segment of his story ended with Nancy Punches on the floating bookcase, rising toward the ceiling. Once she reached it, she would surely drown. Mark put it this way:

> The murky water covered the window, and the light winked out. The water kept rising. Nancy reached up and touched the ceiling.

3. CRISIS

Aristotle wrote of the "peripeteia," or "reversal of the situation," a third-act twist that suddenly plunged the protagonist into dangerously deep water. Most modern story analysts prefer to think of the peripeteia as "the crisis," a broader idea denoting an increase of intensity that brings the story to a head.

For Nancy Punches, the crisis arrives when she reaches up and touches the ceiling and realizes that she's about to drown. The crisis is the point where everything hangs in the balance, where things could go either way.

That's a key point for any storyteller, and not simply because the audience is holding its collective breath and will soon need permission to inhale again. The crisis also poses a crucial dramatic question for you as a writer: Do you begin the story just before the inciting incident and tell it in chronological order? Or do you begin it with the crisis, using the dramatic intensity of that moment to grab readers by their lapels and jerk them into the story?

The Roman poet Horace recognized the dilemma in *Ars Poetica*,[10] a treatise on the ancient world's epic poetry. Homer began his epics in the middle of the action and then flashed backward in time to clue listeners into the essential backstory. He began, in Horace's terms, *in medias res*, or "in the middle of things." Beginning at the beginning, according to Horace, was to start *ab ovo* ("from the egg") or *ab initio* ("from the beginning").

The distinction emphasizes a key point. For a nonfiction story, the narrative arc describes reality, the order of events as they actually unfolded in real time.

In fiction, you follow the same principle, although the arc describes an imagined reality. But in nonfiction or fiction, no law says you have to tell the story in precise chronological order. You can jump around the arc in any number of ways, using flashbacks or flash-forwards. Your plot, in other words, need not follow the narrative arc. The movie *Memento* told an entire story backward, beginning with the last scene and working its way, scene by scene, toward the beginning.

Nonfiction narratives usually move forward through time chronologically but often include a flashback or two that fills readers in on necessary background. David Grann, who has displayed his mastery of narrative structure in best sellers such as *The Lost City of Z* and *Killers of the Flower Moon*, when he wrote his *New Yorker* story on the effort to capture a live giant squid. He built most of his narrative out of the time he spent with Steve O'Shea, an obsessed New Zealand squid hunter. But he used long flashbacks—1,500 words and more—to fill readers in on other efforts to track the elusive squid:

> Last January, before I ventured out with O'Shea, I joined the squid squad of Bruce Robison, one of O'Shea's leading counterparts. Unlike other hunters, Robison has two underwater robots, which have superior imaging capabilities and speed through the water more quickly than divers or most submersibles.

An *in medias res* opening starts with the crisis and then flashes back to the beginning. The writer's narrative line then works its way back through exposition, complication, and rising action. When it arrives at the crisis again, it moves through it and then proceeds on into the new territory that lies in the direction of the climax.

An *in medias res* narrative looks like figure 4.

Mark and I discussed the possibility of an *in medias res* opening for the Nancy Punches story. We could have started with her floating on the bookcase, with just enough backstory for readers to recognize the peril she was in. Leaving her with the ceiling just an arm's reach above would have been a helluva cliffhanger.

On the other hand, opening *in medias res* makes the writing more complicated, and Nancy's story was Mark's first news narrative. Besides, the natural *ab ovo* opening of the narrative arc—the one where Nancy walks down to the Chehalis, sees the rising water, and decides she has nothing to worry about—had an ominous quality with plenty of power for pulling readers into the yarn. My advice followed the KISS ("Keep It Simple, Stupid") principle I learned in

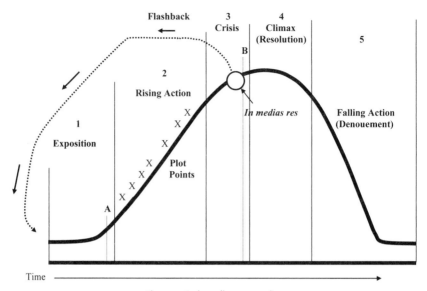

Figure 4. An *in medias res* opening

the army. I advised Mark to begin with something similar to the line he ulti-mately chose: "Nancy Punches stared at the turbulent water."

No matter how experienced you are, you're well advised to apply KISS any-time you consider extensive flashbacks or flash-forwards. *Memento* notwith-standing, the storyteller's usual aim is to keep readers happily lost in story, and jumping out of the chronology threatens that. Flash-forwards are particularly damaging to a reader's sense that he's living the story because they're such pa-tently artificial devices. While we're experiencing the world firsthand, we may recall things that happened earlier, but our consciousness doesn't suddenly jump forward in time. A flash-forward reminds us that there's a writer between us and the story, someone who intrudes on the narrative line by saying, in ef-fect, "Wait a minute here, while I tell you what's gonna happen on down the line."

All of which moved Tom French to write, "Beware the extended flashback, the ornate flash-forward, the so-called expert dragged forward to 'explain.' Stay as close to the action as possible."

———————

The crisis is the peak of the breaking wave that is a narrative arc. When it col-lapses, the wave's force will change things profoundly. In a tragedy, it will destroy the protagonist (Macbeth). In a simple story heavy on action, it will resolve the complication so that the protagonist can return to his status quo. (The ambulance arrives and whisks the woman who was trapped in the burning car off to the hospital.) In a full story with a constructive ending, it will transform the protagonist, producing a permanent psychological change that allows him to move forward in life armed with new insight and knowledge. (Sam Lightner comes to terms with his appearance and chooses to join his classmates in the march toward adulthood.) Aristotle referred to that insight as "the recognition."

A Hollywood action film is usually a mere yarn—the most violent of events leave Dirty Harry unchanged. But when Clint Eastwood moved on to more serious film dramas, the narrative arc inevitably carried the protagonist into new ways of seeing the world. *Unforgiven* earned the critical acclaim that the Dirty Harry movies never did.

Robert McKee says that if you look at the protagonist's situation at the beginning of a film and his situation at the end, "you should see the arc of the film, the great sweep of change that takes life from one condition at the opening to a changed condition at the end."

In a yarn such as the Nancy Punches story, things generally happen too fast for any true psychological transformation. Nancy carried all the persevering resourcefulness she needed into her crisis, and, once it passed, she was essentially the same person she'd been going into it. Most short narratives are similar. Stu Tomlinson's cop wasn't significantly different after he rescued the woman pinned in her burning car. Nonfiction doesn't often offer the opportunity to follow the narrative arc through a profound change in the protagonist's way of seeing the world. So you seldom get a "point of insight," the plot point marked B on the arc.

Count your lucky stars when it does. Having both an inciting incident (Plot Point A) and a point of insight (Plot Point B) means you have a complete story, and that means you have the raw material for a piece of writing with real literary merit.

But even when you don't have a true psychological transformation, it's useful to think of the crisis culminating in a point of insight. Ask yourself, "What event sets up the resolution of the crisis?" Consider that your point of insight. Even if you're writing a news narrative, having such a point helps you visualize its full structure. I'd say that when the firefighters arrived with the jaws of life, that was the point of insight for Stu Tomlinson's burning-car narrative. And when Nancy Punches touched the ceiling, that was the point of insight for her narrative. In both instances, some kind of climax had to immediately follow.

4. CLIMAX

The climax is simply the event—or series of events—that resolves the crisis. When Frodo destroys the ring of power, he resolves the complication that drove the ring trilogy. When the firefighters pried the woman out of the smashed car, loaded her into an ambulance, and sent her to the emergency room, that ended Stu Tomlinson's rescue yarn. And when Nancy Punches nears the ceiling, the next event will determine whether she lives or dies. That, too, will constitute the yarn's climax:

> With only ten inches of clearance remaining, the water's steady rise seemed to slow.
> Then it stopped.
> She had no sense of time, but eventually dusk flickered into the room through the window. The water was dropping. . . .
> Through the night, the water dropped until Nancy could again stand up. She couldn't see, but she managed to get the puppies inside her fleece pullover. She held their warmth against her and wandered the room, hallucinating that the walls were made of glass. A puppy stuck his head out and licked her face, then pulled himself back under the pullover.
> Just keep moving, she thought. Don't give up.

In delirium from hypothermia, Nancy struggles through the night and into the next day. The puppy pops out and licks her face again. Nancy hallucinates, but one of her visions—a little girl near her house—turns out to be true. The girl runs for her father, who breaks down Nancy's blocked door, rescuing her and her puppies. Her complication has been resolved.

Nancy's fortitude and resourcefulness kept her alive, but the water dropped because of natural forces and her neighbor rescued her from her house. Frodo's climax, on the other hand, was true Hollywood because it was of *his* own making. *He* carried the ring to Mount Doom, overcoming everything from Orcs to earthquakes along the way. *He* threw the ring into the only fire that could consume it.

Sometimes true life provides a climax wrought of the protagonist's own struggles, Sam Lightner being a case in point. But true life isn't Hollywood, and that's not always the case. Jason McGowan didn't operate the jaws of life. (Although he did help keep the trapped woman alive until the firefighters could arrive.) Nancy Punches didn't stop the flood. (Although she used her brains and her persistence to stay afloat until the flood crested.) Yet both sets of facts made excellent news narratives. Which raises a central point about nonfiction narrative: You may be a piece or two short of a complete story structure, but the power of a dramatic true story, the reader's knowledge that the story is true, is enough to entice readers through the complete narrative arc.

5. FALLING ACTION/DENOUEMENT

The climax takes you to the story's peak, and from then on you have nowhere to go but down. Hence the notion of "falling action." Intensity fades. The pace slows. Things wind down.

At that point in the story, you probably have some unanswered questions remaining. Did the woman rescued from the burning car live or die? How bad were her injuries? What happened to the guy driving the pickup, anyway?

You deal with such questions in the falling-action phase of the story, which for that reason is also known as the denouement or "unknotting." It is the point in the story where everything becomes clear.

Stu Tomlinson wrapped up his tale of how Jason McGowan led the effort to save Evan Waggoner, the woman trapped in the burning car, this way:

> Within minutes, Evan Waggoner was on her way to OHSU Hospital. McGowan rode to OHSU in an ambulance with Tyson Fortner.
>
> At the hospital, McGowan met Waggoner's family. On Tuesday he learned that her pelvis was broken in three places, her left leg was fractured, and her right leg and jaw were injured. She'll be bedridden for three months and faces numerous surgeries.
>
> The case has been referred to the Multnomah County district attorney's office for investigation.
>
> Evan Waggoner says she hopes to soon see her fiancé, Pfc. James Calkins of the Oregon National Guard, who is in Texas and will be deployed to Iraq early next year.

Keep one thing in mind when you're writing a denouement: Falling action has drained all the dramatic tension from the story. Readers want to know the answers to a few questions, but the powerful engine of story has shut down, leaving little momentum to carry your audience farther forward. So don't push your luck. Wrap things up as quickly as possible and leave the stage. One of the main complaints I heard about the film version of *The Lord of the Rings* was that the denouement dragged on and on, with long good-byes and endless departures.

Once you've answered the necessary questions, you have one remaining task—bring the story to an end with what journalistic types call a "kicker."

A good one will sum up, surprise a little, perhaps bring things full circle, firmly planting your protagonists in their new status quo. It will leave absolutely no doubt that the story has ended.

Stu Tomlinson played on the heroic-public-servant aspect of his rescue story by closing with praise for his protagonist:

> And from her bed, Waggoner talked through a hospital spokesman.
> "Make sure everyone knows," she said, "that I wouldn't be here if it wasn't for that officer."

Mark Larabee's string of incredible storyteller's luck ran right through his kicker. As we sat discussing his story, before he began the writing, he brightened and told me a little more about the puppy that licked Nancy Punches's face. A friend brought the little foxhound to visit her in the hospital while Mark was there interviewing her. She'd decided to keep him, he told me, and as a true flood survivor, she'd named him Noah.

"Noah!" I said. "That's great! What a perfect kicker! Somehow, we just have to find a way to make that the last word in the story."

Mark went off to write. When he came back, he'd nailed it:

> Even before the flood, the prized puppies had been sold. Nancy's a breeder, after all.
> On Sunday, a friend sneaked the little puppy who'd repeatedly licked her face into her hospital room and sat him on the bed. The dog sniffed, looked up and then bounded toward her. He licked her face again.
> Another survivor. She won't sell that one, she says. She's named him Noah.

3

Point of View

When the writer approaches the rough materials of his story, he must always determine the focus of character. . . . He asks, whose story is it?
—Cleanth Brooks and Robert Penn Warren

> At five a.m. on a cool Boston morning not long ago, Elizabeth Rourke—thick black-brown hair, pale Irish skin, and forty-one weeks pregnant—reached over and woke her husband, Chris.
> "I'm having contractions," she said.
> "Are you sure?" he asked.
> "I'm sure."

And so the tale begins. . . . Atul Gawande, the Boston doctor who writes the *New Yorker's* "Annals of Medicine" and best-selling books such as *Being Mortal*, plunges us into a story that is—quite literally—pregnant with the kind of drama that will keep most of us reading. But few readers will consider the point-of-view questions that Gawande faced when he decided to begin his yarn in precisely this way.

Think about it. Who's describing this intimate scene in Elizabeth Rourke's bedroom? Where's the storyteller standing? What can he see and hear? Whose story is it, anyway?

Well, you might say, the writer has us readers right there in the bedroom, standing a few feet from the action. Both Elizabeth and her husband are in the frame, and we're close enough to hear what they're saying. All in all, we're in a pretty good position for watching the story unfold.

But wait! Look what happens in the very next paragraph.

She was a week past her due date, and the pain was deep and viselike, nothing like the occasional spasms she'd been feeling. It seemed to come out of her lower back and wrap around and seize her whole abdomen. The first spasm woke her out of a sound sleep. Then came a second. And a third.

My God! Now we're actually *inside* Elizabeth, feeling her pain and understanding her history.

Over the next couple of paragraphs, we learn more about the soon-to-be mom. This is her first pregnancy. And, as it turns out, she's a doctor herself, a new internist at Massachusetts General Hospital. She's already delivered four babies, one of them in the hospital parking lot. And, in the tenth paragraph of Gawande's article, she miraculously extracts herself from her painful childbirth to tell us that story in her own words:

The father had called, saying, "We're delivering! We're coming to the hospital, and she's delivering!" So we were in the E.R., and we went running. It was freezing cold. The car came screeching up to the hospital. The door went flying open. And, sure enough, there the mom was.

So, we might conclude, this is Elizabeth's story, and she's going to tell it. We'll follow her through her childbirth while she explains what's going on.

Then a strange thing happens. A disembodied voice jumps into the yarn, tells a joke, and drops in background information that seems to come from out of the blue. Something else changes, too. Up until this point, the story has unfolded in third person. But then "our," a pronoun of the first-person plural, pops up. This looked like Elizabeth's story, but all of a sudden *we*—all of us readers and, indeed, the entire human race—seem to be involved in it:

Other mammals are born mature enough to walk and seek food within hours; our newborns are small and helpless for months.

Then, midway through the piece, person shifts again. Gawande himself steps forward and tells about his own research on childbirth and what he discovered about the use of forceps during delivery.

I spoke to Dr. Watson Bowes, Jr., an emeritus professor of obstetrics at the University of North Carolina and the author of a widely read textbook chapter on forceps technique.

And so it goes, on through the entire 8,500 words. We stand ten feet or so away and watch Elizabeth go through her delivery, close to the action, in what feels like real time. Then we move way back, blurring details and rushing through time. Soon we again step close to the action. And every once in a while Elizabeth speaks up and comments on her own experience. Or a hidden narrator interrupts to drop background information into the action line. Then the author takes center stage and tells us his own experience with the subject.

We're trained to think this kind of nonfiction storytelling describes reality. But, in fact, no reality follows this otherworldly pattern of close-up and long shot, real time and historical summary. We can't see inside somebody else's mind, and we can't jump around among characters, seeing the world first through one set of eyes and then another. Narrative nonfiction is a device for fooling us into thinking we're experiencing reality when, in fact, it transcends reality by giving us godlike power. And much of that power comes from the way skilled narrative writers manipulate point of view.

But what, exactly, is point of view?

Alas, hardly anybody seems to agree. Novelist Darin Strauss insists that "point of view is simply the workings of the mind of the character who is telling or experiencing the story." Literary agent Peter Rubie says point of view is "a camera-lens position." Creative nonfiction guru Philip Gerard says point of view can be either first or third person and varies according to how much access the storyteller has to the minds of characters.

The rest of us often use "point of view" as shorthand for the values that influence our understanding of the world. Ayn Rand's enthusiasm for unbridled capitalism dominated her novel The Fountainhead. Carl Sandburg's disgust with unbridled capitalism colored his Chicago poems. How values influence storytelling is an important consideration in nonfiction narrative, too. So important, in fact, that we'll deal with it in the separate chapter devoted to theme.

But for our purposes here, point of view boils down to the answers to three questions: *Through whose eyes do we experience the story? From which direction? From what distance?*

POV CHARACTERS

It has to be *somebody's* story, and one of the first questions any narrative writer has to answer is "whose?"

That's different than the question of who *tells* the story. A third-person narrative may follow a single character from the beginning of the narrative arc until the end without that character ever speaking directly to the reader. But readers move through time with the POV character, seeing what that character sees and hearing what the character hears. Sometimes, readers are even privy to what the POV character thinks.

James Campbell's *The Final Frontiersman* tells the entire story, the saga of a trapper who's one of the last men to support his family alone in Alaska's remote northern interior, from the viewpoint of the trapper. Heimo Korth is out duck hunting one day when:

> A half-mile from the cabin, he heard a sound like a locomotive—the ice rending, struggling to free itself. The sound frightened him, and he ran, nearly sprinting through the melting, foot-deep snow. One hundred feet from the river, he could see water pouring over the bank: flood. By the time he reached the cabin, the water was already up to the front door. What to do first? Don't panic, he reminded himself. Don't panic now.

Exciting stuff. Heimo has a big problem on his hands, and we're right there with him, seeing what he sees and—furthermore—knowing what he thinks.

Heimo is not, however, the narrator. Campbell uses Heimo Korth as the vehicle that carries readers through the story, but the author drives the narrative train, never giving up the throttle for so much as a minute.

Heimo *is*, however, the protagonist. It's the gritty trapper who engages the complication, passes through a series of challenges, experiences a point of insight, and ultimately resolves the story's dramatic tension. Like Heimo, the POV character often is the protagonist. But not always. The best-known example from fiction may be Nick Carraway, the POV character in F. Scott Fitzgerald's *The Great Gatsby*. Nick lives in a cottage next to Jay Gatsby's mansion, a prime position for observing Gatsby, discovering his mysterious past, and witnessing his eventual downfall. But it's Gatsby's story, not Nick's.

Writers may shift point of view through multiple characters. Michael D'Orso's *Eagle Blue* followed the Fort Yukon high school basketball team on its quest for the Alaska state championship. The first chapter introduced the coach. The next chapter focused on one of the players. Chapter 3 was a close look at a former player who typifies adult villagers. The opening chapter titles—"Dave," "Matt," and "Paul"—signaled the shifts through POV characters.

A few point-of-view changes are fine, but don't make readers dizzy by spinning through a dozen viewpoints. In a magazine piece or a podcast, you're wise to focus on no more than two or three principal characters, with just a few supporting characters. A book can support a few more, but even Akira Kurosawa's *Rashomon*, the perennial example of manipulating point of view in film, used only four points of view to spin the same tale from different perspectives.

The use of POV characters is one of modern narrative nonfiction's great strengths. Years ago, long before he hit it big with books such as *Homicide* and

The Corner, David Simon, then a police reporter for the *Baltimore Sun*, argued for abandoning the detached point of view that typifies daily journalism. "Isn't it more likely," he asked, "that a more precious perspective is gained when a reporter understands his subjects enough to tell a story from their points of view? To put a reader in the shoes of a defense attorney, a judge, a jail guard, a police informant, a killer—that's storytelling as Damon Runyon and Herbert Bayard Swope knew it." And, as it turned out, David Simon knew it. His mastery of an intimate view of the world from the POV of his principal characters is the heart of his success with TV series such as *The Wire*, *Treme*, and *The Deuce*. To capture that intimate POV requires sensitive reporting, the kind that attracted Chip Scanlan's attention when he interviewed Kelley Benham French about "The Long Road Home," the powerful *USA Today* story she coauthored with Deborah Barfield Berry. On the four hundredth anniversary of the beginnings of American slavery, French and Berry accompanied Wanda Tucker as she traveled to Africa in search of her roots. In a piece for *Nieman Storyboard*, Scanlan cited this line from the story:

> She boarded the shuttle bus and plopped on a seat, nervously tapping her knee with her left hand, At first she brushed away tears, then ignored them. It was hard to breathe.

Scanlan then asked, "The point-of-view is totally Wanda Tucker's. What kind of reporting made it possible to support it?"

"We asked her," French said. "It's so simple to ask people what they're feeling."

When they weren't able to ask about what was going on in Wanda Tucker's head at a specific moment, French and Berry turned to another reporting tactic. Jarrad Henderson, the photographer who covered the story, would show Tucker video of herself moving through a scene. "Then," French said, "he asked her to talk him through what she saw and felt and thought. Jarrad is a brilliant interviewer, and that move was one I'll be sure to use in the future. He tells me it's called 'photo/video elicitation.' Whatever, it was masterful."

FIRST PERSON

Nonfiction writers also have the option of making themselves the POV characters, taking readers along to experience the narrative through their own eyes. Ted Conover, the ultimate participant observer, throws himself into a role and, like Hunter Thompson before him, writes his way through the entire narrative in first person. Thompson rode with the Hell's Angels. Conover walked the cell blocks as a Sing Sing prison guard.

Other writers jump in and out of first person, depending on the need of the moment. Tracy Kidder wrote the vast majority of *Mountains beyond Mountains* in third person. But at one point he wanted to demonstrate his protagonist's physical fitness. Paul Farmer, the humanitarian doctor at the center of the book, regularly trekked into the Haitian hill country to reach patients. On one expedition, Kidder went along. He made his point by contrasting his physical reaction with Farmer's:

> We went on, deeper and deeper into the mountains, Farmer leading the way. We chatted front to back. I was drenched in sweat. I couldn't see even signs of perspiration on his neck.

The kind of first person Ted Conover and Tracy Kidder produce is quite unlike the self-absorbed first-person point of view that colored so much of the New Journalism, the breakthrough style that transformed American nonfiction in the 1960s and 1970s. New Journalists such as Hunter Thompson and Tom Wolfe brought extremely personal points of view to their material, jazzed up their writing with wild, idiosyncratic style, and often seemed to be writing more about themselves than their subjects. But even though *Newjack*, Conover's Sing Sing book, told Conover's own story, his viewpoint looked outward, at the events happening around him. His unobtrusive prose lacked the look-at-me pyrotechnics of the New Journalism. And unlike, say, Hunter Thompson's *Fear and Loathing in Las Vegas*, it told the story without the author *becoming* the story.

Modern narrative journalism, says David Simon, "can in no way be confused with the 'New Journalism' of an earlier era—a style of writing in which the thoughts and philosophies, visions and verbiage of the writer become as important to the story as the objective reality. Narrative journalism is quite the opposite: It requires a good writer's style and hyperbole to be sure, but at the same time it argues against the writer's unencumbered vision. It is, instead, the vision of those living the reality of the event."

Sometimes, of course, that's the writers themselves. They tell the story in what literary agent Peter Rubie calls "the memoir voice," telling you what they see, hear, smell, and feel while moving along the action line. The approach seems to deliver a special kind of intimacy. It certainly doesn't hurt sales by the likes of Ted Conover, Mary Roach, and Michael Pollan.

SECOND PERSON

You (ha!) won't find much second person in narrative nonfiction. So you'll probably want to save direct address (ha! again) for your work on self-help articles or cookbooks. And because using "you" or suggesting that your readers take a course of action is especially appropriate to guidebooks and instructional manuals, I'll keep using it here.

Second person does occasionally show up in narrative, usually as a stylistic device intended to put readers in a scene. In that context, it's more of a literary device than actual direct address. Jim Harrison sometimes used the technique to good effect. His memoir *Off to the Side* was mostly in first person, as you would expect. He wrote, for example, that he visited Arizona's Cabeza Prieta Wildlife Refuge, "where I've wandered as much as three days without seeing a single other human." Then he moved south to the Seri Coast of Mexico, and advised readers to:

> Make your way slowly from Desemboque to Bahia Kino. . . . Camp on an empty beach or in the desert. Climb a mountain and stare at the Isla Tiburon. Before going read about the ethnobotany of the area, also John Steinbeck's *Sea of Cortez*.

Michael Paterniti, a National Magazine Award winner, used a similar tactic in "The Long Fall of One-Eleven Heavy," his dramatic *Esquire* magazine story on the 1998 crash of Swissair 111 just off the coast of Nova Scotia. For Paterniti, second person was a way to draw readers into the points of view of both victims and survivors. He offered snapshots of their lives just before the plane's ill-fated flight. One of the victims went sailing and stood on deck, feeling the wind on his face. A young woman said good-bye to her boyfriend. Parents parted from their children. And so it went:

> All of these people, it was as if they were all turning to gold, all marked with an invisible X on their foreheads, as of course we are, too, the place and time yet to be determined. Yes, we are burning down; time is disintegrating. There were 229 people who owned cars and houses, slept in beds, had bought clothes and gifts for this trip, some with price tags still on them—and then they were gone.
>
> Do you remember the last time you felt the wind? Or touched your lips to the head of your child? Can you remember the words she said as she last went, a ticket in hand?

THIRD PERSON

Homer described the fall of Troy in third person, and most contemporary nonfiction storytellers follow his lead. When Truman Capote turned his talents with fiction to the real world, laying the groundwork for the explosion of nonfiction narrative that followed, he quite naturally brought the third-person point of view with him. As Capote demonstrated with In Cold Blood, third person offers so many possibilities and advantages that it serves as the nonfiction storyteller's default point of view.

For one thing, first person limits you to your own perspective. You can't slip into another POV character's mind or voice unless you filter his comments through your own experience. A character might tell you what he was thinking at a critical moment, for example, and you can then report the conversation. And, if you want to relate the POV character's experience directly, you can temporarily abandon first person. But your only real refuge is a third-person account that tells the tale from the POV character's perspective.

And why not? Third person offers an incredibly rich vista for viewing an unfolding story. In third person you can turn yourself into a movie camera, using vivid detail to frame external images of scenes and characters. Or you can violate the laws of nature by peeking inside the heads of characters. You can rise high above a scene to report what's going on at the same moment in distant places. You can even claim the prerogative of seeing into the past and future with you-are-there immediacy. Just like Atul Gawande.

Philip Gerard calls the first option—the movie-camera approach—the "dramatic point of view." Because it sticks to an external reality that can be verified by independent observers, it's the most objective and journalistic of third-person viewpoints. Narratives with the dramatic point of view often are structured as a series of relatively pure scenes, divided typographically and—other than brief bits of necessary background—unsullied by digressions. Readers experience the story as any onlooker would, although the writer manipulates the scenic construction to zero in on key moments. It's reality without boredom, pivotal places and times without the often-tedious daily life that connects them. Here's a typical passage from "Mrs. Kelly's Monster," Jon Franklin's Pulitzer Prize–winning narrative for the Baltimore Evening Sun:

> Now, at 7:15 a.m. in operating room eleven, a technician checks the brain-surgery microscope and the circulating nurse lays out bandages and instruments. Mrs. Kelly lies still on a stainless-steel table.

The second option—the third-person limited point of view—gives you more freedom. You mainly report external reality, and you report only the world visible to your POV character. But you also have the right to go inside your characters heads, to convey what they think as that world unfolds around them. Here's a passage from Tom Hallman's "A Life Lost . . . and Found," the story of Gary Wall's efforts to recover from a serious brain injury:

He locked his apartment and walked past his car. Although he'd learned how to drive again, Gary rode the train to work. While other passengers read the newspaper or thumbed through a paperback, he studied his date book.

Gary was worried about the napkins the supplier was supposed to store in a cupboard in the Blue Cross lunchroom. They had started turning up under the sink, and he kept forgetting where they were stored.

But the reach of third person doesn't stop there. Turn megalomaniac if you want. Give yourself the power to see everything, everywhere, anytime you choose. Slip into the ultimate third-person option—third-person omniscient. From this lofty perch, you can gaze down at the whole of creation, reporting on what's happening at any given moment in Sioux City, San Francisco, and Sao Paulo. If you want, jump back a couple of centuries and bring in a bit of background. Speculate about what's likely to happen in the next decade. So long as you take the time to investigate it and accurately report what you find, you're free to include anything that advances the story.

Erik Larson cast *The Devil in the White City* entirely in third person. But he declared himself omniscient from the get-go. He began his yarn on April 14, 1912, with his principal POV character, Daniel Burnham. The famed architect is aboard the *Olympic*, a luxury liner bound for Europe. On impulse, he decides to send a wireless message to Frank Millet, one of his closest allies in the Herculean effort to build the White City, the site of the 1893 Chicago World's Fair.

Burnham signaled for a steward. A middle-aged man in knife-edge whites took his message up three decks to the Marconi room adjacent to the officer's promenade. He returned a few moments later, the message still in his hand, and told Burnham the operator had refused to accept it.

Footsore and irritable, Burnham demanded that the steward return to the wireless room for an explanation.

As Larson very well knows—he's omniscient, after all—Millet is aboard the *Olympic*'s sister ship. And, on the *Titanic*, April 14, 1912, was the proverbial night to remember.

But, for Larson, the first-class dining room on the *Olympic* is merely a convenient and dramatic starting point. He quickly leaps back to the world's fair itself. He mentions the serial killer who stalked young women not far from the White City and who will provide the book's parallel narrative line. Then he

leaps across the Atlantic and back even further in time, to 1889, when Alexandre Gustave Eiffel made his own mark on history:

> In Paris, on the Champ de Mars, France opened the Exposition Universelle,
> a world's fair so big and glamorous and so exotic that visitors came away
> believing no exposition could surpass it. At the heart of the exposition
> stood a tower of iron that rose one thousand feet into the sky, higher by far
> than any man-made structure on earth.

Then Larson slips into his main narrative line as Burnham eagerly waits to
hear whether New York or Chicago will serve as the site for the next world's
fair. He zooms into Burnham and Root, his protagonist's Chicago office, then
rises high above the industrial-age city to describe its collective grittiness:

> Burnham waited. His office faced south, as did Root's, to satisfy their
> craving for natural light, a universal hunger throughout Chicago, where
> gas jets, still the primary source of artificial illumination, did little to
> pierce the city's perpetual coal-smoke dusk.

Then it's another great leap across time and space, to the protagonist's beginnings:

> Daniel Hudson Burnham was born in Henderson, New York, on Sep-
> tember 4, 1846, into a family devoted to Swedenborgian principles of
> obedience, self-subordination, and public service. In 1855, when he was
> nine, his family moved to Chicago.

Then we're back in Chicago, not far from Burnham's office:

> Outside the Tribune building there was silence. The crowd needed a few
> moments to process the news. A man in a long beard was one of the first
> to react. He had sworn not to shave until Chicago got the fair. Now he
> climbed the steps of the adjacent Union Trust Company Bank. On the top
> step he let out a shriek that one witness likened to the scream of a rocket.

We complete this whirlwind tour by dropping back four years, where we
pick up the track of Larson's other principal POV character, the fiendish killer
who contributes the Satanic side of the White City:

> One morning in August 1886, as heat rose from the streets with the
> intensity of a child's fever, a man calling himself H. H. Holmes walked
> into one of Chicago's train stations. The air was stale and still, suffused

with the scent of rotten peaches, horse excrement, and partially combusted Illinois anthracite.

The remarkable thing about all this zipping and zooming across decades and oceans is that we accept it as not only normal, but also great storytelling. *The Devil in the White City* zipped right onto the *New York Times* nonfiction best-seller list and zoomed right to the top.

STANCE

Several years back a fuel tanker on the freeway east of downtown Portland hit a car and burst into furious flames. Smoke boiled into the sky, a dark column visible from my downtown perch in the *Oregonian*'s newsroom. The next morning's newspaper described the smoke rising into the midsummer sky and "obscuring Mount Hood."

The reporter who produced the truck-crash story simply assumed that everybody who saw the smoke viewed it from the same direction. Yes, the dark column obscured Mount Hood if you saw it from the expensive West Hills homes looming over downtown. But newspaper readers east of the crash site saw the smoke obscuring not Mount Hood, but the West Hills. To those readers, the news story's careless confusion over stance may have hinted at bias. In Portland, the West Hills symbolize the city's liberal power elite. Working-class conservatives occupy much of the far east side, and some of those no doubt read the "obscuring Mount Hood" reference and snorted about West Hills snobs, incapable of seeing the world from any angle but their own.

Stance is simply the place you position your camera and the direction you point it, but it reveals worlds about your approach to a subject. The essayist Richard Rodriguez pointed out that "the West" was only west to European Americans on the East Coast. To a Mexican, "the West" was El Norte. To the Chinese, it was "the East."

Bias aside, you ordinarily pick a stance to give readers the best angle on the unfolding story. "Each story can be told from many points of view," said Don Murray, the dean of American newspaper writing coaches. "It is the writer's task to choose the point of view that will help the reader see the subject."

Often stance is simply the position of the POV character. Remember Stu Tomlinson's breaking-news tale about the cop who rescued the woman from the burning car? It began this way:

The pickup blew by, pushing eighty.
Jason McGowan, a Portland police reserve officer whose patrol car

was stopped at Southeast Division and Southeast 142nd Avenue, saw it swerving in and out of traffic.

So Stu's stance—his camera position—is inside the patrol car with McGowan, watching as the pickup crosses McGowan's field of view. But that stance won't work for all the action that follows, and Stu moves his camera several times before he ends the yarn. The best view of the crash that immediately follows his opening is from across the street; so Stu moves his camera there:

> Karen Webb, a Providence Health Systems customer-service rep, was lined up in the drive-through at a Carl's Jr. She watched in horror as a pickup smashed into a Dodge headed for the 7-Eleven across the street. The car and pickup rocketed across the road, smashing through signs and roadside shrubs.

McGowan drove across the intersection, jumped out of his car, and chased the pickup driver, who was by then fleeing on foot. Stu placed his camera so that it could capture this phase of the story from some distance, making all the action visible.

> McGowan ran after him, but Fortner, slowed by injuries suffered in the crash, sank to the ground. McGowan stood over him.

And so it goes, stance shifting to follow the action. Stu moves the camera in close and points it through the window of the wrecked car, showing how the impact pushed the front seat back, trapping the driver. He steps back and rotates the camera to show two more officers arriving at the scene. He sets up the climax by shifting to the firefighters who finally free the victim. And the tale ends with the camera positioned a few feet from the victim's hospital bed. We see her, perhaps propped up against her pillows, as she stares straight into the camera and thanks Officer McGowan for saving her life.

Usually, choosing stance isn't rocket science. The important thing is that you do *choose*. Nonfiction writers unaccustomed to narrative often forget all about stance, and their stories unfold from a bewildering onslaught of directions. To immerse readers in a story, you want them unconsciously secure about their various positions for viewing it. The point is to let them see the action *as though they were there themselves*. That means they need a coherent visual frame, creating a stage for continuous action. You want to avoid what videographers call "jump cuts," sudden breaks in the unfolding narrative that jar viewers by butting inconsistent bits of action together.

Tom Hallman and I spent some time on stance as we polished the first scene in "The Boy behind the Mask." The story opened with Sam Lightner sitting on a living-room sofa, the family cat sitting in his lap, and his siblings playing cards on the floor in front of him. The camera was pointed directly at Sam, but from a position far enough away to include his younger brother and sister in the frame.

Then Sam rose and walked toward the kitchen. Tom's camera slowly rotated as it followed Sam's progress across the room. The boy paused in the kitchen doorway, standing in the shadows and looking at his mom as she washed the dinner vegetables. They exchanged a few words; then Sam stepped into the lighted kitchen, passed behind his mother, and headed up a flight of stairs. Tom's description followed along in the style of a handheld movie camera.

Tom had witnessed the scene, and I hadn't. So, I asked, "What can you see when you look into the kitchen from the living room?" Tom described the arched doorway. He mentioned the kitchen table. I quizzed him about what hung on the walls, the mother's appearance, and the veggies. The scene assumed a more detailed, coherent shape. Not all the details made it into the final narrative, but those that did made sense. As a reader you could imagine yourself there, watching a quiet domestic scene unfold.

> He threads his way toward the kitchen, where his mother bends over the sink, washing vegetables. . . . He stops in the door frame leading to the kitchen and melts into the late-afternoon shadows. He watches his mother as she runs water over lettuce. The boy clears his throat and says he's not hungry.

The conversation about stance also made both Tom and I realize that the view of Sam as he stepped into the bright kitchen was the perfect opportunity to describe the boy's mask, the vascular deformity that powered the story's psychological complication.

> The boy slips behind his mother and steps into a pool of light.
> A huge mass of flesh balloons out from the left side of his face. His left ear, purple and misshapen, bulges from the side of his head. His chin juts forward. The main body of tissue, laced with blue veins, swells in a dome that runs from sideburn level to chin. The mass draws his left eye into a slit, warps his mouth into a small, inverted half moon. It looks as though someone has slapped three pounds of wet clay onto his face, where it clings, burying the boy inside.

To fully experience the power of that sight, you have to *be* there, seeing Sam for the first time. If your stance is clear, the scene pops into vivid life, producing an emotional charge that can power you through the twenty thousand words that follow.

DISTANCE

Once you've chosen POV characters, decided on first or third person, and selected a stance, you have yet another point-of-view decision to make. How close are you going to get to your story?

Remember Atul Gawande's opening in Elizabeth Rourke's bedroom and the way he then moved inside her head to show us the pain of childbirth? That put us extremely close to the POV character's human experience. But, as you step back from the action, you reveal more context, encompassing more abstract elements of reality that involve all of us. Gawande, you will recall, also made quite abstract generalizations about the process of human birth.

Storytelling at different distances requires two different kinds of narrative, each of them essentially a different language. When the distance is great, when you step way back from the action, you write in *summary narrative*. When you shrink the distance, you shift into *scenic narrative*.

The distinction is absolutely critical in any medium. If you don't get it, you can't write narrative.

Here's an example, this one taken from a thrilling tale of death and survival. It's from a newspaper story, but the same point-of-view techniques would apply to radio, magazine, podcast, or book narratives. For that matter, this narrative would also make a dandy film. But identical POV issues come up in almost any kind of story you can imagine.

Several years ago an unexpected downpour drenched the headwaters of the Illinois, an untamed river winding out of the mountains in southwestern Oregon. The Illinois is a whitewater challenge in the best of conditions, which is why it attracts rafters and kayakers from across the country. But the storm whipped the Illinois into a killer that trapped several rafting parties in its canyon. The reporters who worked with me on the story focused on the members of the McDougal party, who managed the first part of their expedition without any major problems:

> After navigating the first ten miles and splashing through thirty-four
> rapids, McDougal's group pulled over at Klondike Creek to set up camp.

But McDougal and his fellow adventurers still faced a fearsome monster known as the Green Wall, a roaring, surging rapid that twisted between the mossy cliff faces that inspired its name. J. Todd Foster and Jonathan Brinkman, who told the tale in the *Oregonian*, dropped into scenic narrative to describe that terrible encounter:

> McDougal and Byars pushed off. They negotiated the fifteen-foot behemoth but were swinging sideways when they hit the next set of waves. The raft capsized, catapulting Byars into the water. McDougal stayed in his seat, virtually upside down. As the raft rose with the next wave, McDougal yanked hard on an oar and righted his boat, a miraculous maneuver.

Both passages describe action. But a fundamental quality divides them, a distinction that accomplished narrative writers never let stray far from consciousness.

Think about the first example and visualize what happened at each of those thirty-four rapids. The men frantically paddling. The rafts plunging up and down huge standing waves. Hissing current, shouts, and sudden alarm as jagged black rocks loom up out of the swirling foam. But Todd and Jonathan chose to *summarize* all that happened over all that time and all those miles in a single sentence. Godlike historians with an omniscient point of view, they told the story as it might have been viewed from far above the canyon, collapsing time and space in a dispassionate account devoid of drama. Because it's an abstract report of what happened, it takes what is essentially a journalistic point of view that's conveyed in a style we know as *summary narrative* or, appropriately, as *historical narrative*.

But when the McDougal party reached the Green Wall, it was showtime. The writers swooped in close, taking readers inside the scene instead of viewing it from far above. Readers viewed the unfolding action as though they were hovering above it, just a few feet away, which is why we refer to this useful and effective storytelling perspective as the hanging-balloon point of view. When they assume it, good storytellers shift into *scenic narrative*, a form that—for obvious reasons—some analysts also call *dramatic narrative*.

At its most fundamental level, the difference between summary and scenic narrative lies in the relative positions of the two forms on the ladder of abstraction (see figure 5). The ladder, one of the most useful concepts for any writer, rises from the most concrete level of any concept through an increasingly abstract series of categories. Think of McDougal, at the instant he dug his oar into the foaming water at the Green Wall, as standing on the first rung of the ladder. On the next rung you might find all four members of his party. On the rung above that, the twenty-two river runners in the canyon. Above that, all river rafters and kayakers, perhaps, and above that all outdoor adventurers. The ladder rises and rises, through ever-larger classes. It passes through the class

Everything
All Living Things
All Human Beings
Outdoor Adventurers
River Runners
Illinois River Runners
Illinois River Rafters
McDougal's Party
McDougal

Figure 5. A ladder of abstraction

that contains all human beings, and the class that contains all living things. It eventually reaches its highest point, as do all ladders of abstraction, in the largest class of all—everything there is.

The lowest rungs of the ladder put you in the scene. Hence the notion of scenic narrative. You see it. You hear it. Sometimes, you even smell it. So you can react as a firsthand observer would. You feel the fear as the Green Wall approaches. You share the horror when Byars's body appears. Emotion originates on the ladder's lower rungs.

As you climb the ladder, the classes of things represented reach further across time and space. A sentence or two applied to them necessarily ignores a lot of detail in favor of a shorthand reference to everything in the category. Hence the notion of summary narrative.

You gain comprehensiveness as you climb the ladder, but you lose the ability to form concrete images. With every step higher, fewer attributes place members within the classes represented. Every aspect of McDougal is relevant to his inclusion in the class containing only McDougal, and if the writer gives you a good description, you can visualize him. But all the rafters on the river have less in common, and you'll have a tougher time forming an image of them. By the time you get up to all outdoor adventurers, the human beings you're talking about are both men and women, tall and short, Black and White, stocky and thin, old and young. Only the vaguest image is possible.

But you've traded specificity for something that also has value. If you can generalize about a larger class, you have knowledge that you can apply in a variety of situations. You might, for example, note that river runners share their genetic attraction to risky behavior with other outdoor adventurers. That might make it possible to predict the behavior of a mountain climber or a sky-diver based on what you know about rafters. So greater *meaning* resides on the ladder's upper rungs.

Reports of the journalistic kind draw mostly on the middle rungs of the ab-straction ladder. The news report of a car crash, for example, will give a fairly abstract description of the wreck and its consequences. It won't rise onto the higher rungs of the ladder to generalize about overall accident rates or trends in auto safety. And, by the same token, it won't descend the ladder to provide a minute-by-minute close-up narrative of the accident. Most news reports, in other words, are not particularly meaningful *or* dramatic.

Once you get in the habit of reporting on the world from the middle rungs of the abstraction ladder, you have a hard time seeing reality in any other way. One of the things that puzzled me most when I started coaching narrative was that journalists, professionals who wrote every day on deadline, often had the toughest time thinking like storytellers.

Why should that be? I knew many of them well, and I can vouch for the fact that they had no trouble spinning yarns around campfires or over beers. When a toddler asked for a bedtime story, I doubt any of them perched on the edge of the bed, picked up the morning's newspaper, and read aloud, in stentorian tones, that "two River City men were killed Wednesday when their car plunged off a Highway 23 embankment and hit a tree, state police said."

"C'mon," the tyke would have wailed. "I said a *story!*"

Stories convey experience. But reports convey information, often great gobs of it. And reports emphasize outcomes. Our hypothetical Highway 23 accident story focuses on the result—the two fatalities—rather than the chains of cause and effect that would produce such a consequence. Nothing wrong with any of that. We need gobs of information to operate in the modern world, and most of the time we don't want to work our way through a narrative to get the main point.

But stories offer rewards beyond raw information, the kind that yield meaning by re-creating life as it's lived. Stories emphasize process, rather than outcomes. So if readers don't need the main point immediately and if a situation offers enough story elements—ingredients such as a protagonist, a complication, and a series of plot points—a narrative might be the better way to go.

To describe the Highway 23 accident scenically, a storyteller might begin not with a summary lead, but with a sequence of specific actions: "A doe trotted out of the woods on the right shoulder, saw the oncoming lights, and bolted across the highway. Mark jerked the wheel to the right. The pickup's tires skidded on the wet pavement."

Storytellers build their tales out of such scenes, the dramatic curtain opening as each scene begins and closing as it ends. Dialogue, which unfolds as characters talk to one another within scenes, is usually more appropriate to the form than the direct quotations typical of news reports. Instead of news values like timeliness and proximity, which reflect broad social concerns, storytellers emphasize dramatic values that concern us as individuals, such as coming of age or coming to terms with our handicaps.

The differences between reports and stories, in other words, are sweeping and profound. No wonder that journalists who've spent their working lives learning one form would have a tough time shifting to the other. And journalists aren't the only writers who've learned to write by crafting reports, rather than by creating stories. Anybody who works in an institutional setting—be it business, law, politics, education, or the military—deals mostly with information. That means reading and writing reports, lots of them. But reports can give you tunnel vision, trapping you on the middle rungs of the abstraction ladder and crippling your ability to tell a good story.

Summary vs. Scenic Narrative

Summary Narrative	Scenic Narrative
Abstract	Concrete
Reaches across Space	Unfolds in One Place
Collapses Time	Seems to Happen in Real Time
Employs Direct Quotations	Employs Dialogue
Organized Topically	Organized Scenically
Omniscient Point of View	Specific Point of View
Deals with Outcomes	Deals with Process
Conveys Information	Reproduces Experience

Most nonfiction narrative writers constantly shift between scenic and sum-mary modes, varying distance with each oscillation. They ignore the writing gurus who harp at them to "show, don't tell," knowing that good writing con-stantly ascends and descends the ladder of abstraction. They show *and* tell.

Note this example from Hal Bernton, a veteran reporter who ventured north on a crab boat long before the Discovery Channel's *Deadliest Catch* acquainted millions of viewers with the terrors of the Bering Sea in February. Hal's as-signment was to explain the economic importance of Oregon's "distant-water fleet," the local fishing boats that roam the Pacific in search of lucrative catches such as Alaska king crab. So soon after he began his story, Hal climbed up the ladder of abstraction to assume a journalistic point of view, telling readers why the fleet mattered:

> Oregon's distant water fleet taps into North America's greatest ocean harvest, a bonanza that each year tempts more vessels north. The fleet employs at least three hundred skippers and crew. They often gross more than triple what they would from fishing year-round off Oregon's coast.

But the statistics told only part of the story. As reality TV has discovered, the Bering Sea in winter challenges human beings like few other places on earth. Daring its ice, wind, and waves to make a hard living on a crab boat demands foolhardy courage, backbreaking work, and a lust for adventure. To capture that part of the story, Hal took his readers aboard an Oregon crab boat called the *Trailblazer*, and adopted a hanging-balloon POV, using scenic narrative to capture the drama all around him:

> Wayne Baker braced himself in the pitching wheelhouse, peering out beyond waves as tall as houses. . . . Winds spiked to sixty mph, licking white plumes of spray from the wave tops. He phoned the galley to summon the crew: One more push for crab.

Good writers rely on the same technique, varying distance by moving up and down the ladder of abstraction, regardless of whether they're producing for newspapers, magazines, books, or for their online equivalents. Here's Susan Orlean, reporting on a taxidermy convention for the *New Yorker*, zooming in close and then stepping back as she shifts from scenic to summary narrative:

> In the Crown Plaza lobby, across from the concierge desk, a grooming area had been set up. The taxidermists were bent over their animals, holding flashlights to check problem areas like tear ducts and nostrils. . . . People

milled around, greeting fellow taxidermists they hadn't seen since the last world championships . . . and talking shop. . . .

That there is a taxidermy championship at all is something of an astonishment, not only to the people of the world who have no use for a Dan-D-Noser and Soft Touch Duck Degreaser, but also to taxidermists themselves. For a long time, taxidermists kept their own council. . . .

For the next several decades, taxidermy existed in the margins—a few practitioners here and there, mostly self-taught, and known only by word of mouth.

The level of abstraction isn't the only thing that distinguishes summary from scenic narrative. Note some of the other differences in the following examples, taken from my former newspaper's coverage of massive floods that inundated Oregon. The first passage, in summary narrative, came from the opening of the main news story:

> Even people who stayed high and dry will pay the price of lost sales, work time, and opportunities. "In some ways we all lose," said Bill Conerly, an economist with First Interstate Bank in Portland.
>
> Already it is clear that damage to property is as broad and deep as the cresting river system. Throughout the region, hundreds of roads and thousands of homes, farms, and businesses were destroyed or are in need of significant repairs.
>
> Government will pick up the tab for streets, highways, and bridges. But thousands of residents may be forced to dip into savings. Only 11,600 Oregonians and 17,400 Washingtonians insure their homes and businesses against floods.

The passage provides plenty of meaning. It's written as though the reporter who produced it hovered twenty thousand feet above the Pacific Northwest, able to see everything that happened across the entire region over the course of a week. From that omniscient viewpoint, it summarizes the storm's effects on thousands of structures. It includes a direct quotation, which was wrenched out of the scene in which it was originally uttered and carried, via the reporter's notebook, to this lofty rung on the ladder of abstraction.

But the summary narrative lacks the specificity readers would need to comprehend the event in their guts. To provide that, a team of narrative writers followed the natural history of the flood as it moved down the Willamette River, tracing the deluge from its origins in a mountain lake to its confluence with the

Columbia.[1] At the Willamette's mouth Tom Hallman found a tugboat captain willing to take him out to where the flood waters poured into the bigger river. What Tom produced was classic scenic narrative:

> Capt. Chris Satalich flips switches, and twin engines on the Lassen, a seventy-foot-long Shaver Transportation Co. tugboat, roar to life. As Satalich checks his gauges, the wheelhouse vibrates.
>
> Satisfied, he nudges the throttles, and the tug moves out of the harbor with the grace of a dancer.
>
> "I've never seen the river like this," he says.
>
> He peers out the wheelhouse windows, thirty-five feet above the water.
>
> "Never," he says.

No statistics. No generalizations. Just the captain standing in his wheelhouse, one man in a scene. And readers are right there with him, immersed not in information, but in experience. They may not know how many cubic feet of water the flood produced, or how many millions of dollars in damage it caused. But they do know something of what it was like to live it.

4

Voice and Style

Voice brings the authors into our world.
—Norman Sims

Mary Roach writes about corpses, cannibalism, and death, which sometimes tests even my well-developed sense of the macabre. During one of my first encounters with her work, the audiobook version of *Stiff* turned to a chapter on how human bodies decay. The subject got so grisly that I almost paused the audio and gave the book up for good. But I talked myself out of it. Mary's just too much fun to abandon.

This is a writer, after all, who described tyrannosaurs as "standing erect as socialites" and referred to the Donner Party cannibals as "resorting to the food that knows no cookbook." In *Spook*, her exploration of the afterlife, she recalled "the raising of Lazarus— depicted in my mother's Bible as a sort of Boris Karloff knockoff, wrapped in mummy's rags and rising stiffly from the waist."

I'd follow Mary anywhere. In "White Dreams," a column that appeared in the online magazine *Salon*, she took me to Antarctica, where she informed me that the folks who work there:

> develop an eye for whites. One day last year, while skidooing the two miles from McMurdo Base to his classroom out on the Ross Ice Shelf, U.S. Antarctic Program survival instructor Bill McCormick spotted a piece of white Styrofoam on the snow. You have to admit it's impressive, an ocular achievement akin to spotting a Wheaty in your All-Bran.

Mary is as droll and clever in person as she is on the page. And John McPhee is a precise, well-ordered Scotsman, as meticulous in dress and manner as he is in his writing. To the extent that Mary Roach is exuberant, McPhee is buttoned down, modest, unassuming. But he's an excellent lunch companion, a quick-witted conversationalist filled with stories and sharp-eyed observations. He was born in Princeton, graduated from Princeton, and teaches at Princeton; so it's no surprise that he writes in the calm, erudite voice of the best professor you ever had. Open *Coming into the Country*, his classic book on Alaska, to a random page, and you'll come across something like this:

> One morning in the Alaskan autumn, a small, sharp-nosed helicopter, on its way to a rendezvous, flew south from Fairbanks with three passengers. They crossed the fast, silted water of the Tanana River and whirred along over low black spruce land with streams too numerous for names. The ground beneath them began to rise, and they with it, until they were crossing broad bench lands and high hills increasingly jagged in configuration as they stepped up to the Alaska Range.

No puns, no gags, no startling imagery. As usual, McPhee's writing unrolls like a carpet, smoothly moving forward to cover the subject. The lack of ostentation pulls the prose aside to reveal the subject with hard-edged clarity. The helicopter is small and sharp-nosed. The Tanana is fast and silted. The black-spruce tundra has a repetitive, anonymous quality that yields a sense of vast, empty space.

On the page, McPhee's voice is as modest as the man himself. Each sentence performs honest labor, contributing to the calm, orderly progression of the narrative. In keeping with its content, each sentence is a sentence, precise and correct, an elegantly simple expression of grammatically flawless English. McPhee is a man in control, and you feel secure when he guides you into some wilderness or backwater. He's the Gary Cooper you'd want guiding your wagon train.

That's no doubt why I read all three of McPhee's books on geology, a subject that holds barely a magazine article's worth of interest for me. The writer makes the subject, and—for me—McPhee makes geology.

What comes through on the page, of course, is not the writer himself, but the writer's voice. Voice plays a key role in attracting and holding readers, regardless of subject. Sometimes it plays the dominant role. It certainly does for Lewis Lapham, the former editor of *Harper's*. "On first opening a book," he once said, "I listen for the sound of the human voice. By this device I am absolved from reading much of what is published in a given year."[1]

Voice is important in fiction, of course. Novelists from Kurt Vonnegut to

Ian Fleming to David Foster Wallace have distinctive on-page personalities that attract devoted followings. Hemingway's voice is identifiable enough to inspire parody.

But voice is critical to nonfiction, too. If we're committing to a guide who promises us a revealing journey through the real world, we want a leader with authority and expertise. And if we're committing to a lengthy trip, we want something more—a personable companion who's going to bring some humanity to the experience. Mark Kramer, founding director of the Nieman Narrative Program and of the Power of Narrative conference at Boston University, argues that voice is the key ingredient in successful long-form narrative, an appealing presence that's absent from the institutional tone of, say, a wire-service report. Voice is the signature of a single human being, and that makes all the difference. "Voice that admits 'self' can be a great gift to readers," Kramer says. "It allows warmth, concern, compassion, flattery, shared imperfection—all the real stuff that, when it's missing, makes writing brittle and larger than life."

But just what is "voice"? The term can be maddeningly elastic, covering a multitude of techniques. "Voice" is so slippery that when I was a callow reporter I dismissed it entirely, figuring it was another one of those empty abstractions that English-lit professors threw around to flaunt their erudition. Now I know better, but I still find it hard to define "voice" with one quick pass over the keyboard. The best all-encompassing definition I've managed to come up with is that voice is the personality of the writer as it emerges on the page.

INSTITUTIONAL VOICE

By definition, institutional writing discourages voice. Teachers write about "outcome-based instructional modalities." Social psychologists publish reports on "cognitive dissonance and social alienation as predictors of antisocial behavior." Cops, doctors, and urban planners all have their way of talking to colleagues, and all suppress their personal voices when they do.

Journalists are among the biggest offenders. I spent decades working with newspaper writers, and one of my biggest challenges was getting them to relax and be themselves. No wonder, they'd been taught just the opposite. Journalism professors—and I was no exception—begin beating individual identity out of the writing produced by J-school students on the first day of Reporting I. In its place, they substitute a timeworn rulebook to make every reporter sound alike, each the faceless voice of a distant, all-knowing institution.

Naturally, the first entry in that rulebook is an aversion to first person, a prohibition that would immediately disqualify Mary Roach or John McPhee from any journalistic post. That prohibition is weakening, but other formulas still reign without significant opposition. Newspapers are going down to their graves filled with a stuffy institutional tone that strips humanity from content. Journalese drowns individual voice in an institutional swamp of passive voice, stilted vocabulary, indirect syntax, and weak verbs. Cops don't catch crooks breaking into a house. Instead, "Police were summoned by a security device early Tuesday and apprehended two suspects attempting to gain entry to a Westside residence."

Bah. Journalists have to cover the news, and every report can't be a long-form narrative. But that doesn't mean reporters must wring the last drop of humanity out of everything they write. David Simon brought a highly personal voice to the *Baltimore Sun*'s police beat. And the ruse of first-person narrative podcasts illustrates the appeal of a personal take on the news. *Serial* topped podcast charts largely because Sarah Koenig's voice as its narrator and chief investigator gave it an appealing personal touch that lured listeners into joining her journey.

FIRST PERSON AND VOICE

For the most flamboyant of the New Journalists, the story was as much about them as it was about the subject at hand. Hunter Thompson filtered everything he wrote through a Hunter Thompson lens. And Norman Mailer was hard to miss in any piece of Norman Mailer nonfiction. All that ego practically demanded first person.

But first person is not voice, and voice is not first person. Even during the heyday of New Journalism, highly voiced writers such as Gay Talese and Tom Wolfe kept the focus directed outward, trying earnestly to capture their subjects' reality instead of their own reaction to it. Modern narrative writers favor that approach, which is essentially ethnographic. Like an anthropologist, they visit a culture, immerse themselves in it, and then describe it for the folks back home. Unlike an actual ethnographer, however, they avoid academese and let their personal voices come through. Sara Davidson, the endlessly ambidextrous blogger, novelist, screenwriter, and journalist, says, "When I first started writing for magazines, Lillian Ross was my model. . . . She never used the word 'I,' and yet it was so clear there was an orienting consciousness guiding you."[2]

Whether or not you use "I" depends on your mission. It's hard to imagine a personal essay without first person. But Erik Larson didn't need first person for *The Devil in the White City*. Tracy Kidder flips into and out of first person as the need arises, occasionally using himself as a foil that illuminates some aspect of his subject. Ted Conover, who actually was trained as an ethnographer, rode the rails as a hobo for *Rolling Nowhere*, worked as a prison guard for *Newjack*, and snuck across the border with illegal immigrants for *Coyotes*. All are heavy with first person. And all clearly convey Ted Conover's voice. But none is, strictly speaking, *about* Conover. That's by careful design. Conover explains that:

> I write about myself, but I don't want the book to be a book about me. It's a big world out there, and I think that, all things considered, there are more interesting things in it than me. That said, I know that my experiences in some of these strange worlds are what will be bring people into them. That is, it's not easy to get the average reader to go into prison. It's not a pleasant place. And a lot of folks are made uneasy by illegal immigration—they don't want to think about it or don't imagine they can know those people. So I sort of become a tour guide, and I try through my voice to provide an entrée into these worlds, a way in.[3]

PERSONA AND POSITION

The humanity that a clear-cut persona brings to a personal essay is one of the charms of the form. By adopting a persona, the writer adopts a distinctive stance toward the material, bringing an identifiable personality to bear on the subject. It may be, as Phillip Lopate points out in *The Art of the Personal Essay*, "mischievous impudence," à la H. L. Mencken. Or essayists may present themselves as loafers, idlers, retirees, or bystanders with the time and the inclination to observe analytically.

Persona is also an essential element of voice. If you want to bring personality to the page, you raise the question, "What kind of personality?"

Naturally, a persona should be as honest as the reporting that expresses it. Still, it's human to have multiple personas. We're one person when we're chatting with an old buddy over a beer, and we're another when we're getting to know a stranger at a dressy cocktail party. Both may be honest representations of who we are, but we intentionally vary them to suit the occasion. The persona a narrative writer brings to a third-person magazine piece or book ought to suit the occasion, too, and it may vary depending on subject and readership. Tom Wolfe adopts personas that reflect the social circles he describes, from teenage girls to astronauts. But, regardless of the subject, we always hear the voice of Tom Wolfe.

Like Wolfe, most narrative writers develop a consistent voice that readers come to expect, one that emerges as writers mature, relax, and become more comfortable with their literary selves. "Gradually," Tracy Kidder says, "I found a writing voice, the voice of a person who was informed, fair-minded, and always temperate—the voice, not of the person I was, but of the person I wanted to be."[4]

Kidder's voice, to my ear, lies in the mainstream of modern narrative nonfiction. John McPhee, too, comes across as "informed, fair-minded, and always temperate." Mary Roach may be giddy, irreverent, and happily bumbling, but she's an exception to the usual nonfiction voice. Ted Conover, Jon Krakauer, Richard Preston, and Jonathan Harr are much more in the temperate zone.

Position is another matter. If you think of narrative as action unfolding on a stage, position refers to where writers stand as they narrate the unfolding story. Some will position themselves in the very back of the stage, barely visible as the action unfolds before them. Some will stand near the audience, occasionally stepping even closer to comment on something that's just happened. Some will plant themselves right in front of the action, keeping the focus on themselves and their commentary on the action behind them.

A journalist such as David Finkel usually stays in the background, letting the facts speak for themselves. But the facts are so deliberately arranged that Finkel's personal take on their meaning comes through clearly. "The Wiz," one of his *Washington Post Magazine* pieces, focused on a high school girl, with little direct commentary on Finkel's broader subject—the lack of women in science. But the girl, an outstanding science student, clearly served as a microcosm. The problems women scientists face are obvious in this description of the girl's interaction with six male classmates:

> It is a loud discussion with overlapping voices, but Elizabeth is a close listener, and she has heard something that needs correcting, or at least elaboration. She also is a patient listener who doesn't blurt out her thoughts, but waits for an opening to fit into. Now, hearing the other voices drop off, she begins to speak, only to realize immediately that she has miscalculated, that the opening has already closed, that she doesn't stand a chance, that she is on the precipice of another of the moments in which, sooner or later, she will end up awkwardly trailing off into silence without having been heard.

Finkel holds his personal take on what he sees in check and reports on the action unfolding in front of him. He's a feature writer, not a hard-news reporter, so he allows a bit of interpretation when he suggests that what we're witnessing is typical of Elizabeth's larger experience. But the focus is on Elizabeth, and Finkel keeps it there while he stands back and tells us what he sees.

Annie Dillard steps a little more into the foreground in this passage from "Encounters with Chinese Writers," which makes a similar point by generalizing—or is it genderizing?—across several experiences:

> Today the usual tea-serving maids do not seem available; so the woman writer pours the tea. There is always one woman. She may have the second-highest rank in the room, or she may have written the novel most admired all over China. It takes her fifteen minutes to pour tea, and she will do this three or four times during the course of the morning. After she serves, she takes an inconspicuous seat, sometimes on the one little hard chair stuck behind the real chairs.[5]

Dillard steps right into the scene and explains how it illustrates what she's seen all over China. And she lets controlled outrage slip into her observation. "This is not—damn it!—an isolated case. There is *always* one woman! And I'm one writer who is personally offended by that injustice!"

Once Finkel and Dillard position themselves as narrators, they tend to stay put, at least for the duration of any individual narrative. But Norman Maclean, the University of Chicago literature professor who wrote A River Runs through It, demonstrated how agile a narrator can be, stepping behind and in front of the action depending on the immediate goal.

Maclean wrote only one piece of book-length nonfiction, Young Men and Fire. But it was an extraordinarily innovative work with a structure I've never seen duplicated. As a narrator, Maclean began far in the background, letting the action carry the story:

> The C-47 circled the fire several times before dropping the crew. The spotter, Earl Cooley, lay flat on the floor on the left side of the open door, with headphones on so he could talk with the pilot; and the foreman, Wag Dodge, lay on the right side of the door so that he and the spotter could watch the country together and talk without the crew hearing much of what they were saying.

But Maclean kept revisiting his subject, the Mann Gulch fire that decimated a crew of Montana smoke jumpers in 1949. Each time he repeated the basic narrative, he layered on more analysis and interpretation. His position as a narrator moved forward with each iteration of the tale until he shifted into full-bore first person. By the end of the book, after reporting on the three years of research that finally solved the puzzle of where two critical events had taken place, he'd positioned himself well in front of the material:

> Three years and two established locations; it doesn't seem like much, even though we had been following a lot of other trails during those years leading to parts of the story of the Mann Gulch fire—trails of experts on death, especially death by fire, and the many trails of Earl Cooley, who with his partner was the first ever to drop on a forest fire from a parachute and who tapped the calf of the left leg of each of those about to die in Mann Gulch to get them on with their last jump. Later I was to see the sad trail of the once majestic C-47 that had dropped its crew into Mann Gulch when the great bird of the sky circled the airstrip in Missoula and disappeared forever into the blue, sold into slavery to an African company. Stories and stories—a storyteller has all kinds of stories going at one time out of which he hopes he can find one story he can tell at one time.

VOICE AND STYLE

Who can say where voice ends and style begins? Some critics use the terms interchangeably; others use only one or the other. But a difference exists, I think, and the distinction is useful.

Every morning we rise with a personality that's essentially the same as the one we went to bed with. But when we walk to the closet to pick the day's clothes, we make stylistic choices that depend on the occasion. If we're planning yard work, we may grab jeans and a T-shirt. If we're headed to the office, we're well advised to don something more formal.

So it is with writing. If voice is the personality of a writer as it appears on the page, then style is the outermost expression of that personality.

The novelist Darin Strauss taps that distinction when he refers to the "linguistic surface" that coats any piece of writing. The term, he explains, "involves diction, syntax, and metaphorical language," traits that will help a fictional character "talk and think in terms that reflect his desire and his significant history." He cites an example from Sandra Novack's novel *Precious*, whose protagonist is a reporter who spots a small building "hiding like an overlooked misprint between jutting office towers."

A nonfiction narrative has a linguistic surface, too. It will reflect the "self" that emerges when a strong narrator takes command of the narrative, but it also will be consistent with the POV characters who are on stage at any one time. The linguistic surface will change, in other words, while remaining fundamentally the same. Art imitates life in that respect, too. Even though they change clothes to suit the occasion, most of our friends have an overall style that we also recognize.

Part of that style stems from the degree of formality they bring to the spoken word, the real-world equivalent of the "diction" that Darin Strauss mentioned. Do they say "you could try" or "one could endeavor"? Do they "spend money" or "allocate funds"? Do they talk about crooks, criminals, perpetrators, or miscreants?

In the world of narrative writing, an author's level of diction is one of the prime markers of his style. Jon Krakauer writes about earthy subjects with surprising formality, as in this passage from *Into the Wild*:

> Truthful responses to these queries were not likely to be well received by the rangers. McCandless could endeavor to explain that he answered to statutes of a higher order—that as a latter-day adherent of Henry David Thoreau, he took as gospel the essay "On the Duty of Civil Disobedience" and thus considered it his moral responsibility to flout the laws of the state.

In contrast, Mary Roach is constantly on her fourth glass of wine with her girlfriends:

> I don't recall my mood the morning I was born, but I imagine I felt a bit out of sorts. Nothing I looked at was familiar. People were staring at me and making odd sounds and wearing incomprehensible items. Everything seemed too loud, and nothing made the slightest amount of sense.

Hunter Thompson never abandoned his quintessential voice, but he always managed to capture a level of diction appropriate to his characters, as when he landed in Louisville during Derby week and met a buffoon in the airport, an encounter he reported in a famed *Scanlan's Monthly* piece titled "The Kentucky Derby Is Decadent and Depraved":

> In the air-conditioned lounge I met a man from Houston who said his name was something or other—"but just call me Jimbo"—and he was here to get it on. "I'm ready for *anything*, by God! Anything at all. Yeah, what are you drinkin'?" I ordered a Margarita with ice, but he wouldn't hear of it: "Naw, naw . . . what the hell kind of drink is that for Kentucky Derby time? What's wrong with you, boy?" He grinned and winked at the

bartender. "Goddamn, we gotta educate this boy. Get him some good whiskey."

I shrugged. "Okay, a double Old Fitz on ice." Jimbo nodded his approval.

"Look." He tapped me on the arm to make sure I was listening. "I know this Derby crowd. I come here every year, and let me tell you one thing I've learned—this is no town to give people the impression you're some kind of faggot. Not in public, anyway. Shit, they'll roll you in a minute, knock you in the head, and take every cent you have."

I thanked him and fitted a Marlboro in my cigarette holder.

Jimbo sounds just like he is. Hunter Thompson is just what he is. Especially when he responds to the homophobic rant by inserting the most macho of American cigarettes into the most feminine of smoking devices.

Syntax, as Darin Strauss pointed out, shapes the linguistic surface, too. Long introductory phrases and clauses that back into long, complicated sentences immediately flag the institutional voice we call journalese. A quick glance at any issue of the *New York Times* yields a typical example: "Throwing the weight of his office behind legislation that still faces considerable obstacles in Albany, Mr. Paterson said he would leverage the personal relationships he developed over two decades in the State Senate to see the bill voted on—and passed."

A great ear for rhythm, on the other hand, marks the kind of style most of us find much more readable. So important is an ear for the music in the words that I included an entire chapter on the subject in my book *Wordcraft*. There I highlighted Bill Blundell's *Wall Street Journal* features for their lyrical appeal, including this beauty of a syncopated sentence: "Nine miles east, Mount St. Helens rises like a white wall, its shattered summit banked in mist."

METAPHOR AS STYLE

Strauss listed metaphor as the last element in the linguistic surface, and it may be the principal element in the stylistic dimension of voice. I began this chapter by describing Mary Roach's distinctive voice, and every one of my examples involved a metaphor, a simile, or an allusion. Figurative language embroiders the cloak of style.

Sometimes a figure emerges as a pure metaphor, simply describing one thing in terms of another. When Erik Larson introduced a Chicago World's Fair architect in *The Devil in the White City*, he noted that "Hunt was fierce, a frown in a suit."

George Plimpton was an elegant stylist who sometimes turned his attention to subjects as unlikely as professional football. But his sense of literary metaphor remained, as in this scene from *Paper Lion*:

> Some of the defense were already kneeling at the line of scrimmage, their heads turned so that helmeted, silver, with the cages protruding, they were made to seem animal and impersonal—wildlife of some large species disturbed at a water hole—watching me come toward them.[6]

Erik Larson's a master of not only pure metaphor, but also of simile, an explicit comparison often introduced with the preposition "like." He noted that the famous landscape architect Frederick Law Olmsted "was not a literary stylist. Sentences wandered through the report like morning glory through pickets of a fence." And he described Minneapolis as "small, somnolent, and full of Swedish and Norwegian farmers as charming as cornstalks."

Similes don't always include "like," however. The key's in the comparison. McPhee described a large, intimidating red-tailed hawk and noted that "his talons could have hooked tuna." He spotted a salamander with coloring "so simple and contrasting that he appeared to be a knickknack from a gift shop."[7]

Metaphor and simile hardly exhaust the figurative possibilities. A real stylist may turn to allusion ("his Alfred Hitchcock physique") or word play (hot dog brands engaged in "grinding competition") or personification. When John McPhee wanted to describe a remote valley for "Travels in Georgia," he wrote that the surrounding terrain "resisted visitors. . . . The north was interrupted by a fifty-five-hundred-foot mountain called Standing Indian. Standing Indian stood in North Carolina, telling Georgia where to stop."[8]

Paula LaRocque once likened such figures of speech to jewels dropped periodically along a path in the woods, luring readers through the writing. That metaphor's apt—you want to space the metaphors out without spreading them so far apart that readers lose sight of those ahead. About one figure for every three paragraphs seems about right.

I started my writing career with a cinder block's sense of metaphor. But I was inspired by an anecdote about Hemingway and Fitzgerald careering through the Spanish countryside in an open car, playing a metaphor game. One would point to a roadside object, and the other had to coin a simile instantly. The penalty for failure was a long pull on a bottle of Spanish red. Developing a sense of metaphor, apparently, could be fun.

I still don't worry much about metaphor in a rough draft, although one occasionally sprouts between my fingers as I write. I'm more likely to find a figure during rewrite, when puzzling over just the right metaphor doesn't interrupt the struggle to get through the first version. As I edit, I stay alert for clichés, which signal opportunity for rooting out hackneyed expressions and replacing them with something fresh.

DEVELOPING VOICE

"Voice," Jon Franklin once said, "is something people worry about only if theirs hasn't changed yet." And it's true that things such as voice and style are the preoccupations of young writers who haven't yet found themselves. As we gain life experience, our personality takes form, in person and on the page.

That said, it's also true that some writers have rich voices and others blend into the chorus. Maybe that's just a reflection of their core personalities, but long experience as a writing coach teaches me that some techniques help writers sing solo.

The best thing any writer can do is to read every piece of writing out loud. When I finish the last line of this chapter draft, I'll go back to the beginning and start reading in a firm, clear voice. I'll hear the false notes, and I'll make dozens of changes. Mostly, I'll cut verbiage and simplify syntax. But I'll add some metaphors, too. And I'll simplify the vocabulary so that it sounds more like me.

But the ultimate secret to letting your voice sound on the page is simply to relax and be yourself. Writing's stressful. Sit down at a keyboard, and unconscious waves of tension ripple through your body. You clench your teeth. You tighten your shoulders. You tap your foot. And the words flowing through your fingers grow rigid and formal, stiffened with the frozen formality of an awkward job interview.

When I'm running a writing workshop, I usually stop the participants halfway through their first drafting exercise. "Time for a tension check," I say, explaining that if their necks, backs, and shoulders are tight, their writing will suffer. They loosen up, go back to work, and the clatter of laptop keys ramps up a notch or two.

That change in pace is important. A relaxed writer is a fast writer, and fast writers sound more like themselves. It only makes sense. Writers who agonize over a rough draft, futzing with every word, will submerge their true selves in nondescript formality. When we speak with the natural rhythms of an at-ease conversation with friends, we reveal who we really are. Writing's not spoken conversation, of course, but the same principle applies. And the beauty of writing is that you can always go back to fine-tune during rewrite.

Relaxed, fast writing is also a lot easier. Plodding through a draft, beset with doubt and plagued by second thoughts, is a mental agony that's fatal to voice. The writers with the most distinctive voices take a different tack, and when they talk about the writing process the word "fun" pops up a lot. Mary Roach says the whole process of narrative is "the weaving of fact and fun." And her advice to would-be narrative writers is "just go with the moment and have fun."[9]

To be honest, "fun" isn't often something I think of when I think of writing. But I do want a little of who I am to come through when I put my thoughts on the screen. So I try to relax, sliding into an easy rhythm that moves ahead quickly and smoothly. The result may not be fun, exactly, but it usually involves a lot less pain.

5

Character

The business of a writer, in the end, is human character, human story.
—Richard Preston

Great narrative rests on the three legs of character, action, and scene, and character comes first because it drives the other two. The personality, values, and desires of a protagonist produce action. And the POV character's wants put her in a particular place, creating scene. "There must be a force which will unify all parts," Lajos Egri said, "a force out of which they will grow as naturally as limbs grow from the body. We think we know what that force is: human character, in all its infinite ramifications and dialectical contradictions." Recent brain research backs up the argument that Egri made nearly eighty years ago. Neuroscientists scanned the brains of subjects as they created stories. "Aristotle proposed 2,300 years ago that plot is the most important aspect of narrative, and that character is secondary," said Stephen Brown, the study's lead author. "Our brain results show that people approach narrative in a strongly character-centered and psychological manner, focused on the mental states of the protagonist of the story."

Think of the great characters from fiction: Mark Twain's spunky Huck Finn. Toni Morrison's determined Sethe. Larry McMurtry's lusty Gus McCrae. The novel rises or falls on the strength of its characters. A work of fiction that has a lasting effect, that somehow changes the way we see the world, does so through the people who live on its pages.

Much nonfiction, in contrast, is filled with ghosts, thin, transparent images that shimmer faintly in the air. They are, to resurrect a quaint nineteenth-century term, mere *shades*, shadows that reveal only the faintest outline of a complete human being.

Pick almost any report from any news source. Chances are it's between six hundred and twelve hundred words long, refers to one or more human beings, and contains a half dozen or so quotations. That's the formula. But those few quotes are all the humanity you're likely to find. Disembodied voices. A few formal pronouncements on the subject of the piece.

Consider a little feature from my part of the world, a twelve-hundred-word story on two skaters scheduled to perform with the Portland symphony. It quotes the skaters six times. "I support myself by waitressing," says one. "They said the tempo would be slightly different," says the other. We also know that the woman is thirty-one and the man is twenty-five. That's about it. The description is so minimal that we can't tell whether the writer actually met the two athletes or merely talked to them on the telephone.

Think about the people you know. If you called them and asked six questions—and allowed six twenty-five-word answers—how much of the real human being would that give you? When it comes to character, magazine writers generally do better than hard-news journalists, especially for profile writing. Still, the vast majority of magazine content is largely informational, too. Specialty forms such as food, wine, and travel writing should be rich in character—the worlds they describe certainly are. But all too often they present readers with the same shades that flit around in the typical news story. Ditto with most podcasts and nonfiction books, especially information tomes such as cookbooks, travel guidebooks, and histories. Even topical current-events books, the journalistic quickies in vogue these days, seldom create more than stick-figure characters. That's a shame, because character is the key to reader interest. Ultimately, we define ourselves in terms of others. What we really want to know is what, how, and why human beings *do*. "Story is about an internal struggle, not an external one," says Lisa Cron. "It's about what the protagonist has to learn, to overcome, to deal with *internally* to solve the problem that the plot poses."

THE RISE OF REAL-WORLD CHARACTER

The genius of modern narrative nonfiction is that it replaced the journalist's who, what, where, when, and why with character, plot, scene, chronology, and motive. The most successful narrative puts character in the driver's seat, where it steers the whole enterprise.

Contrast the ghosts that populate most journalism with the flesh-and-blood character Greg Raver-Lampman created for "Charlotte's Millions," a *Virginian-Pilot* profile of a $21.4 million Virginia Lottery winner. The story introduced readers to a forty-nine-year-old registered nurse named Charlotte Jones and brought her to life with the kind of close-up detail that creates true character.

Over the course of a multipart series, we learned that Charlotte was single and passed her time hunting freebies and bargains. She lived with her sister's family in a two-bedroom house filled with giveaway souvenir mugs, visors, and baskets. She drove an old VW Rabbit. She was an inveterate coupon-clipper who lugged her coupons in an accordion file, "craftily cross-indexed."

Her Rabbit carried a bumper sticker that read "Happiness is yelling bingo," and Charlotte played her favorite game at the Improved Order of Redmen, "Tony Tank Tribe No. 149." Her blue plastic bingo bag contained magnetic bingo wands, bingo daubers, and good-luck charms, including a stuffed Garfield cat. She remembered her first bingo game, in grade school, and the prize she won in it—"a metal wastebasket with a pedal that opened the lid."

Charlotte liked to drive to a Delaware truck stop to buy scratch-off lottery tickets, and she always figured that if she won she could take a trip to Alaska. She played pinball at another truck stop, where she and a pal often cruised through the parking lot so they could see the fancy eighteen-wheelers. At her sister's house, the family liked to eat pizza, hot dogs, and one of her sister's specialties, bread topped with cheese and bacon bits and cooked in the toaster oven.

Get the picture?

Human beings are the sum of their values, beliefs, behaviors, and possessions. They're distinctive because they look a certain way, talk a certain way, and walk a certain way. We know them only when we start to tap the larger context that defines them. Once we got a sense of who Charlotte was, we could understand why sudden wealth undid her, ruining the long-standing relationships and routines that shaped her world.

Character not only drives story. It sometimes *becomes* story. Tracy Kidder's *Mountains beyond Mountains* is one long character study of the protagonist, humanitarian doctor Paul Farmer. What drives this man? Kidder asks. Why would someone with a punched ticket to the American good life live in a hell hole like Haiti, serving the poorest of the poor?

Long character studies such as Kidder's unfold like Russian nesting dolls. The narrative line reveals one layer of character and then probes further, discovering successively deeper layers. Pulitzer-winner Gene Weingarten's "The Peekaboo Paradox" turned the technique to "The Great Zucchini," a children's magician. The *Washington Post Magazine* profile began with a relatively simple question: Why do kids—and their parents—find this guy so compelling?

Well, he has some personal history that explains a few things:

> The Great Zucchini's real name is Eric Knaus. . . . Eric is intelligent, but he is almost aggressively reluctant to engage in self-analysis, even about his craft. What he knows is that he intuitively understands preschool kids, because he's had a lot of practice. He worked at Washington area preschools and daycare centers for more than a decade.

And some of his personal traits don't hurt:

> For all his swagger, Eric Knaus is instantly likable and effortlessly charming. He's got a hitch in his smile that says he's not taking himself all that seriously. His hair is moussed into an appealing, spiky mess, like Hobbes's pal, Calvin. He speaks with a gentle, liquid "I" that tends to put children at ease and seems to work with adults, too. And he is just stupendously great with kids. . . . Eric once had a romance with a single mother he met at a party, but he isn't entirely sure he'd do it again. When they broke up, the child was inconsolable.

But there's a darker side to this guy, something lurking behind his childlike innocence. He can't pay his bills. He has a huge backlog of traffic tickets. He doesn't wash his clothes or furnish his apartment, which is oddly barren.

> Eric's misadventures with traffic tickets are symptomatic of larger problems involving his inability to conduct life as a reasonably mature, moderately organized, marginally integrated member of polite society.
>   Take his apartment . . . please.

And so it goes, more and more of the Great Zucchini coming to light as the narrative advances, each revelation driving the reader forward in the search for more. Ultimately, we reach the innermost doll, discovering that a great children's magician is an undisciplined child himself, a compulsive gambler who's teetering on the edge of self-destruction.

DESIRE

For a storyteller, the critical element of character is the *want* that drives the story. Charlotte is a bingo freak obsessed with finding bargains and freebies. The Great Zucchini wants to avoid adult responsibility. Paul Farmer wants the world to see him as humanity's savior.

The bigger the want, the bigger the story. Charlotte's lust for freebies is about right for a newspaper series. Eric Knaus's addiction fits a major magazine piece. Someone who sees himself as humanity's savior deserves a book.

Really big wants carry an element of danger that fuels the story's drama. "A pivotal character must not merely desire something," Lajos Egri says. "He must want it so badly that he will destroy or be destroyed in the effort to attain his goal."

Ahab's pursuit of Moby Dick comes to mind.

A corollary is that the greater the want, the greater the obstacle to satisfying it. Drama is interesting only when opposing forces appear evenly matched. "A protagonist is pretty much defined by the strength of the opposition (or antagonist) he or she faces," Peter Rubie says. "Ideally, whatever is trying to stop your protagonist from reaching her goal is so formidable that all the way through the book we worry who's going to win the battle."

What tips the scales in the best stories is, once again, character. Typically, the protagonist fails during early attempts to satisfy the central want. Time and again, she confronts the antagonist. Time and again, she loses. Finally, the story reaches a crisis, the point at which—in Egri's terms—the protagonist will destroy or be destroyed. Then she achieves the point of insight, a new way of looking at the world that allows her to finally overcome whatever's standing between her and her want. Climax. Falling action. Denouement. End of story.

The more story you have, the more room character has to grow. The longer your text, in other words, the more important character becomes in the mix of character, action, and scene. In fiction, it's axiomatic that character drives novels while events drive short stories. A short news story allows almost no room for character. A one-thousand-word feature opens things up. A multipart series like "Charlotte's Millions" works best when it makes character a key ingredient. A book-length nonfiction narrative can be all about character, as Kidder's *Mountains beyond Mountains* so convincingly demonstrates.

You don't *create* character in nonfiction narrative, of course—you *report* it. And, unlike a novelist, you can't simply put your lead character into the midst of a crisis that changes character and resolves the story. The unfortunate truth is that adult character changes slowly—if at all—in the real world.

That's not an absolute rule, of course. Drunks dry out, and miscreants find Jesus. Traumatic life experiences—a near-fatal disease, a messy divorce, a wilderness survival—can break through even entrenched character traits. Natural life passages involve change by definition. Tom Hallman found "The Boy behind the Mask" at the cusp between childhood and adolescence, a target of opportunity that he recognized and put at the center of his story.

Which makes a key point: Even though a nonfiction storyteller has no control over the content of a protagonist's character, he *does* control his choice of protagonist. Finding someone who's been through a struggle and experienced a point of insight suggests that you're on to something worthwhile. If you're that lucky soul, think about Charlotte Jones and her reaction when the stars were in alignment. Her word for it was "Bingo!"

ROUND AND FLAT CHARACTERS

Fiction theorists point out that the most fully crafted characters are round, rather than flat. Janet Burroway draws the distinction this way: "A flat character is one who has only one distinctive characteristic, exists only to exhibit that characteristic, and is incapable of varying from that characteristic. A round character is many faceted and is capable of change."

Change is the crux. Sam Lightner was a round character because he was capable of changing from the child who wanted only to look like his classmates into a maturing teen who realized he had to cope with the world as it was. "In the best stories," Jon Franklin says, "the odyssey from complication to resolution changes the character profoundly."

Only narrative can describe that kind of transformation. Profound character change unfolds along an action line that moves through a narrative arc. That's one more reason that—if the material justifies it—narrative trumps a straightforward report for engaging reader interest. We can't resist a well-rounded character.

Not that every character who appears in a story need be fully formed. Many simply exist to advance the plot at some point, or to play off more central—and complete—characters. They're flat characters, the kind E. M. Forster said were "immediately recognizable because they have habitual forms of expression or habitual responses to any situation."[1] They may even occupy center stage, especially if the story is heavy on plot, rather than character. Nero Wolfe may have a round body, but he's a flat character. So is Travis McGee, for that matter, or James Bond.

They're still distinctive. Rex Stout's Nero Wolfe never strays from his part as the brilliant, detached recluse. John D. MacDonald's Travis McGee is forever hard-boiled, with a soft center. Ian Fleming's James Bond lives in a predictable, fully formed world that includes a running flirtation with Miss Moneypenny, a distinctive brand of custom cigarettes, and a recurring faculty for smart-ass comments, perfectly timed.

In the hands of a sharp-eyed observer, even supporting characters can produce rich color. John McPhee's characters may be flat, but they're never dull—as in this encounter from "The Pine Barrens":

> I walked through a vestibule that had a dirt floor, stepped up into a kitchen, and went into another room that had several overstuffed chairs in it and a porcelain-topped table, where Fred Brown was seated, eating a pork chop. He was dressed in a white sleeveless shirt, ankle-top shoes, and undershorts. He gave me a cheerful greeting and, without asking why I had come or what I wanted, picked up a pair of khaki trousers that had been tossed onto one of the overstuffed chairs and asked me to sit down. He set the trousers on another chair, and he apologized for being in the middle of his breakfast, explaining that he seldom drank much but the night before he had a few drinks and this had caused his day to start slowly. "I don't know what's the matter with me, but there's got to be something the matter with me, because drink don't agree with me anymore," he said. He had a raw onion in one hand, and while he talked he shaved slices from the onion and ate them between bites of the chop.

We don't need to know much more about Fred Brown. He's a minor character in an explanatory narrative, after all, and we have no need to see his internal conflicts or his growth as he faces life's complications. His limited, flat self serves John McPhee's purposes just fine.

But a full-blown story narrative needs a rounder character at its center. Human foibles, inconsistencies, and a capacity for change make protagonists sympathetic. It's only when characters reflect the reality of human complexity that they evoke universals readers can recognize. Isabel Wilkerson, a Pulitzer-winning reporter and the author of The Warmth of Other Suns and Caste once put it this way: "It's our responsibility to make our readers see the fullness of the characters we've come up with and to see themselves in him or her and to make them care about what happens to him or her."[2]

That was the whole idea with Hallman's "The Boy behind the Mask." On the surface, Sam Lightner was a kid with a facial deformity. But Tom wanted readers to look past that, to the full, round, human character beyond. The title we chose suggested that behind the deformity was a boy with universal adolescent characteristics, someone who could teach any teen about ignoring peer pressure and accepting yourself. After describing Sam's deformity, Hallman continued his description this way:

> But Sam, the boy behind the mask, peers out from the right eye. It is clear, perfectly formed, and a deep, penetrating brown.
>
> You find yourself instantly drawn into that eye, pulled past the deformity and into the world of a completely normal fourteen-year-old. It is a window into the world where Sam lives. You can imagine yourself on the other side of it. You can see yourself in that eye, the child you once were.

You have to deliver on such a promise. But Tom did, bringing Sam's full character to life in his words, choices, and actions. The measure of the writer's success was the reader response that followed. Sam's classmates wrote to say they'd been unable to see beyond the mask, but that they intended to change that. Older readers recalled their own adolescent agonies, and the painful lessons they'd learned about growing up. Some were quite explicit about the way Tom's rounded character helped them see the story's universals. Remember the comment from chapter 1, the one that illustrated the value of narrative as a source of life's lessons? "I've printed out the story," that reader said, "and I'm going to hold onto it for when my eight-year-old daughter readies for high school and the peer pressure that comes with it."

Bingo!

DIRECT AND INDIRECT CHARACTERIZATION

Janet Burroway's *Writing Fiction* divides the techniques of characterization into two broad types. The first, indirect characterization, is straight commentary by the writer, in the manner of Henry James or other nineteenth-century authors who were a heavy presence in their novels. Burroway quotes James's description of Mrs. Touchett in *Portrait of a Lady*. "She had her own way of doing things," James wrote, and "rarely succeeded in giving an impression of softness."

Nonfiction writers who describe their subjects as timid or brash, forceful or passive, are pursuing the same kind of indirect characterization. They also are writing in a style that largely disappeared from the novel decades ago, and that is particularly inappropriate to the just-the-facts-ma'am style of modern nonfiction.

Instead, the best modern fiction *and* nonfiction writers let a character's visible persona speak for itself, the method Burroway calls "direct characterization." They may occasionally comment on character. But mostly they choose to include details that lead readers to certain inevitable conclusions about the character they are describing. For nonfiction writers, that means an additional layer of careful *reporting*. They fill their notebooks with particulars on a character's appearance, material possessions, behavior, and speech and choose those that reveal the most about the person.

PHYSICAL APPEARANCE

To immerse themselves in a story, readers need enough descriptive detail to visualize characters as they move through the narrative arc. One of the reasons newspaper reports are often so uninvolving is that they're filled with faceless talking heads that defy engagement. Ironically, the best news descriptions often show up in fugitive stories:

> The rapist was between twenty-five and thirty years old. He stands about five-feet-nine inches tall, weighs about 165 and has brown hair. He was wearing a brown leather jacket and a black, full-faced motorcycle helmet. His upper front teeth were straight, but the teeth next to them were crowded and set back.

OK. I can close my eyes and picture the guy. Three or four details will usually do the trick. As Tom Wolfe long ago pointed out, we carry a huge gallery of human images around in our heads. All a written description has to do is trigger one of them. Too many specifics, in fact, will disrupt the process. "Detailed descriptions tend to defeat their own purpose," Wolfe said, "because they break up the face rather than create an image. Writers are much more likely to provide no more than a cartoon outline." Here's Gene Weingarten's description of Karen Ermert, the woman whose murder led to the groundbreaking heart transplant he chose as his leadoff story in his book *One Day*.

> Karen was effervescent, with a broad, intelligent face under feathered blond hair. (Her hairdresser once observed wryly that other clients paid extravagantly for what nature had casually dropped on Karen—multiple shades of blond in captivating layers.) She was conventionally attractive, and a slight chipmunky overbite added a dose of adorable.

If readers know something about the context and if you just need to mention a flat character in passing, you can create a pretty good image by triggering just one connection to a stored archetype. Let the reader visualize an interesting character, in an interesting situation, right away, and then launch action that's pregnant with possibilities. Here's Atul Gawande again, beginning his *New Yorker* story on childbirth:

> At five a.m. on a cool Boston morning not long ago, Elizabeth Rourke—thick black-brown hair, pale Irish skin, and forty-one weeks pregnant—reached over and woke her husband, Chris.
> "I'm having contractions," she said.

Gawande's quick-hit description has yet another virtue—it passes so fast that it barely slows the action line. Long expository descriptions take readers out of the unfolding story. So keep that first image terse. You can drop more descriptive details into the action line later.

MOVEMENTS, EXPRESSIONS, AND MANNERISMS

Most of us have some sense that a full-fledged narrative should show the characters in action. Beginning writers often go wrong, as Robie Macauley and George Lanning point out, when they include insignificant actions just to break up background or dialogue. "Many cigarettes have been lighted," they write, "many noses rubbed, many throats cleared in that endeavor."

The point, as always, is that every word must do some work, and every detail must advance the action line and develop character. You never include detail for its own sake.

Unlike rubbed noses and cleared throats, some gestures and mannerisms can reveal dimensions of character hidden by words. Here's Steve Beaven, a former colleague and author of the book *We Will Rise*, as he once described an aging furniture salesman buttering up a young prospect:

> "I'm just looking at everything," she tells Lou. "I have to talk to my boyfriend."
> Lou looks hurt. This is part of his old-man shtick, a crucial element of his sales strategy. "You have a boyfriend, Amy? That leaves me out."

Details such as Lou's hurt look take almost no space; so they fit in even short news features. In my years as writing coach, I made a point of praising them when they appeared, taking note when a reporter mentioned that a portly television show host "smiled and raised his eyebrows" when he admitted that he cheated on his diet. Or when a former Columbia River Gorge boardhead, banished to the workaday world, spoke in a voice that was "warm and dreamy" as she watched windsurfers skim across the water. And when a drug addict finally got her back up during a counseling session, the reporter was savvy enough to put the direct quotation in the context of a gesture: "'I'm tired of being the one who's always wrong,' she said as she crossed her arms."

STATUS INDICATORS

In a material culture, we reveal ourselves by what we consume, and the great popular novelists write books rich in brand-name details. Characters drive Toyotas or Hummers, wear jeans or Armani suits, and reveal their place in the social structure via their houses, furniture, and jewelry. Stephen Maturin is forever rumpled. Archie Goodwin likes an occasional glass of milk. James Bond drives an Aston Martin.

Of all the nonfiction writers, Tom Wolfe makes the biggest fuss about possessions as a key to character, insisting, like Madonna, that we live in a material world. Here he is at the beginning of his career, describing teenage fans at a 1964 Rolling Stones concert:

> Bangs manes bouffant beehives Beatle caps butter faces brush-on lashes decal eyes puffy sweaters French thrust bras failing leather blue jeans stretch pants stretch jeans honeydew bottoms éclair shanks elf boots ballerinas Knight slippers, hundreds of them, these flaming little buds, bobbing and screaming, rocketing around inside the Academy of Music Theater.

You had to be there, I guess. But strip away the excess, and you'll see that Wolfe was on to something. We're social animals, and we evolved—or not— depending on how well we could read our place in the pecking order of our isolated, constantly threatened band of hunter-gatherers. We still spend a shameful amount of time pigeonholing the folks around us. Are they part of our group, or not? Do they outrank us, or do we outrank them? What can we tell about what they think and behave based on what they wear, drive, or paint on their faces?

Wolfe, who after all holds a Yale PhD in American studies, insisted that status symbols were key to understanding contemporary culture. In his famed introduction to *The New Journalism*, he argued that the power of modern narrative nonfiction rested, in part, on "the recording of . . . the entire pattern of behavior and possessions through which people express their position in the world or what they think it is or what they hope it to be."

"The recording of such details is not mere embroidery in prose," he continued. "It lies as close to the center of the power of realism as any other device in literature."

You often can tap the power Wolfe describes with just a detail or three. A reporter for the *Oregonian* perfectly captured a bachelor farmer's empty life by noting that "He hadn't dated in two years. His nightly dinner consisted of a hamburger patty, instant mashed potatoes, and green beans. His best friend was his black Labrador, Cole."[3]

SPEECH

What we say has a lot to do with our character, and dialogue is a narrative tool so important that it deserves its own chapter. But *how* we say something reveals character, too, perhaps even more profoundly than the actual content of our words. Are we insistent, whiny, arrogant, meek, or gruff? Do we speak the king's English or the fractured grammar of the backwoods? Do we betray our origins with the nasal honk of upper Wisconsin or the liquid sound of a Louisiana drawl? Speech itself is a status indicator. We open our mouths, and we instantly plug ourselves into our particular social niche. The way we talk may be the most revealing detail of all.

An unspoken ban on the use of dialect has long crippled characterization in the standard news story. Bland quotations march on and on through the typical report, conveying nothing beyond the modicum of information they contain. No voice. No emotion. No humanity.

The reluctance to present people as they really speak is, I suppose, understandable. If you quote an uneducated hayseed verbatim, you may look like an arrogant city swell. But isn't it also arrogant to substitute your own manner of speaking for someone else's, as though yours were the only English acceptable in polite company? And isn't the rich patois of an authentic American dialect more likely to convey the color of daily life, the variety of our culture, or honest emotion? Consider the forlorn resolve of this prison inmate:

> "This is the hardest thing I've ever had to do in my life, be away from my family," Cliff Rickerd says from an interview at Oregon State Penitentiary. "And I ain't going to do nothing to get took away from home again, once I get out of here."[4]

And thank God nobody on my newspaper's copy desk "fixed" this wonderful quote from John Lee Hooker, the great Detroit bluesman:

> Since I was twelve years old the blues done followed me, and I'll never get out alive.[5]

ANECDOTES

Top nonfiction writers are masters of the anecdote. For good reason. These stories within stories maintain reader interest by salting a larger article with little narrative arcs, each one pulling the audience inexorably forward. They illustrate important points. And anecdotes are especially persuasive evidence for a writer's take on a character. Not to get too existential about it, but ultimately we are what we do.

John McPhee peppers his explanatory narratives with anecdotes, many of them devoted to character. For "Travels in Georgia," his ramble through the countryside with two wildlife biologists, he took pains to portray one of them as a woman completely at home in the natural world. He cinched the case with this tale:

> I once saw her reach into a semi-submerged hollow stump in a man-made lake where she knew a water snake lived, and she had felt around in there, underwater, with her hands on the coils of the snake, trying to figure out which end was front. Standing thigh-deep in the water, she was wearing a two-piece bathing suit. Her appearance did not suggest old Roger Conant on a field trip. She was trim and supple and tan from a life in the open. Her hair, in a ponytail, had fallen across one shoulder, while her hands, down inside the stump, kept moving slowly, gently along the body of the snake. This snake was her friend, she said, and she wanted Sam and me to see him. "Easy there, fellow, it's only Carol. I sure wish I could find your head. Here we go. We're coming to the end. Oh, damn. I've got his tail." There was nothing to do but turn around. She felt her way all four feet to the other end. "How are you, old fellow?" And she lifted her arms up out of the water. In them was something like a piece of television cable moving with great vigor. She held on tight and carried her friend out of the lake and onto the shore.

Tracy Kidder's *Mountains beyond Mountains* proceeds by establishing humanitarian doctor Paul Farmer's personality and then digging deep to find its origins. Kidder portrays the good doctor as an antiauthority free spirit, someone who defies convention by blithely going his own way regardless. He drives the point home with anecdotes like this one, set in the medical clinic Farmer established in Haiti's backcountry:

> patients were supposed to pay user fees, the equivalent of about eighty American cents for a visit. Haitian colleagues of Farmer's had insisted on this. Farmer was the medical director, but he hadn't argued. Instead— this was often his way, I would learn—he had simply subverted the policy. Every patient had to pay the eighty cents, except for women and children, the destitute, and anyone who was seriously ill.

THE PURPOSE OF CHARACTERIZATION

Human beings are infinitely complex, and no sane writing project attempts to explain even one person entirely. *Mountains beyond Mountains* goes on for more than three hundred pages and focuses on character about as thoroughly as any work of modern nonfiction. But Tracy Kidder still can't hope to unveil every facet of the mystery that is Paul Farmer. Nor would he want to. Farmer may be a Boston Red Sox fan or an acrophobe, but that tells us nothing about his humanitarian work unless it reveals something about his faith in underdogs or the bravery it takes for him to travel the precipitous roads leading to his clinic. *The purpose of character is to drive story.* Any detail of appearance, any anecdote or personal possession, no matter how intrinsically interesting, is a distraction if it fails to move the story forward.

Ultimately, every nonfiction writer who successfully probes human character must develop a theory of personality that guides the reporting. When Tom Hallman and I talked as he reported a story, much of the conversation probed possibilities for explaining action through character:

> A slacker barista decides to cut his hair, buy a suit, and join the mainstream workaday world. Interesting. How does a slacker's character differ from a suit's? What kind of changes must this barista negotiate? How will those personality shifts affect his behavior, appearance, and possessions?
> A brain-injured man has to give up his old identity and find a new one. Interesting. What is identity, anyway? How do we craft our sense of self and find our place in the world?
> A disfigured boy must leave childhood and come to terms with himself as an adolescent. Interesting. How do human beings develop their character so that they can come to terms with who they are and move past unattainable ideals?

One point of story, after all, is to teach us the secrets of successful living. Some values guarantee failure. Some habits and viewpoints increase the odds of success. Difficult challenges call for fresh approaches, shifts in perception that sometimes redefine the very meaning of success and failure. Yes, fate can deal consequences beyond our control. Lightning strikes, meteors fall, drunk drivers come out of nowhere. But great storytelling deals with the world we *can* control, if only we can muster the will to crack the code. And the code is written in character.

6

Scene

While the outline is the structural skeleton of the narrative, the flesh and blood that turns that skeleton into a living thing are not chapters . . . but scenes.
—Peter Rubie

You stroll into the theater, find your seat, and settle in. A hush falls over the audience. An actor walks onto the stage and speaks his first line.

The experience dates to the ancient Greeks, and probably to performances in caves and around campfires. We're hardwired to absorb stories by scenes—even our dreams consist of characters moving across a mental stage. Storytelling is not continuous, and never has been. We spin out narrative in a series of episodes. The curtain opens, closes, and opens again.

As the modern era dawned, we incorporated scenes in newer media. The novel, like the play before it, takes its shape from a series of scenes. A radio drama creates a succession of imagined scenes. The movie is almost exclusively scenic. And when the New Journalists turned the techniques of modern fiction to telling true stories, they built their tales from the same basic building block. In the 1970s, Tom Wolfe listed "scene-by-scene construction" as a hallmark of the form.

It still is. Erik Larson used economical and powerful scene-setting to turn what could have been dry history into the vivid storytelling that powered *The Devil in the White City*. Here's a key moment, 2 p.m. on Tuesday, February 24, 1891, the point at which the committee members charged with choosing designs for the Chicago World's Fair strolled into the library of Burnham and Root, the city's leading architectural firm:

The light in the room was sallow, the sun already well into its descent. Wind thumped the windows. In the hearth at the north wall, a fire crackled and hissed, flushing the room with a dry sirocco that caused frozen skin to tingle.

The three details—the light, the wind, the crackling fire—catapult us back through the decades. The sensory context puts us in the room, feeling the mood of the place, waiting for what happens next.

When you set out to craft a nonfiction story, it doesn't hurt to think of yourself as a playwright. You must, after all, create a stage, a place where the story can unfold. Once you have a story space, you can people it with characters. Then, with a snap of your fingers, the characters can breathe, move, act. You launch your plot and complete the storytelling tripod created when you combine character, action, and scene.

But remember: The scene is never an end in itself. In a story, the ultimate point is to reveal character through *action*. The wants and needs of the characters drive the plot forward through a series of scenes, each making larger points essential to the story's overall message. You use each scene to frame the action, gripping your audience in the developing drama. As Paula LaRocque, longtime writing coach at the *Dallas Morning News* put it, "Setting is the gift wrap; story is the gift." Or, as George S. Kaufman, of Broadway musical fame, put it: "You can't hum the scenery."[1]

Erik Larson exhaustively searched diaries, newspapers, and court records not because he wanted to take us sightseeing in the past, but because he wanted to tell a *story*. He included the scene in Daniel Burnham's office because it provided a setting for the genesis of the Chicago World's Fair. And, with the scene established, action inevitably followed. In the Burnham and Root library, the committee members joined some of the country's best-known architects. The new arrivals, fresh from Chicago's wintry streets, filled the room "with the scent of cigars and wet wool." The architects started the show:

> One by one they walked to the front of the room, unrolled their drawings, and displayed them upon the wall. Something had happened among the architects, and it became evident immediately, as though a new force had entered the room. They spoke, Burnham said, "almost in whispers."
>
> Each building was more lovely, more elaborate than the last, and all were immense—fantastic things on a scale never before attempted.

The White City, one of the wonders of its age, was complete in the mind of man. Now all that remained was creating it in fact, a tour de force of construction that an army of workers would complete in less than two years. For Erik

Larson, the fairgrounds then became a scene within a scene, the space he used to tell the story of a fiendish serial killer. The White City had its devil, and Larson had the narrative arc that would drive his book to number one on the *New York Times* best-seller list.

TAPPING THE SCENES WITHIN

Scene-setting takes its power from its ability to put us into a story, to let us ride the narrative arc ourselves. We filter the details the writer provides through our own experiences, which is why great storytelling can coax such strong emotions out of us. The facts are the writer's. But the emotions are ours, as potent as the love, anger, fear, and rage that wash over us when we tangle with reality firsthand. "Images drive the emotions as well as the intellect," says Steven Pinker, who goes on to call images "thumpingly concrete."[2]

As Tom Wolfe pointed out, that's consistent with what we know about brain physiology and the process of memory:

> If students of the brain are correct so far, human memory seems to be made up of sets of meaningful data. . . . These memory sets often combine a complete image and an emotion. The power of a single image in a story or song to evoke a complex feeling is well known. . . . The most gifted writers are those who manipulate the memory sets of the reader in such a rich fashion that they create within the mind of the reader an entire world that resonates with the reader's own real emotions. The events are merely taking place on the page, in print, but the emotions are real. Hence the unique feeling when one is "absorbed" in a certain book, "lost" in it.

"Lost" is the operative word here. David Lean, who created film classics such as *Lawrence of Arabia* and *Doctor Zhivago*, said that his real breakthrough as a director came when he realized his job wasn't to re-create reality, but to immerse viewers in a kind of dream. The novelist and critic John Gardner mined a similar vein when he talked about a storyteller's ability to create a "fictive dream."

The idea of narrative as a dream transformed the way I thought about storytelling in general and scene-setting in particular. The writer's mission, I realized, is not to describe what's out in the world in all its detailed complexity. The mission is to tap what's already in the reader's head by carefully selecting a few details that stimulate existing memories. In *Red Harvest* Dashiell Hammett described "a brown and red room with lots of books in it." That was all I needed to imagine the room and the action Hammett described in it. That was all it took, in other words, to ignite the fictive dream.

The same terse scene-setting works for narrative nonfiction as well. The details must be absolutely accurate, of course, but they need not be exhaustive. All they need do is stimulate readers to fill in the blanks. My former colleague Marty Hughly, sent out to cover a circus parade, established the setting with the thinnest slice of the noisy, busy, complex reality he actually experienced:

> The smell of fresh circus wafted on light winds. Traffic stopped, and shopkeepers, passers-by, and parents with children in tow took to the streets. Big beasts marched in line.

John McPhee tapped the power of metaphor by evoking the unplanned hodgepodge of Anchorage with this single reference to the kind of sprawl most of us know in our hometowns:

> Almost All Americans would recognize Anchorage, because Anchorage is that part of any city where the city has burst its seams and extruded Colonel Sanders.

CHOOSING SCENES

The reporting for even a five-thousand-word magazine article usually produces enough material to produce a dozen or more scenes. But a five-thousand-word narrative needs only three or four. How do you choose?

Like most things in life, it depends. In this case, it depends on the kind of narrative you're writing. In an explanatory narrative, each scene holds some of the larger, more abstract points the writer wants to make about his topic. One of John McPhee's aims for "Travels in Georgia" was to show how development destroyed wildlife habitat. A scene that described a power-shovel operator tearing up a prime wetland was a logical jumping off point for a discussion of how government policies and development pressure made life tough for frogs.

Scene selection gets more complicated in a story narrative. Each scene should unfold along the narrative arc, propelling the action line through the phases of story. You'll want to open a story narrative with a scene suitable for exposition, which in an opening means introducing the protagonist and providing the backstory necessary for understanding the complication. If the first scene doesn't contain the inciting incident, the next scene should. Then a series of scenes will proceed from plot point to plot point, moving upward through the rising-action phase of the story. The crisis will unfold in one of the story's key scenes, as will the climax. A single scene may be enough for falling action and denouement.

Peter Rubie, the literary agent who wrote *Telling the Story*, reminds writers to choose scenes that keep the focus on protagonists and their struggles to overcome the opposition that stands between them and resolution of the complication. A good scene, he says, will:

cause a subsequent scene to occur, creating cause and effect.
be driven by the main character's needs and wants.
explore various ploys by the character to get his own way.
include action that changes a character's position, relative to the end of
the story.

Robert McKee underscores that last point in his advice for screenwriters, noting that each movie scene must change what he calls the protagonist's "value charge." The phrase refers to the degree to which a character is up or down relative to the ultimate goal of resolving the complication. In a survival yarn, the protagonist may fall into icy water, a mishap that sends his value charge plunging. That's worth a scene. When he snares a rabbit and eats it, his value charge climbs, and that's worth a scene, too.

And don't forget Mel McKee's notion that "a story is a war." Conflict lies at the heart of all good storytelling, and it therefore lies at the heart of good scene selection as well. "Is there opposition in the scene?" Peter Rubie asks. "Forward momentum is the overcoming of opposition." If a scene you're considering lacks conflict and emotion, he adds, don't bother with it.

REPORTING FOR SCENE

Novice narrative writers sometimes grasp the notion that scene-setting is essential to the form, but fail to understand that descriptive detail must serve some larger purpose. The young reporter who wrote this unintentional parody of "it was a dark and stormy night," one of the most ridiculed lines in the English language, is a case in point:

There was a slight breeze and the skies were clear in the early hours of Friday, July 13. Through the darkness, the bright moon cast long shadows.
One fell across the life of a twenty-six-year-old North Portland woman that morning.
She was raped.

Maybe the bright moon had something to do with the assault, although the writer never explained what. It's hard to imagine that the slight breeze had anything to do with the story. This was a story about a rape, not a kite. And, as Bill Blundell has pointed out, the main point of description is story progression.

That means details must be meaningful, and it is in the selection of meaningful detail that print and audio storytellers enjoy one of their great advantages over their counterparts in film and photography. Photos show everything, but everything can be a confusing distraction. Not that visual storytellers don't have their own techniques. Great photographers work hard to direct our eyes to significant details with composition and focus. Master filmmakers penetrate the confusion with tricks like the camera pan that lingers on a significant detail, singling it out as the "ominous object" that Hitchcock used to such good effect. When the camera swept over a room and paused on a paperweight, you knew the paperweight would figure in the tale.

But a print writer needn't resort to fancy techniques. Just mention the paperweight and the implication is that it will play a part in the action that follows. Readers expect writers to follow Chekhov's Rule—"One must not put a loaded rifle on the stage if no one is thinking of firing it."[3]

REVEALING DETAILS

Every good narrative has a larger point, and every good narrative writer is constantly primed to spot les petits vrais—"the little truths" of life. Not every detail contributes to scene building, but the best not only create the stage that holds the action, but also help make some larger point.

Lisa Cron, who reviewed the latest brain research and used it to write Wired for Story, notes that there are three main reasons for any sensory detail to be in a story:

1. It's part of a cause-and-effect trajectory that relates to the plot.
2. It gives insight into the character.
3. It's a metaphor.

David Grann met all three tests when he walked into Steve O'Shea's personal space and spotted the evidence that he was dealing with a man crazed by a single-minded pursuit:

> We then headed to his university office, where he had to gather various things for the expedition. It was in an attic-like space, and seemed entirely devoted to what he described as his "lunatic obsession." Pasted to the walls and stacked on tables were pictures, many of which he had sketched himself, of giant squid, colossal squid, broad squid, warty squid, leopard squid. In addition, there were squid toys, squid key chains, squid journals, squid movies, and squid-related newspaper clippings ("Warning! Giant

flying squid attacking vessels off Australia"). On the floor were dozens of glass jars filled with dead squid that had been preserved in alcohol, their eyes and tentacles pressing against the glass.

Tracy Kidder's "Small-Town Cop" was utterly devoted to his job, which was all he'd ever wanted to do, a fact Kidder drove home with this observation:

> In crayon on the wall inside his bedroom closet on Forbes Avenue, Tommy had written,
>
>> Tom O'Connor September 29, 1972
>> I want to be a policeman.
>> I am in the sixth grade.

COLLECTIVE DETAILS

Images from the bottom of the abstraction ladder have the sharp focus that convinces readers they're dealing with the real thing. But stepping a couple of rungs up the ladder to describe groups, neighborhoods, or even whole cities is also consistent with the way we see and understand our surroundings. Gay Talese once described New York as "a city of things unnoticed. It is a city with cats sleeping under parked cars, two stone armadillos crawling up St. Patrick's Cathedral, and thousands of ants creeping on top of the Empire State Building."

Like most skilled nonfiction writers, Tracy Kidder zooms in tight and then pulls back with his narrative camera. He characterizes groups with *collective details*, the status indicators that place human beings in social context. Here's his small-town cop again, surveying his domain with a knowing eye:

> Tommy would glance, and glance again, at the little knots of costumed youths loitering in Pulaski Park and by the information booth— skateboarders with their baseball caps turned backward, homeboys with baggy pants and gold chains. Goths in torn black clothes adorned with spiky jewelry.

SPACE

A stage is three dimensional. And if you want readers to immerse themselves in the story, to get right on stage with the characters, you must give them a sense that they exist in every one of those dimensions. "You have to set a scene so the reader gets a feeling of volume, space, dimension," Mark Kramer says, "and has sensory experience there."

Here are Deborah Barfield Berry and Kelley Benham French again, describing Wanda Tucker's entry into Luanda, Angola's capital city:

> Low adobe huts blurred past, roofs held down by concrete blocks. Then came peeling high-rises with rusty air conditioners. Wash lines with colorful clothes hung from balconies. The city bustled with people, but few of them seemed in a hurry. Children headed to class in white uniforms. On the sidewalks, people prayed, bounced babies, grilled yams, crammed bus stops, peed against walls, braided hair, carried strings of fish.

Notice how the passage creates a sense of space—long shots of high-rises, mid-range images of clothes hanging from balconies, and tighter views of adobe huts. Lots of perspective-rich images can do the same thing—a road winding into the snowy woods, a long stairway ascending in front of you, railroad tracks. Seize on such devices to help flesh out the stages you create. And a sense of movement adds to the illusion of immersion in space—from the protagonist's point of view buildings blur past, people bustle on the street, bouncing babies, peeing against walls, and carrying strings of fish.

You also can create a sense of narrative motion by describing the approach to a scene, moving from the long view to the scene itself. As Tracy Kidder did when he first described Paul Farmer's Haitian medical clinic:

> In daylight, in an all but treeless, baked brown landscape, Sanmi Lasante makes a dramatic appearance, like a fortress on its mountainside, a large complex of concrete buildings, half covered with tropical greenery. Inside the walls, the world turns leafy. Tall trees stand beside courtyards and walkways and walls, artful constructions of concrete and stone, which mount the forested hillside.

The initial view is from a distance. The clinic sits isolated in the brown landscape. But then Kidder zooms into the leafy green world of the clinic itself, duplicating the experience you would have if you visited Sanmi Lasante yourself.

ESTABLISHING SHOTS

The need to create a sense of surrounding space transcends print. Podcast narrators can describe the spaces they enter as they follow their narrative lines. Television and movie storytellers often use "establishing shots," wide-angle views that take in the entire setting that will contain a sequence of actions. Kidder's description of Sanmi Lasante established the spatial context for the action that followed in the clinic. And he opened "Small-Town Cop" with an even broader establishing shoot, one that embraced the entire stage on which his policeman would operate:

> From the summit of Mount Holyoke, in western Massachusetts, you look out on the valley of the Connecticut River, a broad landscape of cultivated fields and of forest sweeping away across the horizon, and, at the center, the old town of Northampton. It nests within natural boundaries. To the east the wide river bends around fields, planted mostly in corn. To the north and west, the foothills of the Berkshires rise up in the distance, higher than Northampton's many steeples. . . . From the summit it seems, like the corn fields beside it, a dream of perfect order, entirely coherent and self-contained, a place where a person might live a whole life and consider it complete, a tiny civilization all its own. Forget the messiness of years and days—every work of human artifice has a proper viewing distance. The town below fits in the palm of your hand. Shake it and it snows.

The rest of the story takes place within the town. But because Kidder began with a mountaintop view of the setting—the perfect establishing shot— readers continue to experience the town as it exists in the surrounding landscape. And that surrounding landscape has everything to do with the feel of the place as a small town, which is central to understanding the small-town cop who's the focus of the story.

TEXTURE

I once served on a Poynter Institute workshop faculty with Gerald Carbone, a Pulitzer winner from the *Providence Journal*. For his part of the workshop, Carbone marched us outside and told us to describe the scene in terms of *texture*. Look for the elements that contrast with one another, he said. You'll give your readers a richer experience if they can see something other than sameness. I turned my back on Tampa Bay and looked back toward the institute's lavish building. The cross-hatched pattern of the red tile roof shimmered against the blue sky. Palm fronds undulated against the building's geometric lines. I could see exactly what Carbone meant.

My own best example harks back to a long-ago trip to New York. It was the bad old days, before the city's rebirth in the 1990s. Great wealth stood in sharp contrast to crime, poverty, and degradation. I walked up Fifth Avenue and paused at Tiffany's, peering through a small window and staring at a $200,000 diamond tiara. The window was filthy. To look through it, I had to lean over a bum asleep on the sidewalk. Perfect!

ATMOSPHERE

Not only do savvy writers surround readers with textured space, but they also give them a sense of mood so palpable they can inhale it. Steven Pinker points out that "mood depends on surroundings" and suggests that you "think of being in a bus terminal waiting room or a lakeside cottage."

In fiction, Thomas Mann is past master of *atmosphere*. In nonfiction, *New York Times* reporter Anthony Shadid did an equally impressive job. Here's his description of Baghdad during a dust storm:

> On the storm's second day, the city of more than five million was coated in a film of dust, blown in from Iraq's deserts. The sky turned from a blinding yellow at dawn to blood-red in the afternoon. A dusk-like brown was followed by an eerie orange at nightfall. An occasional vegetable stand provided the city's few glimpses of color in its onions, tomatoes, eggplant, and oranges. Rain fell throughout the day, bathing Baghdad in mud.

Note the texture supplied by the vegetable stand. "It just struck me that the vegetable stand was the only color in the city being overwhelmed by dust," Shadid told Keith Woods, that year's editor of *Best Newspaper Writing*. He himself was a little surprised that something "so inconsequential as a vegetable stand somehow helped you describe what the city looked like at that point."

Carefully chosen details like the vegetable stand add up to create atmosphere. When Erik Larson evoked the feel of life in 1890s Chicago, he took a literal approach to creating atmosphere by describing the yellow glow of hissing gas lamps in the city's "perpetual coal-smoke dusk."

That, when combined with similar details, added to the overall sense of early Chicago as a gritty cesspool of industry, which made the White City all the more wondrous in comparison. Atmosphere served as a key element in the storytelling, a critical component of the core message. Larson had the good sense to ask not only "What happened?" but also "How did it feel?"

SETTING

Sometimes scenic details serve an additional function, one that gives narrative an added dimension. By evoking a particular time and place, they take readers on the road or into a time machine . . . or both. Erik Larson's 1893 Chicago is one example. So is the Alaska described in John McPhee's *Coming into the Country*. I just opened the book at random and plunged into a bit of action that describes a character's visit to the remote village of Eagle:

> Cook was anxious to get back to Donna. So, less than a week after breakup, with ice running heavy, he borrowed a canoe and started for the river with his dogs. He might have used the quiet eddy at Eagle's boat landing, a short distance upstream, but that would have meant taking the dogs through town, and Cook did not wish to create a disturbance. Several dozen dogs are chained to stakes beside cabins throughout Eagle, and Cook's loose ones, running amok, could be counted on to start fights and drive the tied ones berserk. So Cook, whose base in Eagle is a shack on some land he owns, led his dogs through woods and down to the river just below the town.

The passage reeks of Alaska's interior. "Breakup" is the term Alaskans use to describe the annual ice thaw on the state's big rivers, an event so important that they run a huge annual betting pool predicting the date. Dogs chained outside cabins, shacks, canoes—every detail adds to a sense of Alaska as a unique and special place. Cumulatively, they add up to what literary critics refer to as "setting."

Setting takes on special importance in regional narrative, a genre that takes much of its character from the place where it unfolds. In the strongest regional writing, setting is a constant presence, and place steps into the foreground with such insistence that it almost becomes a character in its own right.

Robin Cody captures my part of the world, the Pacific Northwest, as well as anybody does, largely through the sights, sounds, and smells that give a strong sense of setting. His *Northwest Magazine* story on gyppo loggers, the independent cusses who run their own operations in the region's big timber, wove setting into a strong action line, as in this description of a gyppo logging "show":

> A sharp bleep—the signal from choker setters to the tower—splits the drone of diesel engines at the landing. The skyline slackens, dropping its rigging to the canyon floor. Three choker setters, like toy soldiers in the distance below, scurry to hook up another batch of logs. Setting choker is dangerous, more dangerous on the steepest slopes. Imagine a game of

giant Pic-up Stix, hooking cables under and around the right sticks when they lie crisscrossed on a forty-degree incline. Poison oak, nettles, and wasps are minor irritants to the choker setter. The big bad dream is a cable snapping or one of these logs moving the wrong way.

With chokers set, the men scramble to a safe distance and radio a piercing two bleeps back to the tower. The skyline comes taut, lifting its load with the crack of dry branches and logs spinning off dust and bark as the haul-back cable pulls them to the landing.

Log trucks move in and out. The loader lurches steadily from log pile to truck. The overhead cables continue their busy dance against the gray morning sky. The smell of fresh timber, pungent fir and raw hemlock, mixes with the exhaust of straining engines. From below rise the syncopated bleeps of the choker setters, and from the next ridge comes the whine of a cutter's chain saw.

Robin is a best-selling writer in these parts, and one of the reasons for that popularity has to be his skill with setting. He's always spot-on when plucking geographically significant details out of the landscape, something this North-westerner can certify. I've seen gyppo logging shows, and I can testify to the fact that Robin captures that one-of-a-kind setting perfectly.

BRINGING SCENES TO LIFE

Ultimately, the point of description is to create scenes that seem absolutely real, and vivid details are the most important elements in living scenes. A sense of space helps, as do texture and atmosphere. But the frosting on the scenic cake is the illusion that we're seeing a scene through the eyes of particular characters as they move through their own worlds. Tom Wolfe articulated the idea that modern nonfiction should tell stories through POV characters, and that applies just as much to scene-setting as it does to other elements of story. When Tracy Kidder described skateboarders, homeboys, and goths, he did it through the eyes of his protagonist, police officer Tom O'Connor. Deborah Barfield Berry and Kelley Benham French used the same tactic when they described their 1619 protagonist finally arriving at her African destination:

Wanda Tucker stepped off the plane to a sky so gray it blended into the tarmac.

She inhaled, balanced her new bag with the straw handle, then step-by-step-by-step made her way down the metal stairs.

It had been 40 hours since she left Virginia. Her 61 years had caught up.

Something about flying over that wide, dark water, watching the low tin roofs rise to meet her, had brought home the reality of what she had come here to do.

The plane hissed. The faces around her were brown like hers, but their words were a scramble of sound.

Such descriptions gain added authenticity because they're woven so seamlessly into the action line. We see the world as the POV characters move through it, and the most involving scenes pass by as though we're walking or driving through them with those characters, not as though we're staring at them from a theater seat. Tracy Kidder described the road to Paul Farmer's remote medical clinic with lurching, jolting motion and snatches of what the POV characters saw along the way:

On the other side of the Plaine du Cul-de-Sac, though, at the foot of the mountains, the road turned into something like a dry riverbed, and the truck began pitching and rolling, scaling its way up the cliff—look down over the edge and you saw a bone yard of truck bodies. No one talked much from then on, not even the friendly, chatty Haitians in the front seat.

SCENIC CONSTRUCTION

The technique Tom Wolfe listed as most basic to the New Journalism—"scene-by-scene construction"—is also the technique that most distinguishes narrative nonfiction from expository forms of nonfiction. It is, in other words, a characteristic that separates reports from stories.

We organize reports by topic. And, if we want to get formal about it, we follow the roman numeral outline Ms. Grundy taught us in the fourth grade. Just about any news story or news feature fits the pattern. Take the concluding story in my newspaper's coverage of a classic Western "all-hat-no-cattle" con man. This character seduced innocent investors into a tax dodge based on limited partnerships in what was supposedly a large ranching operation. In fact, he owned only one bunch of cows that he hustled around to multiple corrals, giving the impression of vast herds. The final story in our trial coverage followed this topical outline:

I. Courtroom Anecdote
  1. Con Man's History
  2. Sentencing

A narrative, in contrast, proceeds through a series of scenes carefully selected to tell the story. One of my all-time favorites is Barry Newman's "Fisherman," a *Wall Street Journal* feature about the odd British sport of coarse fishing. It's a decidedly blue-collar enterprise, organized in pubs and targeted at the trash fish found in old canals, stagnant ponds, and other water that would instantly asphyxiate a respectable trout.

Barry's scenic structure begins as the narrator pulls up in front of Kevin Ashurst's house. You get your first hint that coarse fishermen are something other than tweedy gents with bamboo fly rods when Barry points out some dead sheep lying in the yard, rotting away. Ashurst is raising maggots, his preferred bait.

From there, Barry's narrative line follows a typical coarse-fishing experience. And, because "Fisherman" is an explanatory narrative, each scene allows the author room for a little discourse on the subject. When Barry mentions the sheep, he explains what coarse fishing is and how it works. When he takes us inside Ashurst's farmhouse for a cup of tea, he tells us something about the maggot farmer's background and the competitive drive that explains his status as a champion coarse fisherman. A trip to the pub shows us how a drawing assigns fishermen to various pieces of backwater. The next scene puts us alongside Ashurst at his assigned spot on a canal, where we learn something about his fishing strategy. Then it's back to the pub, where we learn that Ashurst has once again taken the top prize. The little yarn closes with Ashurst in bed back at the farmhouse, worrying about how he can improve his technique for the next competition.

Barry's simple scenic outline looked like this:

Novice narrative writers sometimes have a hard time adapting to the episodic nature of scenic construction. But each of Barry Newman's scenes is substantially removed from the others in time and space. One scene ends, and another opens somewhere else down the narrative arc. And in most print narratives typographical devices—typically star-line breaks, bullets, or drop caps—separate each major unit in the overall structure. That's not a problem because readers are used to the curtain opening and closing, and they've been especially well trained by the dramatic scene changes that characterize motion pictures. Podcasters usually make their most dramatic scene changes between episodes, but can also signal time or locale changes within episodes with time tested "meanwhile-back-at-the-ranch" audio cues from the narrator.

Once you get used to thinking of stories as a series of scenic episodes, plotting the scenic structure becomes the natural first step to planning the narrative. Nothing does more to clarify a story in your own mind. And, as a result, nothing does more to simplify the reporting and writing.

I found the process enormously helpful as I worked with newspaper and magazine journalists steering through big narratives, often under challenging reporting conditions and tight deadline pressure. Consider the case of the *Taki-Tooo*, an Oregon fishing boat that went down on a Father's Day outing in the early 2000s. The story had all the elements for great narrative. It would have worked in a national magazine, as an interactive online presentation, as a podcast, or as a television documentary. We grabbed it for my newspaper.

The boat's owners ran charters out of Garibaldi, a tiny Oregon Coast fishing town on Tillamook Bay. Seventeen fishermen showed up for an early spring bottom-fishing expedition into the Pacific Ocean. But the tide was low, the waves were high, and the Coast Guard had warned charter-boat captains about treacherous conditions on the bar at the mouth of the bay.

Several charter captains canceled the day's fishing. But four boats, including the *Taki-Tooo*, gathered just inside the bar and waited for a chance to run for it. Three boats made it through huge breaking waves. The *Taki-Tooo*'s captain gunned his engine and headed into the maelstrom. The boat dropped into a trough and sloughed sideways just as a wave of up to twenty-five feet slammed into it broadside.

The *Taki-Tooo* rolled, and then rolled again. The violent motion threw the deckhand, the captain, and some of the fishermen into the water and trapped others in the cabin, where they struggled to escape through blocked windows and hatches. The deckhand and some of the fishermen swam for the beach. The captain died in the water, one man never made it out of the cabin, and others drowned in the open sea. The breakers eventually threw the boat's battered hull onto the beach, where rescuers cared for the survivors and collected the eight dead.

The *Oregonian* covered the tragedy as major news, beginning with A1 stories on Sunday, June 15, and continuing with follow-up stories through the week. But by Tuesday we were thinking about what's known in the business as a tick-tock, a narrative reconstruction of the entire episode. Only narrative could give readers a sense of what it was like to be there, from the charter office to the dock to the bar to the beach. Reexperiencing the whole sad chain of events would help them understand what happened in a way bald facts never can. And the dramatic force of a tick-tock might force reassessment of the policies that contributed to the tragedy—the federal government's failure to dredge a dangerous bar, the rules that make life jackets optional when crossing the bar, and the policy that gives captains the option of disregarding Coast Guard warnings about dangerous bar conditions.

On Wednesday I assembled six reporters in a conference room. Half of them had been on the spot-news team that covered the sinking, and they were familiar with the sources that might be useful for a tick-tock. I stood at a flip chart and wrote down names while the reporters called out twenty-three suggestions. Then we assigned a reporter to each source. I ripped the big sheets of paper off the pad, taped them to the wall, and turned back to the flip chart, using a Magic Marker to sketch a large narrative arc. We walked through the sequence of events as we knew them, and I positioned each of those on the arc. Assembling on the dock and pushing off at 6 a.m. Waiting while the three other boats left the harbor. Attempting the bar at 7 a.m. Capsizing and struggling for survival until the whole sorry business ended on the beach about 9:20 a.m. Once we'd finished that, the arc went up on the wall next to the list of sources.

Then we talked about the key scenes, the episodes that would best help us tell the story from the viewpoints of the characters in the best positions to view them. We came up with a list of nine, and I sketched those as a series of boxes

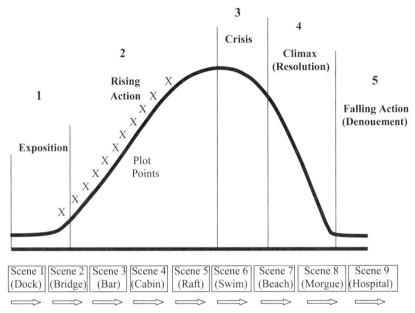

Figure 6. Sinking of the *Taki-Tooo*: A narrative arc with scenic construction

on yet another page of the flip chart. At that point, we had all we needed to sketch the structure of the entire story. Combining the arc and the list of scenes produced a blueprint that looked like figure 6.

We would begin the story on the dock, which would give us a chance for the necessary exposition. We'd introduce the captain and the deckhand and several of the key characters among the fishermen. We'd describe the boat, the bay, and the bar, with all its dangers. In the next scene, we'd continue the exposition on the boat's bridge as the captain waited in the staging area inside the bar, the place where he made his fatal decision. Then we'd detail the run for the sea and the capsizing before moving to the horrific scene in the inverted boat's flooded cabin, followed by a scene on the single life raft and another detailing the struggles of those thrown into open water. We'd begin the falling action with a scene on the beach, where bystanders dashed into the surf and pulled both bodies and survivors ashore, as well as a separate scene from the viewpoint of Coast Guard rescuers who arrived in helicopters and plucked some survivors from the water. We'd end in the hospital, with survivors talking about their experiences.

Underneath the boxes designating the scenes, I wrote a few words describing the action that would end the scene with a cliff-hanger, an action portending drama in the next section. The deckhand pushing off the dock. The captain hitting the throttle as he surged toward the bar. The deckhand shouting as the big wave loomed over the boat.

And what, exactly, did she say? Nobody had any idea at that point; so I made a guess, writing "This is it!" on the flip-chart page, which I saved and which sits right next to me as I write this. But you can't guess in a true-life narrative. Clearly, the reporter who interviewed the deckhand would have to ask. She did, and that turned up the deckhand's actual words. "Oh shit!" she said, just as the monster wave was about to hit. And, because it was so appropriate to the scene, I had no problem including the profanity in the final story. Not a single reader complained.

That little incident illustrates the value of planning each scene and sketching out the scenic blueprint for the entire narrative. The process guides the reporting that follows, focusing the questions and zeroing in on the story's key moments.

The group decided on two reporters—Michelle Cole and Katy Muldoon—to do the actual writing. We went through the chart, assigning half the scenes to each. The remaining reporters could then feed information to the appropriate writers as it turned up. The six reporters, excited by the possibilities the planning had revealed, copied the flip-chart sheets hanging on the walls and left the conference room, their heads abuzz with plans for the interviews they'd conduct to complete the narrative. They had two days—I'd need substantial editing time, and the deadline for the first weekend edition was midnight Friday.

Once they got back to reporting, they turned up terrific opportunities for dramatic scene-setting. A Garibaldi pastor and his wife had watched much of the action from their home, high on a hill overlooking the bay. The boat's owner had watched the capsizing from the jetty. A freelance photographer had videotaped the rescue efforts from the beach. As it turned out, he was willing to sell us the tape, and every witness we contacted was willing to talk, some from their hospital beds.

The new information changed the structure slightly. We collected good material from the charter-boat owner about the day's 5 a.m. beginning in the company office; so we made that Scene 1 and moved the dock scene to the second position. The pastor and his wife had such a compelling story that we decided to make them POV characters for a scene of their own. And so it went. But, by and large, the original structure served us well. We made deadline for first edition with a jaw-dropping narrative that began at the top of page one and jumped to two open pages inside, complete with great photographs and a color graphic that explained the whole sequence of events. Six reporters, photographers and photo editors, graphic artists, and a story editor had managed to coordinate their efforts to produce a polished seven-thousand-word narrative in two days.

But the result wasn't just good luck. We'd carefully worked through our scenic construction, and, as always, fortune favors the prepared mind.

7

Action

Narration is not a still life; it's a moving picture.
—Ted Cheney

Put yourself in a movie theater. The action film you've paid so dearly to see has reached the point that story theorists call "the crisis." Our hero, at the wheel of a bright-red sports car, screams up a hill and flies through the intersection at the top, airborne. A dogged villain, driving a black SUV, crests the hill behind. Tires squeal; horns blare. The bad guy T-bones a garbage truck, glass shattering and metal screeching. A second villain roars past the flaming wreckage, bursts through the smoke, and glimpses his prey rounding a distant corner. He floors it.

OK. You get the picture. Now take yourself back to your quiet house, fire up your printer, and punch out the five pages you wrote today. Pick them up. Flabby featherweights, aren't they, limply hanging from your fingers? Spread them on your desk. Notice how they just lie there. No color, no noise, no nuthin'.

Print is the least sensory of all media. Radio fills our ears with voices and music. Television and movies transport us to scenes filled with action. Online graphics sweep and soar, zooming in and out, throbbing with color. A podcast fleshes out a story with the voices of the characters who lived it. But print is inert, silent. And if you want to turn those passive squiggles of ink on a page or electrons on a screen into something that competes with a chase scene on a big movie screen, you have your work cut out for you. Re-creating the lush, palpable stuff of human existence is the ultimate challenge of the writer's craft.

But it's a challenge you must meet. Action, after all, is story itself.

Fortunately, print storytellers have spent hundreds of years developing techniques that give their medium way more power than you'd expect from such a weak channel. Learn their craft, and you can create powerful life on those flabby pages.

THE NARRATIVE LEAD

The importance of action suggests that you should get moving right out of the blocks. *Something* should happen in the first line of your narrative. Ted Cheney, one of the first scholars to take narrative nonfiction seriously, concluded that "good, dramatic nonfiction openings . . . have life within them, life that moves, that gets somewhere."

But where? Aimless action gets you nowhere, and readers expect an opening that takes them from one intriguing development to the next.

From story theory, we know that the narrative arc first rises when a protagonist engages a complication. So it follows that first lines should knock key characters out of the stable orbits they enjoyed before some comet flashed through their private solar system, loosing forces that will produce irreversible change. Which is why Lisa Cron urges writers who introduce us to a protagonist in a stable orbit to, as soon as possible, "fling her out of her easy chair and into the fray. A story is an escalating dare, and your goal is to make sure your protagonist is worthy of her goal."

Lajos Egri, the playwriting guru, said, "A play should start with the first line uttered." An ideal "point of attack," he added, zeros in on a moment where something vital is at stake. That might be:

"exactly at the point where a conflict will lead up to a crisis."

"at a point where at least one character has reached a turning point in his life."

"with a decision that will precipitate conflict."

Once the doors close and the curtain opens, a theater audience is trapped, at least through the first intermission. So the playwright has a little time to catch its interest. The readers of a narrative piece in a news source, book, or magazine, on the other hand, have far more freedom. Bore them for an instant, and they'll move on. So first lines in the popular print media must immediately demand attention, crackling with enough energy to turn heads. They should serve, in other words, as "narrative hooks."

Remember the opening Stuart Tomlinson produced for my newspaper, the one about the cop who rescued a woman from a burning car? It opened this way:

> The pickup blew by, pushing eighty.
>
> Jason McGowan, a Portland police reserve officer whose patrol car was stopped at Southeast Division and Southeast 142nd Avenue, saw it swerving in and out of traffic. Then it nearly hit him.

The truck, operated by a man with multiple drug and driving convictions, swerved into oncoming traffic and smashed into a passenger car. The impact pinned a young woman in the car, which burst into flames. McGowan captured the truck driver and battled the car fire, keeping the woman alive through a series of crises until firefighters arrived and pried her out of the wreckage. The whole episode was a perfect little narrative, with a hero and a happy ending. Readers wrote to say how much they appreciated a newspaper story that, for a change, recognized a public servant for doing his job selflessly and well.

You'd be hard-pressed to beat the energy generated by "The pickup blew by, pushing eighty." But, in most cases, you don't have to. To snag a reader's interest, you have dozens of tricks at your disposal. Like countless successful storytellers before you, you can, for example, tease your readers, making them wonder what happens next. A local doctor flew his parasail into a tall cedar tree near a cliff on the Oregon Coast, and teetered precariously on a branch, one wrong move short of a fatal fall. Rescuers arrived, but their equipment couldn't reach him. Somebody thought of a well-known former logger, a tree-topper skilled at climbing the highest evergreens. The call went out. The logger answered. And Larry Bingham's lead read:

> Becky Saari listened to her husband on the phone and grew more intrigued with every word.
>
> "What is stuck in the tree?"
>
> "Who?"
>
> "Doing what?"

Hmmm. Guess I'll read a few more lines to discover the answers to those questions. And to see our logger arriving at the accident scene, easily climbing the tree, roping up the terrified doctor, and bringing the tale to a happy conclusion.

Stuart's and Larry's leads made for great narrative hooks, which is all the more remarkable considering that each writer worked on a tight deadline. But, in retrospect, I think my editing should have included advice to start each story from the protagonist's point of view. Telling a story from the perspective of the key player helps put readers in the scene, where they can recognize the coming challenges as though they themselves were facing them.

Keeping in mind the importance of action *and* point of view, the default option for any narrative opening is to begin with the name of the protagonist and to immediately follow that with a strong verb. Stuart might have written that "Jason McGowan saw the pickup blow by, pushing eighty." Larry might have begun with the logger arriving on scene and eyeballing the physician teetering far above.

You have a thousand ways to begin any story, of course, and the protagonist-verb form of opening sentence may not always be the best. But it does remarkably well in a variety of situations. *Oregonian* reporter Joe Rose launched one of his most successful police-beat stories with both attention-grabbing action and the point of view of a key player. The story unfolded in a funky all-night doughnut shop frequented by college students and downtown hipsters. The action began when a thief tried to make off with "the sacred doughnut," a giant foam facsimile hanging on Voodoo Doughnut's wall. Like peasants in a Frankenstein movie, the joint's late-night crowd pursued the thief through downtown streets, eventually rescuing the sacred doughnut and bringing the thief to justice. It all began, according to Joe's story, when "Fryer Jay heard the crash in the Voodoo Doughnut kitchen and turned away from a Monday night rush of college kids."

Not every narrative opening demands slam-bang action. Quieter stories call for quieter openings. But it's still essential that something is happening. When the great *Philadelphia Inquirer* medical and science writer Don Drake reconstructed the first scientific recognition of a horrifying new disease called AIDS, he calmly described the key researcher arriving for the breakthrough conference: "The research immunologist entered the dark lounge of the small hotel opposite the Centers for Disease Control and ordered a martini." When Dave Hogan launched a poignant story about a young boy who watched his father die from a heroin overdose, he began with a bystander encountering the child: "An eight-year-old boy stood alone on a Northwest Portland sidewalk Monday night as people filed out of the Mission Theater & Pub. Dried tears streaked his face." And when Tom Hallman launched the three-part series that would win him the feature-writing Pulitzer, he focused on a quiet scene that introduced his protagonist: "The boy sits on the living-room sofa, lost in his thoughts and stroking the family cat with his fragile hands."

CONTINUOUS MOTION

Motion is the beating heart of story. Narrative strings events together through time. Yes, sometimes you have to punch the pause button while you explain things. And occasionally—*very* occasionally—you may want to speculate about the philosophical implications of something that just happened. But readers won't cut you much slack for what old newshounds derisively called "navel-gazing." So once you launch it, keep the action moving.

Not every narrative mimics an action movie, of course. Nonstop chase scenes will fill your audience with nothing but testosterone-poisoned adolescent boys. But more serious films rely on their own varieties of less in-your-face action. And even chick flicks, the kind of romances that leave guys like me complaining that "nothing ever happens," have their own quiet style of constantly building action, although it may focus more on shifting human relationships than airborne pickup trucks. And, despite their name, concept books, the extended narrative essays that explore subjects like codfish, salt, or the color red, succeed only when they keep things in motion.

Mary Roach, one of the most successful concept-book writers, has a thing about death. She's hit the best-seller lists with *Stiff*, an extended first-person concept book on dead bodies, and *Spook*, a similar treatment of the afterlife. Neither subject lends itself to slam-bang action. But Mary didn't attract huge audiences by letting her topic lie there, as dead as its subject matter. Motion enlivens almost every passage. At one point in *Spook*, she joins an Indian doctor on a visit with a villager who, word has it, carries the reincarnated spirit of a local man. Mary exploits the doctor's domineering personality for comic effect, and she taps that vein as she joins him in a car bound for the village. Notice how, at the same time, she keeps the narrative moving:

> What he likes best about this particular car is the driver. "He is submissive," Dr. Rawat says to me, as we pull away from the curb. "Generally, I like people who are submissive."

Pulling away from the curb is not explosive action, but it keeps the story rolling forward. It tells you what happened next.

THE LANGUAGE OF ACTION

"News," Jimmy Breslin once said, "is a verb." What the hard-boiled New York columnist meant was that news, like story, hinges on action. If the cat's still stuck in the tree it climbed yesterday, where's the news? If the firefighters arrive in a ladder truck and pluck the kitten from the very top branch, you have the makings of a story.

Breslin made a linguistic point, too. Verbs signify action. And, if you're going to keep a story moving, you'll need lots of good ones. That seems like a simple enough order. But far too many would-be narrative writers dilute their impact with flabby verbs and weak sentence syntax. A writer who doesn't know his verbs can turn the most dramatic events into a snooze. A journalist who documented the long struggle of a wounded soldier described the attack that shattered his body this way:

> Then there was a flash and a loud bang, followed by a mushroom cloud of dust and debris. A roadside bomb had ripped through the lead Humvee.

The writer had all the ingredients, but he cloaked their impact with a weak verb, an expletive, and an unnecessary perfect tense. If he'd followed a few basic guidelines for re-creating action, he might have written this:

> A roadside bomb flashed, ripping through the lead Humvee and erupting in a cloud of dust and wreckage.

Years ago I taught several one-week narrative workshops for the Haystack Program in the Arts, which operated in a charming little town on the Oregon Coast. One summer the workshop's adult students wrote about the tidal wave that smashed into the town decades before. On other summers different groups of students reported a dramatic charter-boat sinking and a disastrous Coast Guard rescue attempt on the Columbia River's dangerous bar. While working those actual stories, they learned about story theory, point of view, characterization, and scenic construction. They also learned about other key skills for writing forceful narrative, the kind I covered in *Wordcraft*, the companion to this book.[1] One of those skills involves choosing the right verbs.

One of my Haystack students, Jan Volz, finished the course and took a job at a small Central Oregon newspaper, where she quickly proved that even a beginning narrative writer, equipped with the right tools, can produce gripping stories. Jan ran into a story that she might have blown off in one standard journalistic report, with this sort of lead: "A car carrying four Redmond residents skidded into the Crooked River yesterday afternoon, leaving a twelve-year-old girl in critical condition."

Instead, Jan stuck with the story and, a month later, came back at it with a narrative that began this way:

Winona Dmytryk-Graham's shoulder-length hair *whips* around her face as her maroon Ford LTD *purrs* steadily toward Paulina.

"Hey, somebody put in 'The Shake,'" Tashina Hickman *calls* from the back seat.

Winona *smiles*. Her twelve-year-old daughter loves the new tape by Neal McCoy. But as she *glances* at the dashboard clock, the smile disappears.[2]

Great! Jan's grabbed our attention by putting us in the middle of an active, vibrant scene filled with verbs such as "whips," "purrs," and "glances." But, as is usually the case, she needed to slow down briefly for some exposition— backstory that explained why the characters were on that highway, rushing from Redmond to Paulina. So she wrote:

It's 12:20 p.m., and her fourteen-year-old son, T.J., and family friend Tyson Reedy, eighteen, *are* scheduled to ride the bulls at the annual Paulina Rodeo.

They're going to be late.

Fair enough. For exposition, you usually need a few linking verbs such as "is" and "are," both forms of "to be," the most common linking verb. But Jan never strayed from the action for more than a paragraph or two. As soon as she explained who Winona and her passengers were, why they were on the highway, and what the country around them looked like, she put us right back in the thick of things. She described Winona rounding a bend, spotting a pickup truck parked in the middle the highway, and slamming on the brakes. What happened next unspooled in a series of vivid verbs.

The car *jerks* left as the air *fills* with curses and carnival-ride shrieks. Hitting loose gravel on the side of the road, the car *lurches* back hard to the right. Gravel and dirt *fly* through the open windows.

Verbs such as "jerk," "fills," "lurch," and "fly" are active, muscular action words that fit sudden violence. Unlike linking verbs, they describe motion. They get us out of exposition and back into narrative.

The car plunged into the river. Winona and the boys escaped and made it to shore. Tashina passed out, trapped underwater, and when rescuers pulled her toward shore nearly ten minutes later she lay motionless, apparently dead, her lips blue and her skin translucent. An elk hunter arrived in a flurry of strong verbs. (He "slams" on his brakes, "abandons" his car, and "stabilizes"

Tashina's neck.) The girl was past the point at which brain damage usually occurs. But CPR produced a couple of ragged breaths, and paramedics rushed her to the hospital. Maybe because the cold water slowed her metabolism, she slowly recovered, a testament to the value of public-spirited citizens willing to get involved with CPR and quick action. Jan's narrative line ended a month after the accident. After Tashina recovered and left the hospital, she and Winona returned to the accident scene, overcome with emotion as they remembered the day the girl almost died.

TIME MARKERS

A narrative is a sequence of actions, and readers must always have a clear understanding of what's happening when. But they're easily confused by flashbacks, flash-forwards, multiple narrative lines, and all the other departures from straight chronology we use in print storytelling. Feedback from baffled readers long ago taught me to make sure a final draft made a story's chronology clear.

Often, time markers can be relatively subtle. You might simply note the fall colors on the trees when you open a new scene that jumps ahead from summer to autumn. Or you could slip in the height of the sun in the sky when a character walks out of a building.

But some narratives demand more. The *Oregonian* reporters who reconstructed a rafting disaster on their state's wild Illinois River needed not only highly specific time markers, but also other measures of the unfolding action. Their narrative cut between multiple rafting parties, all of them moving down the river's canyon. And the situation grew more and more dire as the river's flow, expressed in cubic feet per second, grew more and more uncontrollable. We talked the issue over and decided to head each new scene with the basic information—time, place, and cfs figure. The scene headers looked like this:

Miami Bar, 9 a.m. Saturday, March 21. River flow 2,002 cfs.
Klondike Creek, 6 a.m. Sunday, March 22, River flow, 6,020 cfs.
The Green Wall, noon Sunday, March 22, River flow 10,177 cfs.
Deadman Bar, 12.5 miles downstream from the Miami Bar launch,
    12:45 p.m. Monday, March 23, River flow 15,684 cfs.

PACE

Imagine that you're listening to Homer himself as he tells the story of the Trojan War. He calmly describes the Greeks disembarking from their home cities, and hurries them to the walls of Troy, skipping over the details of the voyage across the Aegean. He wants you on the battlefield, where he can dig into the real action.

A story is a journey, and journeys can be tedious or fascinating. A day spent at a steady seventy miles an hour on a freeway arrowing across a featureless plain can drive you bonkers. A drive through rolling countryside, with frequent stops to explore quaint little towns, can make for a deeply satisfying Sunday. As a writer, you want to include plenty of highlights, and you want to move readers quickly between them. "Each scene will have a climax," says narrative literary agent Peter Rubie, "and one definition of pace is how rapidly a narrative moves from climactic point to climactic point." As Nathan Bransford, put it, "Pacing is the length of time between moments of conflict."[3]

Elmore Leonard, as is his wont, focused on the payoff of good pacing when he famously said, "I try to leave out the parts that people skip." Once you reach the high points of a narrative—the parts that nobody skips—you slow down. Accordingly, when Homer gets the Greeks to Troy, he gives you time to appreciate the drama. Achilles surges forward to take his fatal wound, and you're in the moment. Homer slows, his voice fills with intensity, and he tells you every detail. "Intensity," Jon Franklin says, "is a measure of how closely the storyteller focuses his narrative camera on the story's participants and scenery."

On one level, the blind poet has merely shifted from summary to scenic narrative. But he also has engaged your deeper interest by manipulating the apparent speed of the story. Control over pace is one of the storyteller's most powerful narrative techniques.

In a sense, the successful storyteller inverts life. The tedious parts of our existence move with excruciating slowness. But, as the cliché has it, time flies when you're having a good time. Tom French, who won a Pulitzer Prize at the *St. Petersburg Times*, says he tries to do just the opposite. "The paradox is that when you're in the boring stuff, that's when you need to speed up and when you're in the best stuff where things are really moving rapidly, you slow down. The reason you slow down is so that the reader can really feel and process and really enter that scene."

Tom's a great student of the movies, and he often applies cinematic terms to narrative technique for print. So it's not surprising that he refers to the descent into scenic narrative—and the reduced pace that results—as "zooming in."

"And how do you slow down?" Tom asks. "You allow more space on the page. You allow more sentences. You literally write in shorter sentences. You get more paragraph breaks. You use space. You find pauses inside the scene that occur naturally that you would normally skip over."[4]

Part of what gives scenic narrative its power is the way it hesitates just when something important looms, creating what Tom calls "that delicious sense of enforced waiting." As is often the case with narrative, the technique runs contrary to journalistic instinct, which dictates that you rush to the main point.

Tom's own writing beautifully illustrates the technique. His story "A Gown for Lindsay Rose," about a nurse who sews clothes for stillborn babies, reached its emotional high point when Lois Beneshtarigh prepared a dead child for burial:[5]

> Tuesday afternoon, when Lois brought the Spittka baby into the back room of the nursery, she knew what to do.
>
> First, she rolled a screen in front of the window, so none of the other mothers in the unit would see. Then she weighed and measured the baby. She was four pounds, four ounces, and seventeen inches long. Lois took the girl's tiny feet, pressed them to an inkpad, and made two sets of footprints, one for the hospital's records and one for the parents to take home. Lois placed a pink basin in a sink and filled it with warm water. Then she stepped outside and asked if one of the other nurses would witness the baptism.
>
> A nurse, an older woman with grown children, watched as Lois lowered the child into the warm water, immersing her completely except for her face.
>
> "I baptize thee in the name of the Father, the Son, and the Holy Spirit," said Lois, dabbing the girl's forehead.
>
> The other nurse was mesmerized. Over and over, she noted how perfect the child was. "She's such a beautiful baby," she said.

The scene continued, slowly unfolding in a series of closely observed details. Lois carefully washed the body. She thought of her own children, and the things about growing up that the stillborn baby would miss. She prayed. Then:

> Lois washed the child's hair and the rest of her body with Johnson's Baby Shampoo. Then she dried her with a towel and rubbed her feet and her back with Johnson's Baby Oil. She wanted those two scents—and all the associations that come with them—to reach the family when it came time for them to hold her.

With the baby in her arms, she walked over to the shelf and got the pink-trimmed gown.

EXPOSITION

Exposition—the backstory readers need to understand what's going on—is the enemy of narrative. It slows the action, rips readers out of scene, and destroys the dreamlike state that immerses them in the front story.

But you invariably need exposition. For one thing, story revolves around motive, and readers need to know *why* characters do what they do. That requires that you drag information into the story that goes well beyond the action occurring at that point in the narrative line. When *Wall Street Journal* reporter Bill Blundell headed out to a working cattle ranch to show his readers, most of them urban business types, what cowboys really do, he had to explain why anybody would tolerate such brutal, discouraging work for such meager pay. So he wrote this:

> But the cowboy knows he is only a speck on the vast plain, his works insignificant, his power to really control the land almost nil; nature herself is the only manager of the Rafter Eleven or any other ranch. So the cowboy learns to bow humbly before the perils and setbacks she brings, and to try to appreciate her gifts.
>
> A big buck antelope squirms under a fence and sprints over the plain, hoofs drumming powerfully. "Now that's one fine sight," murmurs a cowboy.

Or maybe you need to explain *how* something's done so that readers can appreciate its difficulty. Note how Mary Roach slipped background into a knife-throwing narrative:

> I raise the first blade. "Hold on," says Adamovich. "We're forgetting the most important thing." The most important thing in knife throwing turns out to be a tape measure. For a half-spin throw, one that rotates 180 degrees in the air, you stand eight feet from the target. For a full spin, twelve feet. If your stance is more than a few inches off, your knife will hit at the wrong point in its revolution, clanging broadside into the target and dropping to the ground. Because of this precise geometry, knife throwing is not something you can easily do on the run or on an impulse. Only in the movies can someone successfully nail a target by whipping out a knife. . . .
>
> Adamovich says, "Monkey see, monkey do," and hurls five knives, one

after another, into the bull's-eye. Then he hands them to me, whereupon nothing like that happens.

So, given that some amount of exposition is necessary, what can you do to limit the damage it does?

First, write no more than absolutely necessary. "You try to minimize all explanation," Blundell says. "If someone asks you what time it is, you don't tell him how to make a watch. The internal explanations of things that are going on are often pretty dull. It may be necessary, but you want to get rid of them in a hurry and get back to the action. The key thing is to keep the story moving."

When you find yourself writing exposition, step back, clear your head, and ask yourself, "Do my readers really need this to understand what's going on?" If not, desist. The only necessary exposition serves dramatic purposes. It allows the reader to understand why the protagonist must overcome a complication. Or it enhances drama by explaining why the challenge is so daunting.

If you do leave the action line, don't leave for long. Bill Blundell says his rule of thumb is to never digress from the main narrative for more than two paragraphs.

When I was editing *Northwest Magazine*, Spike Walker brought me the story that launched a national obsession with the dangers of Bering Sea crab fishing. Spike turned the magazine piece into a book, and the book inspired *Deadliest Catch*, the hit Discovery Channel reality series.

Spike's original story focused on a young fisherman named Wallace Thomas, who somehow survived after abandoning ship in the Gulf of Alaska. Given the material—towering waves, prowling polar bears, daring helicopter rescues—almost nonstop action powered the tale. But in those days few readers knew much about how crab boats operated in some of the earth's most dangerous waters; so Spike needed occasional explanations that briefly diverged from the main action line. Here's how he dealt with the all-important survival suit:

> A few of the other crewmen ducked into the galley, glanced at the destruction, then quickly scrambled out of the room. Doc turned white-faced to Wallace, "We're going to put on our survival suits. This storm is getting out of hand."
>
> Wallace felt a sickening fright rush over him. He didn't own a survival suit. Without one, he knew he didn't stand a chance in the icy seas. During his short career at sea, he had never worn one, but he knew all about survival suits and their lifesaving and buoyant qualities. He had

been a wilderness survival instructor back in Florida and he knew it was hypothermia—loss of body heat—not drowning, that was the more likely to take lives of sailors forced to abandon ship in the icy-cold ocean. A survival suit looked similar to a diver's wet suit, except it was loose-fitting and allowed a sailor to climb into it quickly while still wearing boots and clothing. It zipped up the front and had an attached hood that sealed tightly around the face to prevent the cold, penetrating water from seeping in. A leaky survival suit usually results in fatal loss of body heat.

The life raft, remembered Wallace. If the ship went down, it would be his only chance. He grabbed a flashlight and ran out on the back deck.

Sometimes, you don't have to leave the action line at all. Instead, you drop exposition into action sentences via subordinate clauses, modifiers, appositives, and other incidental elements. Reserve the main clauses for action alone.

Note how this example from the story about the soldier badly wounded in Iraq abandons the main action line to insert expository elements wrapped around weak verb constructions such as "that's how" and "to be."

That's how, on Nov. 28, 2005, Cpl. Sandoval came to be on a stretch of hilly, barren terrain in northern Iraq that baked under the midday sun. He manned the .50-caliber machine gun on a Humvee.

But the scene itself wasn't static. Picture it. The corporal gripped the machine gun. He scanned the hills. The Humvee rolled forward.

You can't make things up, of course, but the Humvee had to get to that point on the map, and it at least seems safe to describe it in motion. So how about this version?

On Nov. 28, 2005, the Humvee, with Cpl. Sandoval manning the .50-caliber machine gun, rolled into a hilly, barren patch of northern Iraq.

Skilled writers develop a subtle faculty for slipping backstory into main clauses without even alerting readers to what they're doing. Note how much Rheta Grimsley Johnson, the great Southern journalist, blended into one line she produced for a story in the *Memphis Commercial Appeal*:

The women wore tentative smiles with their Dacron finery and carried patent-leather bags on arms the Mississippi sun had mottled.

Think about how much that single sentence reveals. The tentative smiles tell us the women are uncomfortable. The mottled arms tell us they're of a certain age. The finery reveals that they're at a formal occasion, but the Dacron and patent leather tell us they're working class. The Mississippi sun tells us where they live.

But no matter how skilled you are slipping bits of exposition into action clauses, sometimes you have to break free for Bill Blundell's two paragraphs of more extended explanation. You can minimize the damage by reassuring readers that the digression is just a pause in ongoing action. Go back to the Mary Roach example and note how she plugged the explanation into an action-filled scene. She raises the knife, prepared to throw. Her instructor stops her at that pregnant moment, creating a little cliff-hanger. Then Mary, in a short aside, addresses us directly and reveals the secret of successful knife throwing. The instructor resumes the action, grabbing the blades and punching them into the target. Bill Blundell calls that the sandwich technique. Action's the bread. Exposition's the filling. They work together to make an appealing whole.

When it's consistently repeated, the technique trains readers to stick with you as you digress. They quickly learn that even though you've abandoned the action, you'll soon be back in the thick of things. And Bill reinforces that lesson by placing especially memorable action right after any expository digression, creating little rewards that lure readers relentlessly forward. Remember how that buck antelope squirmed under a fence and sprinted across the plain, hooves drumming?

FIRSTHAND ACTION
One of the unspoken traditional rules that hobble conventional print journalists—though not other narrative writers—is that they never can say anything on their own authority. A police reporter may be hanging around the cop shop when a patrolwoman hauls a car thief in and books him. But then her story dutifully reports that "a twenty-two-year-old man was arrested and charged with grand theft auto Tuesday, *police said*." If she sees a tornado rip through town the next morning, she can't trust her own eyes. She must track down a witness. "It was twisting and writhing," said Elaine Bowser, of 2376 SW Cedar Street. "I saw it coming, and I ran for the cellar."

Presumably, the reluctance to offer anything firsthand makes the journalist sound more objective. By keeping herself out of it, a reporter cloaks herself in a veneer of scientific detachment. Just the facts, ma'am. I'm a disinterested observer, and what I think happened is irrelevant. Here's what everybody else has to say about it.

This reticence drives some reporters into passive voice, the ultimate refuge for dodging personal responsibility. "Mistakes were made," said Richard

Nixon as he tried vainly to squirm his way clear of any role in the Watergate break-in. And, in similar fashion, reporters excise themselves from their own reporting. They don't admit that they themselves saw anything. But it's OK to note that certain things *can be seen.*

> In the glow of the camera light, the registered nurse anesthetist can be seen sitting just next to Steverson's head, carefully monitoring his vital signs and his breathing.

Secondhand action is fine for a report on a city council meeting. Or in just about any report, for that matter. But the last thing you want in a nonfiction narrative is detachment achieved by filtering all content through some third party. For the great majority of narrative, your aim as a storyteller is to put readers into a scene where they can experience the action *as though they were there witnessing it themselves.*

One of the pivotal points in Erik Larson's *The Devil in the White City* arrives as Chicago's citizens learn they've won the competition to stage a world's fair. For Chicago, the news that arrives by telegraph in the offices of the *Chicago Tribune* is a big deal, an affirmation that it's arrived as a world-class city. Larson conveyed that by describing the crowd that gathered to hear the news, a scene that he found via a contemporary newspaper account. He could have quoted the original news story. Instead, he took his readers there directly, describing the long-ago scene firsthand:

> Outside the Tribune building there was silence. The crowd needed a few moments to process the news. A man in a long beard was one of the first to react. He had sworn not to shave until Chicago got the fair. Now he climbed the steps of the adjacent Union Trust Company Bank. On the top step he let out a shriek that one witness likened to the scream of a skyrocket. Others in the crowd echoed his cry, and soon two thousand men and women and a few children—mostly telegraph boys and hired messengers—cut loose with a cheer that tore through the canyon of brick, stone, and glass like a flash flood. The messenger boys raced off with the news, while throughout the city telegraph boys sprinted from the offices of the Postal Telegraph Company and Western Union or leaped aboard their Pope "safety" bikes.

8

Dialogue

Remember that dialogue is not talk but action; it is what people do to each other.
—Don Murray

When the New Journalism burst onto the American scene in the 1960s, narrative nonfiction took a quantum leap forward. Writers such as Joan Didion, Gay Talese, Truman Capote, and Norman Mailer borrowed sophisticated stylistic devices from fiction. Among them was dialogue, long an essential plot- and character-development device in the novel. But instead of inventing conversations between fictional characters in imagined scenes, the New Journalists went out into the world and reported them, recording the actual words that real people exchanged among themselves in the process of their ordinary lives. In "The Feature Game," his introduction to *The New Journalism*, Tom Wolfe included dialogue on a short list of essential elements in the powerful new nonfiction emerging all around him. "Dialogue," he wrote, "involves the reader more completely than any other single device."

The old journalists had, of course, been using the real words of real people for centuries. But they relied mostly on the direct quotation, individual comments produced in interviews and then dropped into expository news reports. When a journalist included the words of Charles Lindbergh in a report of the Japanese attack on Pearl Harbor ("We have been stepping closer to war for many months. Now it has come, and we must meet it as united Americans."), that was a direct quotation. When Gay Talese reported a squabble between Broadway director Joshua Logan and temperamental actress Claudia McNeil, he used true dialogue.

"CLAUDIA!" Logan yelled, "Don't you give me that actor's vengeance, Claudia!"

"Yes, Mr. Logan," she said with a soft, sarcastic edge.

"I've had enough of this today, Claudia."

"Yes, Mr. Logan."

"And stop Yes-Mr. Logan-ing me."

"Yes, Mr. Logan."

"You're a shockingly rude woman."

"Yes, Mr. Logan."

The transition from direct quotations to dialogue is especially challenging for old news hands or any other writers used to working in straight-ahead expository reports. News journalists, in particular, are addicted to the direct quotation, and pro forma news feature stories often consist of little more than a string of direct quotes broken up by transitions. For traditional reporters, quoting directly is a habit that's ingrained in the entire writing process, from gathering information to structuring a report. At the end of a game, a sports reporter heads for the locker room to get his quotes. And feature writers often prowl for a good "kicker quote," a pithy comment just right for a closing line.

I just called up the Metro section of my morning paper, and every one of the six main reports contains a direct quotation in the first five paragraphs. A bar owner says he's going to fight charges that he runs a disorderly joint. ("We are taking every single alleged violation, and we are going to defend ourselves.") An organization announces a beach cleanup. ("All 362 miles of coastline, every inch that's accessible, will be cleaned.") A parachute rigger says he can tell if a chute found in the woods belonged to a notorious skyjacker. ("I packed it; I put it together. So I would know it.")

Each of those quotes serves a useful purpose, and there's no denying that the direct quote has its place. Good ones lend authority, tell us what others think, and add colorful voices. Indeed, this book is filled with direct quotes, most of them either examples from published work or comments from writing experts who bring expertise to the subject.

Magazine and book writers, as a rule, are more willing to step out with a strong personal voice and an authoritative narrative style, which often gets them away from quoting directly. But that doesn't mean they use dialogue instead. Much magazine and book content is purely expository, summary narrative that tells you how to find a fishing hole or prune a pear tree. Other than the author's, it often contains no human voices whatsoever. That's fine. If my pear tree's looking gnarly and a master gardener wants to tell me about pruning, I'll pay close attention to his voice alone. But if you want to tell a true *story*, your readers should hear your characters talk to one another.

One of the secrets of the modern podcast's success, of course, is that members of the audience *can* hear characters talk to one another, at least if the reporter is savvy enough to capture authentic dialogue as it unfolds among the characters she's covering. Print reporters have a tougher time getting the feel of a real conversation, but the best manage beautifully.

Here's an example from McPhee's "Travels in Georgia," this one drawn from the stop at the stream-channelization project marked on McPhee's spiral graphic, the one I included in the chapter on structure. Two wildlife biologists strike up a conversation with the operator of a huge power shovel. The man's tearing up prime wildlife habitat, but the biologists nonetheless display the flattering charm they use to get information out of the locals.

"Howdy," said Carol.

"You're taking some pictures," he said.

"I sure am. I'm taking some pictures. I'm interested in the range extension of river frogs, and the places they live. I bet you turn up some interesting things."

"I see some frogs," the man said. "I see lots of frogs."

"You sure know what you're doing with that machine," Carol said. The man shifted his weight. "That's a big thing," she went on. "How much does it weigh?"

"Eighty-two tons."

"Eighty-two tons?"

"Eighty-two tons."

"Wow. How far can you dig in one day?"

"Five hundred feet."

"A mile every ten days," Sam said, shaking his head with awe.

"Sometimes, I do better than that."

"You live around here?"

"No. My home's near Baxley. I go where I'm sent. All over the state."

"Well, sorry. Didn't mean to interrupt you."

"Not 't all. Take all the pictures you want."

"Thanks. What did you say your name was?"

"Chap," he said. "Chap Causey."

Note how McPhee mixes physical action—"the man shifted his weight"— with the dialogue, reinforcing the sense that you're there watching the scene unfold and hearing old Chap firsthand. And after a digression on stream channelization, the Soil Conservation Service, the traditional rationale for such projects, the ecological damage they do, and the growing opposition, he quickly returns to physical action:

> After heaving up a half-dozen buckets of mud, Causey moved backward several feet.

Of course, dialogue isn't an end in itself; it has to do some real work. It can advance action as characters encounter and struggle with obstacles, such as an antagonist who resists a character's progress in resolving a complication. It can help shape a scene as characters comment on objects in their environment, such as the clothes one of them wears.

For all its strengths, dialogue does a lousy job of exposition. Savvy fiction writers have long understood that you should never make your characters say something they would already know, as in this imaginary snippet:

> "Say, Zeke, are ya plannin' to take those ponies up ta the corral ya built last winter before old Nellie got sick?"
>
> "Well, Hank, I figgered I'd jus' drop them mares off onna my way down to see Miss Vickie, who—as ya might remember—is the tall, golden-haired woman we seen in the saloon jus' outside your hometown a Wichita last week."

You're not likely to encounter such obviously contrived dialogue in the real world, of course. Actual human beings seldom explain what everybody involved in a conversation already knows. Sometimes they do voice useful background information, but you're still well advised to let that pass. Supply the background yourself in your role as narrator. Reserve dialogue for the things it does best.

Paraphrased dialogue is something else. As the narrator, you can approximate what the parties to a conversation are saying while you slip in background information as a kind of stage whisper to the audience. Richard Preston repeatedly uses the technique in *The Hot Zone*:

> Immediately afterward, Joe McCormick got up and spoke. What he said remains a matter of controversy. There is an Army version, and there is another version. According to Army people, he turned to Peter Jahrling and said words to this effect: Thanks very much, Peter. Thanks for alerting us. The big boys are here now. You can just turn this thing over to us before

you hurt yourselves. We've got excellent containment facilities in Atlanta. We'll just take all your materials and your samples of virus. We'll take care of it from here.

In other words, the Army people thought McCormick tried to present himself as the only real expert on Ebola. They thought he tried to take over the management of the outbreak, and grab the Army's samples of virus.

C. J. Peters fumed, listening to McCormick. He heard the speech with a growing sense of outrage.

Because we reveal so much of who we are by how we speak, what dialogue does best of all is develop character. Tracy Kidder captured much of the character of a small-town cop, as well as the daily reality of police work in a tight community, via the ongoing dialogue his subject had with friends and acquaintances:

He spent a larger part of every evening shift making friendly greetings, beeping at old friends and the parents of old friends in passing cars, waving to an old classmate, now a reporter for the local paper . . . , calling "Good evening, Your Honor" to the mayor as she walked out of city hall: He spotted a lawyer, one he liked, on a sidewalk and called to him through the cruiser's PA system, his amplified voice echoing off the buildings, "Charlie! It's good to see you wearing men's clothes again!" He turned down a side street and called to a staggering drunk, "Hey Campbell! You told me you weren't gonna do anything stupid. Go home and go to bed!"

It's not just *what* a character says that gives dialogue its power. Remember, dialogue happens in the context of a scene. The other action that's unfolding in the scene yields meaning, too. So when you're observing an unfolding scene, you want to record more than conversation. Remember when McPhee's power-shovel operator shifted in his seat? And notice how Kidder, in *Mountains beyond Mountains*, uses a sudden blush to reveal something important about Paul Farmer, the humanitarian doctor who serves as the book's protagonist. Here's Farmer, a warm, compassionate man who's embarrassed by praise or personal recognition, chatting with a Haitian friend:

"They had to tie up the dogs in the village, you walked around so late to see sick people," Ti Ofa declares. "I would like to give you a chicken or a pig."

Ordinarily, Farmer's skin is pale, with a suggestion of freckles underneath. Now it reddens instantly, from the base of his neck to his forehead. "You've already given me a lot. Stop it!"

Ti Ofa smiles. "I am going to sleep well tonight."

"Okay, neg pa,"—"my man"—says Farmer.

If you choose to write a nonfiction narrative in first person, you become a character in your own story. So your own conversations with other characters become fair game. They're not the kind of traditional interviews that yield direct quotations. They're casual exchanges that sound like real life, and they help advance the story by moving the action line forward or developing character. And, unlike an interview, the dialogue you report includes your part of the conversation and the action that contains it. So the other character's responses appear in a context that makes them much more meaningful. Gene Weingarten used the technique in "The Peekaboo Paradox," the *Washington Post Magazine* profile of a children's magician with a secret life as a compulsive gambler. The exchange not only probes the magician's character, but also reveals Weingarten's developing relationship with his subject:

> On the turnpike, en route to Atlantic City, I was doing eighty mph when I whipped past a state trooper. He followed me into the next rest stop, lights flashing.
>
> As we waited for the trooper to check my license, Eric said, quietly, "You know, if I had been driving, I would have been in real trouble."
>
> I smiled, relieved. "I know," I said. "Your court date is November 21."
>
> "How do you know that?"
>
> "I ran your police records," I said.
>
> For a moment, there was dead silence. Then: "So you didn't buy that I just really like to talk to cabdrivers, huh?"
>
> The cop may have been twenty feet behind us, but I suspect he wondered why two guys he'd just pulled over for speeding were busting a gut laughing.

INTERNAL MONOLOGUE

The movies can deliver slam-bang action in vivid detail. But film directors don't hold all the cards, and in some respects print enjoys a huge advantage. The movie camera only reveals external realties, the things that are visible to an outside observer. But print can explore the terra incognita of the human mind.

Remember the distinction between a mere string of events and a true story. As Joseph Conrad, Janet Burroway, and many others have pointed out, narrative in and of itself doesn't produce story. Only when narrative combines with motive does it become plot. So what's going on in the mind of your characters advances plot. It's an essential backdrop that explains action.

Travel with Tracy Kidder as he not only takes you along as his small-town policeman makes his rounds, but also takes you inside the cop's head when what the policeman sees sparks old memories:

> He drove through the old industrial neighborhood called Bay State, past what used to be the Clean Bore factory, and in his mind's eye the summer evening turned snowy. He remembered following footprints in the snow from the factory's front door and along the bank of the Mill River. He was an almost brand-new cop. It was getting dark when he saw the burglar up ahead.

Powerful though it is, traditional journalists often find the technique suspect. "Mind reading," they call it, with disdain. They've spent their professional careers learning how to avoid assumptions while sticking to verifiable facts. No wonder they find internal monologue troubling. Gay Talese had an answer for them. After *Honor Thy Father*, his book on the Bonanno organized-crime family, was published, he made the rounds of the talk-show circuit. The book is heavy with internal monologue, and one scene reveals what the family patriarch, Joe Bonanno, was thinking on a particular morning as he drove across the Brooklyn Bridge to appear at a Manhattan court proceeding. His host asked how he could possibly know what Bonanno was thinking at that exact moment. Talese replied calmly. "I asked him," he said.

Zing!

Walt Harrington, the former *Washington Post Magazine* reporter who's one of the strictest ethicists in the business, says his simple rule is that he won't tell you what someone is thinking "unless they tell you what they're thinking."[1]

Yes, most of us have a hard time remembering what we were thinking ten minutes ago, let alone years in the past. And yes, we all fudge our recollections a bit to make ourselves look better. And double yes, psychologists have demonstrated that there is such a thing as selective recall. So internal monologue is inherently suspect.

You can do certain things to improve your chances of getting it right. For one thing, you interview as soon as possible after the event, before memories degrade. Tom Hallman used a good deal of internal monologue in a series he did on neonatal nurses and the psychological strains they faced working on a level-three neonatal ward where many of their tiny patients died. But he limited himself to thoughts he probed on the scene, right as an event was unfolding. When a nurse stood outside an enclosure while a young couple held their dying baby, Tom was standing right next to her. He asked her what she was thinking, at that moment. Chances are, what she told him was exactly right.

You also can evaluate your source's recollection for internal consistency and logical probability, what scientists call "face validity." You can triangulate one account by interviewing multiple witnesses to an event or multiple participants in a conversation. You cross-check with documentary sources. (If your source says she was depressed by the rain that day, you check with the weather service to make sure it was raining.) If you're not absolutely sure about what was said, you paraphrase, rather than pretending you have the exact words by using quotation marks. And you limit your reconstruction to things that happen at dramatic highlights, the relatively rare points in a human life when the experience is so intense that memory kicks into high gear.

Reasonable writers might disagree about how much—if any—internal monologue to allow. But one thing most will agree on is that some sort of attribution should tell readers how you know what you know. In the story about the neonatal nurses, Tom Hallman attributed any internal monologue to the memory of the source. When you're reporting thought or conversation based on more distant memories, you can attribute with phrases such as "he recalled thinking" or "his memory is that," or "as he would later remember."

RECONSTRUCTED DIALOGUE
Reconstructed dialogue is especially suspect, and an ethical nonfiction writer will be extremely leery of putting remembered conversations from long ago inside quotation marks.

But, despite the obvious hazards, I've always been willing to accept some bits of reconstructed monologue when they reflect what somebody was thinking in a pivotal moment of the kind that sticks with us for a lifetime. Remember "A Ride through Hell," the story of an Oregon couple kidnapped by two desperados that was adapted for the television movie *Captive*? The writer, Barnes Ellis, included substantial passages of reconstructed dialogue *and* bits of internal monologue throughout the story. But they seemed reasonable to me. The couple had an experience that was seared in their minds. They were far more likely to remember what they said and thought during certain critical moments than you or I would recall from last week's trip to the supermarket. I have no doubt, for example, that the pair—Paul and Kathy Plunk—were exceedingly alert when the two fugitives showed up at the couple's Oregon Coast motel. The desperados whipped out handguns and demanded money. They were furious when the Plunks reached into the office cash drawer and came up with less than a hundred dollars. Kathy Plunk remembered what happened next:

> "There might be more upstairs," she said, thinking of unpacked boxes in the couple's living quarters. If only she could give them enough money, she thought, maybe they would leave.

The bit of dialogue is simple enough, and Kathy Plunk probably remembered it well enough to justify the quotation marks. Her memory of what she was thinking at the time makes sense, too.

For the same reasons, it's fair to think Mrs. Plunk was accurate when she recalled what she was thinking the first time she endured multiple rapes by one of the outlaws:

> "Is there anything here to be aroused about?" she wondered, trying to avoid panic through conscious objectivity. She saw a man filled with anger and rage.

And the strategy she devised to help her survive made perfect sense, too. One of the fugitives, a young man named Frost, seemed more vulnerable and needy, more likely to forge an emotional bond that would create empathy and fend off violence:

> "If I could get closer in some way to Frost," she thought, "and develop some kind of connection, or something, that might help our cause."

Journalistic strict constructionists might disagree, but I seldom waste much time questioning other short bits of dialogue or internal monologue taken from intense moments. Remember the deckhand on the *Taki-Tooo*, the woman who shouted "Oh shit!" as a huge wave was about to broadside the boat, sinking it and killing half the passengers? I have no problem accepting those as her exact words. After all, under the same circumstances, that's exactly what I'd say.

9

Theme

Narrative is a kind of back door into something very deep inside us.
—Ira Glass

Before Gary Wall's accident, he'd been a claims analyst for Blue Cross, the health-insurance giant. He'd seen the world in the navy, he'd dated pretty women, he'd rafted rivers. Then a car crash caused a catastrophic brain injury. He was in a coma for a week, and when he woke he didn't speak for two months. He couldn't remember how to swallow or control his bladder. He fell out of chairs. He couldn't recognize everyday objects such as forks, toothbrushes, and shoes.

Tom Hallman would eventually spend eighteen months, off and on, following Gary Wall's struggle to rebuild his life. He was there when Gary lost his Blue Cross job, and when he connected with a brain-injury rehabilitation program. He followed Gary's progress weaning himself off the Post-It Notes he used to remember the simplest task. He watched as Gary landed a job as a stock clerk at Target, began dating again, and established new friendships. And, through the entire year and a half, Tom and I talked regularly about the most fundamental issue in narrative nonfiction: *What does all this mean?*

I had the same conversation with dozens of narrative writers over the years, and it was always the most interesting part of my job. What could be more rewarding than puzzling out the life lessons that emerge from the struggles of our fellow human beings? As Ted Cheney argued in *Writing Creative Nonfiction*, this kind of narrative "doesn't just report the facts—it delivers the facts in ways that move people toward a deeper understanding of the topic."

So just what did Gary Wall's struggle reveal? Tom and I kept coming back to a computer metaphor Tom mentioned not long after he launched his reporting. Gary Wall's brain injury, he said, had erased his hard disk. The old Gary was gone. If he hoped to live out the rest of his years in ways that were at all rewarding, he would have to build an entirely new existence. But how do you do that? What is identity, anyway? The question had implications for virtually all readers. The answer would help Tom and me find what we routinely called "a universal"—a life lesson useful for virtually all potential readers.

Finding universals is what gifted storytellers know they must do to create work that rises above a routine report. It's what Deborah Barfield Berry and Kelley Benham French were after when they crafted a theme for "The Long Road Home" and expressed it in what they—in a nod to the old *Wall Street Journal* nut graf—called a nut section. Chip Scanlan asked them what the section accomplished. And French said that it links the specific story she and Berry were telling about Wanda Tucker's trip to Africa and a true universal. In it, French explained, "We need to lay plain Wanda's connection to Angola and say why her story matters. We need to make clear that the story is not just hers, but part of a much larger American story. This is the section where we need to really ring the bell at the top of the ladder of abstraction."

So what bell did Tom and I need to ring at the top of the abstraction ladder? Tom's computer-disk metaphor was key to finding a universal meaning to Gary Wall's life that would touch nearly every reader.

Genetics aside, we reasoned, we all start out like a blank computer disk. And, through life, we build a unique self that defines who we are, where we live, what we do. How do we do that in a way that satisfies our needs, that gives us pleasure and a sense of accomplishment?

As Tom and I talked, I recalled my grad-school study of philosopher George Herbert Mead's "looking-glass self," the idea that we build our self-identity from how we perceive others reacting to us. If our acquaintances treat us with pity, we'll think of ourselves as pitiable. At some level, Gary seemed to understand that. When he applied for a job as a stock clerk, his therapist offered to accompany him on his interview. No, he said, he'd go by himself. He didn't want the interviewer to hire him because of his disability, but in spite of it.

Tom and I dug deeper. What Gary seemed to be doing, we concluded, was deliberately acting to define a new self. Time and again he overcame fears and anxieties to reach out for a new place in the world. He was terrified when he first asked a woman out for coffee, but he did it. He devoted his free time to studying Target's product inventory so that he could interact with customers, another scary act of reaching out. He cultivated new friendships. Day by day, he was positioning the mirrors that would reflect a new looking-glass self.

The talks Tom and I had created a framework for elevating Gary's narrative to more than a sequence of facts. It gave us the ingredient that's missing from so much of journalism, the void that leaves facts empty of meaning, emotion, and inspiration. They gave us a *theme*. And a theme, Steven Pinker says, "is what your story reveals about human nature."[1]

THEME STATEMENTS

In a fully realized story, the action line—what we call "plot" in fiction—exists to serve the theme. Theme gives the audience a sense of time well invested. (What's the point of reading unless reading has a point?) Story scientists argue that one reason we are so attracted to stories is that their life lessons have survival value—which was why the brain evolved its built-in story wiring.

But a clear theme also focuses reporting and writing. So when Tom and I started talking about Gary Wall, we immediately began work aimed at finding a theme. Eventually, we settled on "action creates identity."

That theme statement gave Tom a guideline for his reporting. He'd focus on Gary's increasing assertiveness, the way he pushed himself outward as he recovered. When Gary overcame his isolation by forcing himself to take part in a church singles dance, Tom knew that was central to the theme. He made a special point to be there, and I made a special point of making sure a photographer was there, too.

As the story took shape, the text reflected theme at every opportunity. The lead emphasized Gary Wall's barren, postaccident existence:

> A bed, a dresser, and an overhead light. The bedroom was as barren as a thirty-dollar-a-night motel room.

And it established the idea that the room's occupant had lost his previous life:

> The only personal touch was a photograph taken during a rafting trip on the Clackamas River. The picture showed him grasping an oar and standing between three men and two women. He was smiling. He kept the picture because it was his last link to a lost life.

Tom reinforced the lost-identity motif again at one of the most important points in any newspaper or magazine story, the last word before the jump to an inside page. He described Gary lying in bed after awakening, trying to remember if he'd dreamed the night before. He hadn't.

There had been no dreams in six years, not since the day he died.

Bang! The opening spread ended on "died." The story continued on the inside pages as Gary rose, worked his way through the chores listed on the sixty yellow Post-It Notes in his apartment, and prepared for his bus trip to work at Blue Cross. Kathryn Scott Osler's opening photos showed him looking at himself in a bathroom mirror, adorned with a Post-It Note, and hunched over his breakfast table, surrounded by similar reminders. The loss-of-identity motif continued:

> What frightened him, though, was that he had lost the essence of himself. His sense of humor was gone. Subtleties in conversation and gestures were lost on him. He realized that he was missing the things that had made him Gary Wall. One by one his friends stopped calling. The man they had known no longer existed.

Then Gary's rebirth began, and Tom began driving home the core theme, that one by one your actions define your identity. Gary's therapist told him:

> You have a brain injury. But you can have a life. A different life than most of us, but still a life. It will be up to you to determine what kind of life you find.

Gary had dinner with his mother, who recalled that she'd divorced her abusive husband when she was twenty-nine and responsible for four young children. She started work as a hospital clerk.

> Eleven years later she was an assistant supervisor in charge of forty employees. "I know all about starting over," she told her son. "Don't let yourself be pushed down, Gary. Try. You will fail. But try again. You will make it. You are my son, and I believe in you."

Gary struck up a friendship with another brain-injured man, taking the initiative to find things they could do together. When a woman spoke to him at his athletic club, he asked her to coffee. ("This Diane Foster awakened something in Gary Wall, something he thought was dead.") He trained for a job search, interviewed for the Target job, and got it. ("And so his new life began.") He attended a singles dance and met a woman named Susan. She liked him because, among other things, he carried no baggage. ("Gary, she said, had no past. Yes, he admitted, he was starting over.") Gary thrived at Target and received a raise. He turned forty, and received another raise. His mother threw him a birthday party. Susan attended, and so did several of his new friends. Then a sour note: Susan found a new boyfriend and moved on. Gary reached his point of insight:

> He sat alone in his apartment and wondered what he had done wrong. If there was something he could have changed. He realized there was nothing. He had sought a life and found one. He had rediscovered that a life is filled with hope and disappointment, of dreams and realities, of joy and pain.
>
> That was life. Now he had to go live it.

Tom closed with Gary dressing to attend another singles dance. He splashed on some cologne—you never knew whom you might meet at a dance. He headed for the door, turning out lights as he went. All the Post-It Notes were gone, save the one on his door:

> "Believe," it said. "Don't doubt."

PUTTING YOURSELF INTO IT

A literary theme inevitably springs from the writer's personal values, his or her highly individual understanding of cause and effect in human lives. Lajos Egri, the playwriting guru, referred to the theme of a play as its "premise," the foundation on which the whole drama is built. And in his view you find the premise inside yourself, not flitting around somewhere in the external world. "It is idiotic to go about hunting for a premise," he wrote, "since . . . it should be a conviction of yours."

Or, as Nora Ephron put it, "All storytelling is a Rorschach."[2]

Every one of those conversations Tom and I had about theme—on the Gary Wall story and every other project we took on over the years—was an exploration of our beliefs about the world and how it worked. One of the reasons we made a successful team was that we shared basic understandings about reality. We believed in free will, the notion that you were master of your own fate. We thought credit belonged to those who earned it through their own actions. We thought human beings needed to come to terms with who they were, put greed and jealousies aside, open their hearts to others, and take chances. And we figured that if you gave it a shot, you'd often succeed, even if your standard of success changed along the way.

All that's fairly sappy, predictable stuff. A batch of clichés, really. But that's

OK. Thousands of years of human experience have given us just a few basic principles for living a good life, and they're bound to be a little shopworn. Predictable and obvious, even. Willa Cather, a real reductionist when it came to these things, is famous for having said, "There are only two or three human stories, and they go on repeating themselves as fiercely as if they had never happened before."[3]

Academic experts agree. Patrick Colm Hogan, professor of English and comparative literature at the University of Connecticut, argues that the three prototypes that account for two-thirds of story narratives are concerned with three basic topics: struggles for power, romance, and food. Other experts list more topics, but still confine themselves to a relative few. "As many scholars of world literature have noted," Jonathan Gottschall notes in The Storytelling Animal, "stories revolve around a handful of master themes." He listed sex, love, fear of death, the challenges of life, and power. Others come up with more. In The Book on Writing, former Dallas Times-Herald writing coach Paula LaRocque rattled off nearly five times as many: "Some of the obvious theme or action archetypes," she wrote, "are quest, search, journey, pursuit, capture, rescue, escape, love, forbidden love, unrequited love, adventure, riddle, mystery, sacrifice, discovery, temptation, loss or gain of identity, metamorphosis, transformation, dragon-slaying, descent to an underworld, rebirth, redemption."

"Loss or gain of identity," eh? I guess those Gary Wall conversations weren't all that original. But, as I've been saying, thematic originality is no virtue. As Jon Franklin pointed out, clichés may be an embarrassment at the sentence level, but they are at the heart of theme. "At the conceptual level," Franklin wrote, "the cliché undergoes a strange metamorphosis: It becomes an eternal truth."

Connecting with readers means finding the context that links the lives of your protagonists with their own.

When my colleague Doug Binder told the story of a man who found new love after his wife died, dozens of readers wrote to thank him. Many of them echoed the reader who wrote, "Possibly it moved me so much because it touched much that has happened in my own life, but I think only a good writer can do that—find a commonality with his readers."

If your protagonist lives a life that seems especially alien to your audience, you must take special pains to demonstrate connections. The Charlotte Observer's Tommy Tomlinson once wrote about a mathematician's solution to a problem that most of us would find arcane, but Tommy still managed to find a larger lesson in the quest: "He knows now that figuring out the mysteries of giant number fields isn't that different from working out the problems of everyday life. You break them down into small steps. You leave them alone now and then so you can come back fresh. Mainly, you trust what your instincts tell you."

When you think about it, every theme incorporates a lesson. That's the value added that draws an audience to a story in the first place. The bigger the lesson, the more value added. The biggest have the enduring quality we associate with great literature.

Paula LaRocque touched on the instructional qualities of story themes when she wrote that "archetypal tales, from fairy tales and *Aesop's Fables* to *Madame Bovary* and *The Sweet Smell of Success*, are in their essence moral or cautionary tales. In contemporary art, they are sophisticated and subtle extrapolations of universal patterns. They seek cause, consequence, reason, and order."

And, she added, "So does humankind."

If all humanity is the subject, then all human beings—not just celebrities—are possible subjects of our storytelling. And, indeed, one of the main characteristics that distinguish narrative nonfiction from conventional journalism is the fact that so much of it tells tales not of potentates and publicly acclaimed heroes, but of ordinary folks facing the challenges of ordinary living. Steve Weinberg, writing in *Columbia Journalism Review* about the rise of nonfiction narrative, noted that "a cornerstone of this journalism trend is an emphasis on noncelebrities. They could be called 'ordinary people,' except that journalists choosing them believe part of the job is to find the extraordinary in the ordinary."

Weinberg went on to quote the historian Will Durant, who's often cited where narrative nonfiction writers gather. Durant wrote:

> Civilization is a stream with banks. The stream is sometimes filled with blood from people killing, stealing, shouting, and doing the things historians usually record; while on the banks, unnoticed, people build homes, make love, raise children, sing songs, write poetry, and even whittle statues. The story of civilization is the story of what happens on the banks. Historians are pessimists because they ignore the banks for the river.

FINDING THEMES

I suspect that even fiction writers find that their themes emerge from their material. They start with interesting characters, disturb their tranquility with a good complication, and let 'er roll. The way those characters resolve the complication emerges from the author's beliefs about how the world works.

Nonfiction writers *must* find their themes in their material. The world delivers the facts, and nonfiction specialists have to make some sense of them. "By meaning," Jon Franklin once said, "I really mean the shape of the story and what the shape of the story says. It's not something that you bring to the story. It's something that you find in the story and extract from the story."[4]

Several tricks of the trade can help you find that something. Tom French says he often zeroed in on a theme when he was struggling to write a title. "I'm always looking for an overall title," he said, "as well as titles for the various parts and chapters. It's a way of orienting your brain toward the essence of the story, also its structure and drive."

For the *Oregonian*, I usually worked with the writer and the copy desk to come up with titles and subtitles, and those helped us target the theme even more directly. We organized the Gary Wall story around the idea that "action creates identity," and Gary Wall illustrated the point because he'd lost his old life and took aggressive action to build a new one. For the main title we came up with "A Life Lost . . . and Found." For the subtitle, we wrote, "To Build a New You, You Must First Build a New World."

Tom French may plunge directly into his search for a title, but I like the process Hallman and I followed with Gary Wall. First, we come up with a theme statement, and we use that to find both the title *and* the shape of the story.

We're in good company. Several gurus of narrative—Jon Franklin, Lajos Egri, Bill Blundell, Robert McKee—endorse the idea of a theme statement. And they're in remarkable agreement about the shape it should assume. "A true theme is not a word but a sentence," McKee says, "one clear, coherent sentence that expresses a story's irreducible meaning."

A sentence must, of course, contain a verb, and that's key to writing an effective theme statement. Franklin strives for active verbs. I'm even more persnickety. I want transitive verbs, the variety that takes direct objects. Because they answer the question "what?" sentences built around transitive verbs show causality. And causality is the essence of a theme that tells readers how the world works and how they can influence it. Hence, "Action creates (what?) identity."

Lajos Egri, you may remember, referred to the theme as "the premise." And his formula for stating a premise suggests how a good theme statement helps you discover the shape of your narrative. "Every good premise," he said, "is composed of three parts, each of which is essential to a good play. Let us ex-

amine 'Frugality leads to waste.' The first part of this premise suggests character—a frugal character. The second part, 'leads to,' suggests conflict, and the
third part, 'waste,' suggests the end of the play."

So the theme statement suggests your structure. It guides your reporting. It
helps you find a title. If you have to cut, it tells you what can go and what must
stay. In one way or another, it affects every phase of the writing and reporting
process.

Because a theme statement is so valuable, the first word I write on any project
is always the same. I open a new computer screen and type "T-H-E-M-E." Then
I hit the colon key and sit there for a minute, puzzling over just the right noun-
verb-noun structure for my statement. As I write this, the first line on this computer file reads "THEME: Stories wring meaning out of life."

Once I have a theme, I do a little outline—topical or scenic, depending on
the material—that will guide me through the theme's development. Then I'm
off on the writer's journey, secure in the knowledge that I know my destination.
When I arrive, I erase the theme statement and outline.

A theme statement is a kind of elixir that even helps writers work with editors. Hashing one out together provides common ground, a shared standard
for making decisions about a story. When I'm coaching a story, I often suggest
that the writer come up with a theme statement fairly early in the process. Then
the two of us work together to polish it, eventually arriving at something that
synthesizes our two sets of values.

That's what Hallman and I did on the Gary Wall story. Tom did most of
the work, of course. But I have to think that the way we worked together as
writer and editor had something to do with the story's ultimate outcome. And
we must have done something right. "A Life Lost . . . and Found" swept the
feature-writing categories for our state and regional writing awards. Patsy
Sims selected it for Literary Nonfiction, an anthology of top American newspaper, magazine, and book narratives that included work by Tracy Kidder,
John McPhee, and Tom Wolfe. And it was one of three finalists for that year's
Pulitzer Prize for feature writing.

10

Reporting

The crucial part that reporting plays in all storytelling, whether in novels, films, or nonfiction, is something that is not so much ignored as simply not comprehended.
—Tom Wolfe

Decades ago I served a stint as a police reporter for a midsized daily. I'd stop by the newsroom each morning, salute the city editor, and stroll to the sheriff's office, just a couple of blocks away. "Anything happening?" I'd ask the desk sergeant. "Just what's there," he would say, waving a hand at a box of press releases. I'd sift through them, scan the previous night's activity log, and jot a few notes. From there, I'd head to the county jail, where I'd repeat the process before heading out for stops at another three or four police and fire departments. Then it was back to the newsroom for a determined attack on my typewriter. Some days, I'd grind out five one-source wonders—short, superficial reports that were typical of newspaper work in that era.

A decade later, Tom French tackled "South of Heaven," one of his first major narrative efforts at what's now the *Tampa Bay Times*, and helped change the rules of the game. To better understand the challenges of modern public education, Tom tracked a half-dozen high school students who represented everything from academic overachievers to potential dropouts. He spent a year reporting and writing the story.

The newsies who'd been trained my way, with pro forma beat reporting and a checklist of official sources, were skeptical of the narrative approach. After "South of Heaven" appeared, Tom French's editor—quite aware of the raised eyebrows all around the newsroom—scheduled him for a sort of internal book tour. Tom visited his newspaper's various departments and bureaus to explain how he'd managed to spend so much time on one story. I saw the same attitude in my shop. When narratives began appearing in the *Oregonian*, hard-boiled old beat reporters whispered among themselves. "What's this foo-foo literary stuff?" they'd ask. "Where's the reporting?"

In fact, what they were seeing was reporting that went way beyond the superficial fact gathering of conventional news coverage. Reading press releases, checking statistics, consulting experts, attending meetings—all that's no more than a preliminary scouting expedition for a narrative story that explores life as it's actually lived in the real world.

To be sure, reporting for narrative is dramatically different from the reporting that produces a standard police-beat story. It may involve large amounts of time simply hanging around, watching and thinking. It often ignores conventional information-gathering techniques such as sit-down interviews. It goes beyond public utterances to probe the psychology that explains action. It explores social context, cultural values, and identity. When we began experimenting with narrative at the *Oregonian*, its reporting protocol was so alien to traditional methods that some old hands didn't even recognize it for what it was.

But it was—and is—hard-nosed reporting.

And, as *New York Times* reporter Steven Holmes said after working on the Pulitzer-winning "Race in America" series, "Reporting is the key to good journalism, and it makes no difference what kind of journalism you're talking about."[1]

IMMERSION

Being there and watching. And listening, and smelling, and feeling. That's immersion reporting. And, although not all narrative nonfiction involves immersion reporting, the technique is a hallmark of the form. Norman Sims discovered that John McPhee traveled 1,100 miles of highway with his wildlife biologists to write "Travels in Georgia." "You've got to understand a lot," McPhee said, "to write even a little bit."

Ted Conover may be the ultimate practitioner of narrative immersion and has even written a guidebook, *Immersion*, outlining his techniques. The author of *Newjack*, *Whiteout*, *Coyotes*, *Rolling Nowhere*, and *The Routes of Man* slips into the worlds he writes about so thoroughly that he, in effect, assumes a new identity. For *Newjack*, he spent almost a year as a Sing Sing prison guard, walking the cell blocks, hanging with the other guards, and drawing a regular paycheck.

As far as the cons and staffers knew, he *was* a prison guard. His membership in prison culture gave him access to a world inaccessible to quick-hit feature writers. "Patience is a huge part of it," Conover has said. "Being able to live 'without knowing' is crucial to the method."

The approach echoes ethnography, the branch of anthropology devoted to comparative descriptions of the world's cultures. Not surprisingly, Ted Conover studied ethnography at Amherst and wrote an ethnographic undergraduate thesis on the time he spent as a railroad hobo, the experience that he turned into *Rolling Nowhere*. But, instead of describing Micronesians or Maori, narrative journalists penetrate the subcultures of our own society, sending back dispatches to those of us who lack the time and reporting skill to discover parallel universes on our own.

But there's one big difference between ethnographers and immersion reporters. In *The Literary Journalists*, Norman Sims points out that, "like anthropologists and sociologists, literary journalists view cultural understanding as an end. But unlike such academics, they are free to let dramatic action speak for itself." When Tom Hallman told Gary Wall's story, he never once stepped back and baldly stated that "action creates identity." The story unfolded naturally, showing rather than telling. The theme, emerging as it did from the flow of life, had much more power than a pronouncement from a soapbox.

Cynthia Gorney, a veteran narrative journalist who got her start at the *Washington Post*, has developed a kit bag of immersion-reporting techniques. Gorney, who has published in an impressive array of national magazines and taught at the University of California, Berkeley, journalism school, says she approaches her reporting by asking questions such as what it's like to actually be her subjects and looking for the most interesting or surprising aspects of their worlds. She says she answers those questions by:

1. "Breathing their air."
2. Quietly observing, hanging around."
3. "Understanding the rhythm of their typical work."
4. "Learning their vocabulary."
5. "Reading their literature"—texts, guidebooks, professional publications.
6. "Finding their gurus."

One of Gorney's projects for the *New Yorker*, "Chicken Soup Nation," explored the publishing phenomenon built on the sappy success of *Chicken Soup for the Soul*. Spin-offs from the original now include more than 250 titles and staggering total sales of more than 110 million books. Gorney interviewed publishing company execs. But she also hung around at the publisher's Santa Barbara offices, watching the receptionist open submissions for new "Chicken" books. She likens such reporting to the police ride-alongs that beginning reporters typically take to craft one of their first feature stories. Unfortunately, police ride-along stories are almost always a cliché, and the practice stops with one night in a squad car. Gorney urges more. "Police ride-alongs," she says, "ought to happen in lots of different fields."[2]

The time invested in becoming part of a subculture pays rich dividends because it gets writers past the roadblocks that usually bar entry to outsiders. We all keep our guard up around strangers. But familiarity breeds trust, or at least indifference. The "fly-on-the-wall" technique operates on just that principle. Once something gets familiar enough, it disappears into the background. Only then, the theory goes, will the subjects of an immersion reporter's interest relax and become themselves.

Of course, a fly on the wall won't go unnoticed with a camera crew in tow or if it's flitting around with a microphone. Documentary film and podcasting lack the subtlety of print reporting with a notebook stuck inconspicuously in a hip pocket. Nonetheless, stick around long enough and even a bulky TV camera will sink into the background. In 1971 PBS aired *An American Family*, a gripping bit of immersion reporting that documented the breakup of the Loud family. The omnipresent crew shot three hundred hours of film to produce twelve one-hour episodes, becoming such a constant in the lives of family members that they essentially forgot the cameras were there. At one point Pat Loud demanded—on camera—a separation from her husband, Bill.

Some critics argued that the cameras encouraged the Louds to perform—to do things they wouldn't otherwise have done. The same criticism has been leveled at print reporters as well, of course. In the end, only the honesty of reporters can minimize the effect of their presence. And, in the end, *An American Family*, ended up on *TV Guide's* list of "The 50 Greatest TV Shows of All Time," For better or worse, it also won widespread credit as the first reality TV show.

Regardless of occasional controversy, there's no doubt that immersion reporting can be deeply revealing, uncovering layers of meaning hidden to conventional journalists. Sometimes, it's the only way to get at a subject. Ted Conover tried the standard approach when the *New Yorker* asked him to write about prison guards, but the authorities wouldn't give him the access he needed. A year in the trenches produced *Newjack*—an insider's view of prison life and its problems that standard reporting never would have brought to the surface.

Likewise, Tom French's immersion in a year of high school produced an understanding of the problems of modern education that never would have emerged from school board meetings, PTA workshops, or conventional interviews with teachers, administrators, and students.

Sometimes interviews aren't even an option. In 1965 Gay Talese headed to California for an *Esquire* profile of Frank Sinatra. The singer had the sniffles and refused an interview. Talese hung out, talking to Sinatra's acquaintances and members of his entourage, gathering tidbits and biding his time. He spent every minute he could following Old Blue Eyes around, a fly on the wall observing the phenomenon that occurs when a temperamental pop icon becomes his own industry, the center of a solar system of orbiting musicians, music-business honchos, rat-pack wannabes, and assorted hangers-on. The story began with an engaging scene-setter:

> Frank Sinatra, holding a glass of bourbon in one hand and a cigarette in the other, stood in a dark corner of the bar between two attractive but fading blondes who sat waiting for him to say something. But he said nothing; he had been silent during much of the evening, except now in this private club in Beverly Hills he seemed even more distant, staring out through the smoke and semidarkness into a large room beyond the bar where dozens of young couples sat huddled around small tables or twisted in the center of the floor to the clamorous clang of folk-rock music blaring from the stereo. The two blondes knew, as did Sinatra's four male friends who stood nearby, that it was a bad idea to force conversation upon him when he was in this mood of sullen silence, a mood that had hardly been uncommon during this first week of November, a month before his fiftieth birthday.

"Frank Sinatra Has a Cold" was an early masterpiece of the New Journalism, a reporting tour de force that *Esquire* still touts as "one of the most celebrated magazine stories ever published." Sinatra had been one of the most remote, guarded celebrities in American pop culture. Talese ripped away the veil, allowing *Esquire* readers to see him close up, in unguarded moments, behaving as naturally as a lion running free in the Serengeti. And all because the great man refused an interview.

ACCESS

You can't just knock on a door, walk into a stranger's house, and assume your fly-on-the-wall observation point. Somehow, you have to talk your way in.

Successful narrative reporters have developed techniques for overcoming the resistance of reluctant sources, and they share personality traits that disarm resistance.

Reporting for narrative defies the stereotype of the brash, aggressive, in-your-face reporter. The top narrative writers I know have uniformly mild, polite dispositions, nonthreatening in every sense of the word. Tom Hallman is boy-ish, wide-eyed, and endlessly interested. Rich Read oozes bottomless sincerity. Anne Saker bubbles with contagious enthusiasm.

Furthermore, they're genuinely *interested* in what their sources have to say. They flatter, in the best sense of the word, honestly putting average folks in a celebrity spotlight that makes them feel special. When you speak, they look you in the eye, taking in every word, nodding, leaning forward, their faces echoing your emotions,

Notice the startling uniformity among narrative stars when they talk about their approach to sources:

Truman Capote: "But, above all, the reporter must be able to empathize with personalities outside his usual imaginative range, mentalities unlike his own, kinds of people he would never have written about had he not been forced to by encountering them inside the journalistic situation."[3]

Lane DeGregory: "When we open our eyes and ears, stop being snobs, realize we haven't heard it all before, and allow ourselves to witness other worlds with honest wonder, stories emerge."[4]

Leon Dash: "If you have a judgmental reaction in your eyes during an inter-view, or a judgmental nuance as you pose a question, people will close down."[5]

Ted Conover: "I'm the interested listener who is seldom disputatious. . . . I often try to position myself as a student to their teacher. I am a person who doesn't know much: Can you help me?"[6]

Richard Ben Cramer: "The thing is that people *want* to tell their stories. But only if you're interested in them, which I am. . . . Their wives and girlfriends have long since tired of hearing about him, and here comes this kind of wooly guy who *really wants to know.* All the stuff they know about this amazing guy, but have never been given the opportunity to really explain, is finally going to be heard. They're in heaven."[7]

Mary Roach: "Magical things happen when you're obviously fascinated by a topic."[8]

Not that good narrative reporters are credulous pushovers. Barging into other people's lives takes quiet confidence and relentless determination. If you fail once, you try again. And again. "Stubbornness really helps," says Tom French, "being really, really stubborn."[9]

So do persuasive tactics. At the *Oregonian*, we did a lot of tick-tocks, narrative reconstructions of major news events. Typically, these were tragedies, accidents, and disasters that cost several lives. The survivors, shaken and paranoid, had been assaulted by intrusive television news crews and terse wire-service reporters. That's when I advised reporters to use the "it's-your-one-chance-to-get-history-right" argument. Anyone who's been swept up in major news knows that preliminary reports of the event are often shallow and misleading. So survivors often welcome a chance to set the record straight. As a narrative reporter setting out to reconstruct the entire event, you tell them—quite honestly—that you're going to give their story the time and attention it deserves. The rest of the world will finally understand how such a thing could happen, and why survivors did the things they did. You'll strive for absolute accuracy. Everything will be in context. And they will have a complete record to pass along to the grandchildren.

The pitch almost always works, especially if the reporter making it approaches with the kind of humility and sincerity that typifies the narrative writer. Tom Wolfe, extravagant as always, parodied "the continual posture of humiliation" involved in such reporting:

> The reporter starts out by presuming upon someone's privacy, asking questions he has no right to expect an answer to—and no sooner has he lowered himself that far, than already he has become a supplicant with his cup out, waiting for information or for something to happen, hoping to be tolerated long enough to get what he needs, adapting his personality to the situation, being ingratiating, obliging, charming, whatever seems to be called for, enduring taunts, abuse, even the occasional roughing up in the eternal eagerness for "the story"—behavior that comes close to being servile or even beggarly.

Yep. I've been there. You put on your reporter's hat, and you slip into another personality, one that gives you license to do and ask things that you would never consider in your nonreporting life. But it's not really an act. Those of us attracted to this game naturally fall into the role of quiet outside observer. We often come from middle-class or lower-middle-class backgrounds. We somehow manage to get decent educations that give us analytical skills and the cultural context needed to find meaning in the mundane. We grow up crossing the usual cultural barriers, learning how to talk to longshoremen, steel workers, bureaucrats, and college presidents.

Nora Ephron, one of the most self-reflective practitioners of the narrative craft, nailed the personality type in the introduction to her essay collection *Wallflower at the Orgy*. Reporters, she said, were the kind of people who seemed most comfortable on the sidelines, hanging back with a certain kind of detachment while they watched others play the game of life. "I always seem to find myself at a perfectly wonderful event," she wrote, "where everyone else is having a marvelous time, laughing merrily, eating, drinking, having sex in the back room, and I am standing on the side taking notes on it all."

OBSERVATIONAL AND RECONSTRUCTIVE NARRATIVE

Nothing beats seeing the action firsthand. If you can tell readers you saw it with your own eyes, you carry the kind of credibility that's admissible in court. And observational narrative—the kind generated by full-body immersion—projects authority. Your writer's voice naturally sounds more confident when it's not undermined by attributions and speculation. "Listen to me, pal," you seem to be saying. "I was there, and that's the way it was."

But immersion reporting is a huge risk. You could spend a year or more on a book that sells poorly. Or a month on a magazine piece for a fee that averages out to minimum wage. An editor who lets a reporter chase a big narrative story takes a valuable staffer out of the daily mix for weeks with no guarantee that the result will pay off with readers. As Norman Sims put it, "Literary journalists gamble with their time."

The risks are especially high with narratives that need all the essential story ingredients—a sympathetic protagonist, a complication with universal applications, rising action, climax, and resolution—to work. But the real world doesn't necessarily work like a perfectly formed story. You might follow an athlete for months only to have her drop out just before the championship match. Or a love-conquers-all yarn may end with rejection and disappointment. As the bumper sticker has it, "Shit Happens."

But even if it does, there may be a way around it. Yes, I've occasionally commiserated with disappointed reporters as they sat in my office, shoulders slumped, while we pulled the plug on a story that took weeks of work. But every story development says something about life, even if it wasn't part of the original theme statement, and you often can pull a story out of the hat even if it isn't the one you thought you had. Tom Hallman and I figured Sam Lightner's story, the one that won the Pulitzer, was going to be about the lengths that Americans will go to look like everybody else. Sam's surgery nearly killed him, all right, but it didn't do all that much to change his appearance. So Tom and I looked for other lessons in Sam's experience. The way he came to terms with a bad situation gave us something much more powerful—and universal—than our original approach would have produced.

The risky element in observational reporting suggests one of the advantages of taking the opposite tack—reconstructing a past event by interviewing witnesses, searching documents, and retracing the action line. Because you're working backward from a known destination, you guarantee yourself a satisfying outcome. You just have to pick the right story in the first place.

When we decided to go after "The Green Wall," the reconstructive narrative I described in the chapter on point of view, the curtain had already closed on the entire drama. After several days of spot-news coverage, we knew that some of the rafters trapped by an unexpected storm on the Illinois River had lived, and that some had died. We had good access to the survivors. So, going in, we knew that story had everything we'd need to tell a dramatic tale.

A dogged researcher can reconstruct a surprisingly lifelike narrative of events decades in the past. G. Wayne Miller's *King of Hearts*, an amazing reconstruction of how Walt Lillehei pioneered open-heart surgery a half century before, pulsated with vivid, detailed action.

> Asleep, Gregory was stripped of his gown and left naked under the glare of hot lights. How small he was—smaller than a pillow, smaller than most laboratory dogs. His heart would be a trifle, his vessels thin as twine.
>
> All set? Lillehei said.
>
> The people with him were.
>
> Lillehei washed Gregory's chest with surgical soap. With a scalpel, he cut left to right on a line just below the nipples.
>
> Observers in Room II's balcony leaned forward for a better look. On the operating-room floor, a crowd of interns and residents climbed up on stools.
>
> Lillehei split the sternum, the bone that joins the ribs, and opened a window into Gregory with a retractor.

Nestled between his lungs, Gregory's plum-colored little heart came into view. It was noisy; with his hand, Lillehei felt an abnormal vibration.

Wayne Miller was nothing if not dogged in his pursuit of such detail, and his forty-one pages of source notes and bibliography reflect a savvy and persistent research effort. For his account of little Gregory Glidden's case, for example, he tracked down two of the little boy's nurses and discovered that they'd kept a detailed diary of his entire hospital stay.

Miller had the advantage of some surviving witnesses. But Erik Larson tackles subjects beyond the reach of any living memory. Nonetheless, he used letters, newspaper accounts, court records, diaries, memoirs, and collections of private papers to craft *Devil in the White City* as vividly as though he were actually there for the 1893 Chicago World's Fair. "No document," he says, "is worth overlooking."

For *Isaac's Storm*, an account of the deadly Galveston hurricane of 1900, Larson turned up a city of Galveston insurance map with a schematic on every house—building material, stove location, and so on. He notes that searchable databases now exist that are built from eyewitness accounts describing specific locales in several cities, such as one for London during the period 1890–1900. I once ran across a similar database, produced by a consortium of universities and Google Earth, to re-create Rome as it existed on June 21, 320 AD, during the reign of Constantine the Great.

It's surprising how often modern technology produces records that good reporting can weave into a you-are-there narrative line. Cell-phone and surveillance cameras capture scenes that would have been lost not many years ago. The ubiquity of good-quality video cameras means that bystanders often produce detailed visual records of dramatic events. When the fishing boat *Taki-Tooo* went down on the Tillamook Bay bar, my reporting team was able to get video from a television freelancer who shot the rescue and recovery operation. When I assigned a narrative class to the sinking of the *Sea King*, a fishing boat that went down on the Columbia River bar, we discovered a trove of contemporary documents. The Coast Guard report contained a verbatim record of the radio traffic between the boat, the Coast Guard station, and the rescue boats on the scene. The National Transportation Safety Commission investigation included a score of eyewitness accounts. But the real jewel was even better than an eyewitness account. On the day the *Sea King* got into trouble, the Coast Guard was testing its brand-new motor lifeboats on the bar. As luck would have it, one of the crewmen was shooting video as the boats battered their way through the surging breakers. After a Coast

Guard vessel took the *Sea King* under tow, the crewman recorded the entire scene: The cutter that tried to shield the foundering boat from the raging sea. The helicopters that dropped Coast Guard rescue swimmers onto the fishing boat's deck. The sudden, sickening motion as the *Sea King* wallowed and went beneath the waves, killing one of the fishing crew and a brave young Coastie.

INTERVIEWING

Even if you practiced total immersion for a story narrative, observing every step of the action line, you'd still have to do some interviewing. Tom Hallman came close to the immersion ideal for "The Boy behind the Mask," but he still interviewed friends, parents, teachers, nurses, and doctors. What's the point of following a doctor around, observing her every move, when she's doing paperwork or making hospital rounds? You observe a doctor when she's treating *your* patient. You interview her when you want general information about a disease or a treatment.

An informational interview for a narrative differs little from interviewing for a conventional journalistic report. Early in his reporting, Tom might have asked, for example, fairly abstract questions about Sam Lightner's condition, medical history, and prognosis. But an interview to reconstruct a narrative line you haven't seen yourself is a different animal altogether.

I learned how challenging such interviews could be early in my career, when I was researching *The Information Empire*, my history of the *Los Angeles Times*. Many of the key players in my story were still living, and I interviewed them at length. As a young reporter, I was shocked by the foibles of human memory. My interview subjects either couldn't remember significant events or carried only the foggiest recollections of them. Or, worse yet, they remembered significantly different versions of the same thing. Often those memories were self-serving, inflating their own contributions or ignoring the contributions of others. Victory really does have a thousand parents, while defeat remains an orphan.

Part of my problem was my own fault. I simply wasn't a very sophisticated interviewer in those days, and my questions failed to produce the kind of vivid detail and authoritative evidence I needed to write an engaging narrative. Since then, I've learned a bit.

First of all, it helps to let your sources know exactly what you're trying to accomplish. And that's especially true if they're public figures who are used to conventional media interviews, the kind who will give you quotable sound bites devoid of vivid detail. It helps to tell them that you're *not* writing a standard report, that you're trying to re-create the story as it looked, sounded, and felt like as they were living it. You might tell them to think of their experience as a series of scenes, as in a movie, and to describe the details that fill each scene.

Mark Kramer, says, "When I need to include a scene that I didn't observe but must glean from interviews, I say to the people I'm interviewing: 'Listen, the next fifteen minutes of our conversation will be hard work, not normal conversation. I want you to work with me, please, as though we are two carpenters. I need parts to assemble.' They aren't haplessly yammering while I take things down but become complicit helpers in building the scene. They create the story *with* me."

When it comes to remembering specifics, one memory can trigger another. So it's often helpful to remind sources of where they were and what was going on when critical events took place. "The office log says you attended a meeting at the state capitol that morning. The university president resigned that afternoon, probably when you were driving back to campus. Do you remember when you first heard about it? Was it on your car radio? Where were you then? What kind of car was it, anyway? What color?"

One thing you owe your sources, whether you're interviewing or silently observing, is an up-front discussion that explains the rules of the game. Traditional journalistic ground rules work well, regardless of whether you're writing a book, shooting a documentary, recording for a podcast, or interviewing for a blog. Consider each of them an ironclad contract. Once you and a source agree to a ground rule, you're bound to it unless you renegotiate. The standard ground rules are:

> On the Record: You can use an accurate version of the conversation without restriction.
> On Background: You can use the information for developing your story, but you can't attribute it to your source, even if you cloak the source's identity. If you want to publish the information, you must get it on the record from another source, and you must publish with attribution to that source.
> Not for Attribution: You can use the information, but any attribution must be to a mutually agreeable cloaked source. For example, if you plan to attribute a quotation to a "source close to the president," your source must sign off on that description.
> Off the Record: You can't use the information unless you get it on the record from another source and publish with full, uncloaked attribution to that source.

The ground rules aren't frozen in the tundra. They're open to negotiation and subject to wide variation. Maybe a source doesn't want you to describe or photograph a particular room in her house. Or doesn't want you asking about a nasty divorce. Accept the deal or not, depending on how important the issue is to you. You may decide that you can't agree to a demand without distorting the essential truth of your story. But if you accept a condition, stick to it unless you can renegotiate later.

I've found that sources often ease up on their demands once they see not-for-attribution or even off-the-record information in the context of a story. I write up a version that includes it and let them read it. "This seems pretty harmless to me," I say. "Are you sure you don't want it included?" Chances are they'll relent.

Politicians and other sources used to public scrutiny will be familiar with the customary ground rules—and they'll hold you to them. But the kind of folks who often show up in narrative nonfiction probably won't be that savvy, and you owe them thorough explanations and appropriate reminders. The most important caution is that everything is on the record in the absence of any agreement to the contrary, even in situations ordinarily considered private. Once a source walked into the men's room, stepped up to the urinal next to mine, began his business, and started discussing some sensitive information. Reluctantly, I said something like, "That's on the record, right?" As I remember, he asked me to forget what he'd just said and quickly changed the subject.

Although they're probably less important than *how* you interview, the old journalistic arguments about audio recorders, note-taking, and interview locales do pop up when narrative writers talk shop. I'm not sure it matters all that much. It doesn't make much sense to run audio recorders through long observing sessions because you'll end up with hours of recording holding almost nothing of value. I see no reason not to record conventional interviews or rich moments of dialogue, although a long-ago experience with a twisted tape taught me to *always* back up tape recordings with notes. Today's digital recorders and smart phones are much more reliable, but I still think backing up with notes is a good idea. In any event, I don't share the fear that audio recorders inhibit sources, producing a kind of Heisenberg effect that alters their words and behavior. If they did, all narrative podcasts would be suspect. Besides, modern recorders are quiet and inconspicuous, and sources get used to them in the same way they get used to fly-on-the-wall observers. And smart phones are so ubiquitous these days that they disappear into the landscape. In any event, sources forget both the reporter and the recorder.

Still, a lot of narrative writers try to keep recorders and notebooks to a minimum when they're in a scene with a source. Gay Talese occasionally pulled out a notebook for an especially juicy quote, but he also took notes when a source was out of the room. And, like Ted Conover and many others, he would type up more complete notes at the end of the day. Conover was essentially undercover for *Newjack*, his chronicle of life as a Sing Sing prison guard, and he couldn't just whip out a reporter's notebook. But, fortunately for him, prison guards carry small notebooks in their breast pockets so that they can document rule violations and the like. Conover attracted no suspicion when he jotted down descriptions of intense moments on the cell block.

If you record a telephone conversation electronically, be sure to let your source know you're recording. That's the honest thing to do anywhere. But if you record secretly in states with a two-party consent statute, you'll be breaking the law if you don't. That's why Apple doesn't allow phone-recording apps on iPhones. There are ways around that limitation on some recording apps, and recording phone calls is easier on Android devices. But the legal restrictions still apply in states that require two-party (or all-party) consent.

Most good reporters agree that face-to-face interviews are best and that informal settings help to loosen up sources. I've always tried to avoid sitting across a desk from a source, even for a conventional news interview. Richard Ben Cramer doesn't like interviewing in living rooms, because "that's where you sit with your hands folded." He asks sources if they can move to the kitchen table. Good idea. And, in my experience, beer helps.

CHARACTER, SCENE, ACTION, AND THEME

When writers come to me for coaching, I always spend the first couple of sessions learning how they operate. I quiz them about how they organize their material, find structures, and write drafts. One of the most revealing exercises is a look in their reporting notebooks. If they're newsies, the chances are that I'll find page after page of direct quotations.

The quote-filled notebook promises dull writing for conventional news stories, and it's death for narrative. How can you tell a real story if you lack the raw material you need to build character, create scenes, describe action, or develop themes? A narrative writer's notebook—or even the notebook for a good feature writer—should be filled with visual details, anecdotes, action sequences, smells, and the like. The best even include reporting on the reporter, noting any questions, emotions, or other internal reactions that occurred during observation. All those can help guide the writing.

As reporting proceeds, these notes will become more and more focused on traits that reflect the larger themes beginning to emerge. You immerse yourself in your POV character's world, taking it all in and thinking hard about what it all means. Cynthia Gorney once said she created raw lists of things she saw and heard during that early phase, zeroing in on more limited categories of detail as she discovered which were especially meaningful.[10]

Character drives story, and a narrative writer's notebook should be especially rich in scribbled observations of physical appearance, facial expressions, gestures, tone of voice, and all the other elements of direct characterization. Taking such notes is especially important when you're observing dialogue—for conveying meaning, the nonverbal cues are often more important than the actual words. During a standard interview, an old reporter's trick is to ask a question you don't really care about so that you can jot down details of physical appearance, clothing, and surroundings while the source drones on.

Remember that a story begins when somebody wants something. So reporting for a story narrative should focus on motivation. For a major project, Jon Franklin conducts what he calls a "psychological interview" that may go on for hours. He starts by asking about childhood memories, looking for the genetic and behavioral roots of motive. Then he works his way through the protagonist's life, targeting key decisions and the elements that went into them.

Most narrative reporting isn't nearly that elaborate, but for anything but the most basic yarn you still need a theory of personality to guide information gathering. Alden Whitman, the New York Times obituary writer profiled in Gay Talese's "Mr. Bad News," was calm, methodical, and matter-of-fact, with a romantic streak. So Talese focused on details—Whitman's pipe, his bow tie, his morning cup of tea—that reflected that personality. Tracy Kidder dug deep into Paul Farmer's past to find out why the humanitarian doctor, who was plenty competitive and ambitious, didn't display the usual American drive for wealth and comfort. The details of Farmer's chaotic childhood—part of it spent on an old boat moored in a swamp—revealed worlds.

The details build your theory, and your theory guides the search for more details. Once you conclude you're dealing with a neat freak obsessed with order, ask to peek in his sock drawer. If all the socks are rolled up, arranged in rows, and sorted by color, you've made your case.

The same back-and-forth between theme and observation guides the selection of visual details and pieces of the action line. To write nonfiction narrative, Truman Capote said, "It is necessary to have a 20/20 eye for visual detail—in this sense, it is quite true that one must be a 'literary photographer,' though an exceedingly selective one."[11]

A character's social structure is almost always relevant to motive. We usually want what our friends and colleagues value, or what we think is valued in the social circles we'd like to join. So one way you probe motive is by noting the "status indicators" that Tom Wolfe sees as so revealing. Does your character drive a Prius or a Hummer? Does the rack in his garage hold cross-country or downhill skis? Does she drink bourbon or scotch, wine or beer?

Because it shows a human being actually expressing personality in the world, nothing reveals character like an anecdote. Remember Carol, John McPhee's wildlife biologist, reaching into a semi-submerged hollow stump to pull out Sam the Snake?

Some of the reporters I worked with brought home great anecdotes all the time, and some had about as much hope of bagging a revealing little story as they did of harpooning a blue whale. My old University of Oregon teaching colleague Ken Metzler, author of *Creative Interviewing*, supplied the hint that explained why. "To get stories," he said, "you have to tell stories."

That's it! Somebody tells us an agonized tale of a disastrous travel delay, and we respond by dredging out our own misery-loves-company yarn of missed connections or lost baggage.

To get anecdotes, you prime the pump by telling a story—either on yourself or your protagonist—and asking for another. "X is quite the neat freak. He showed me his sock drawer, and the socks were all rolled and sorted by color! I bet he does things like that at the office, too."

Careful selection ensures that even small details and relatively mundane personal stories have impact. "You really need to have faith in the power and importance of tiny, tiny moments," Tom French says. "Newspaper reporters are trained so that we are really good at big moments. But the longer I do this, the more I learn to have faith that in those times when it looks like nothing is happening. In front of me something very important is happening. I just need to learn to pay better attention."

If readers know that you have a point, that you're not just aimlessly flopping around among the sights, sounds, and facts of personal history, then they'll pay close attention to the details you've selected. "It's like a Tiffany's window," Mary Roach says. "If there's only one thing in there and if you really set it up, you can really make it shine."[12]

When it comes to finding that gem, the quality of the setting is far more important than the quality of the stone. And the quality of the setting reflects the quality of your thinking as you proceed through the reporting process. "What does this mean?" you constantly ask yourself? "Why did she do that?" "What does this say about the challenges we all have to face?"

If you keep asking, you'll keep finding, even if what you find is not what you expected. "The odds are overwhelmingly against the prepared scientist making any particular discovery," Jon Franklin says, "but it's a foregone conclusion that he'll discover *something*. . . . The same process is at work when a skilled writer stalks the true short story."

AN EYE FOR STORY

Once you learn how to break the world down into the universals of story, you start seeing stories everywhere. Look for a good conflict, and chances are you'll find a good story. Recognize a good protagonist, and chances are you'll find a challenge that will interest an audience.

Ken Fuson sharpened his vision by looking for characters with everyday desires. "I really try to narrow the focus down to what does this person want and are they going to get it?" he said. "Are they going to win the game or get the award or give the speech without passing out?"[13]

Tom Hallman focuses on complications, too. Once he spots someone facing a challenge, he sticks close, gambling that he's found a protagonist who will eventually resolve his complication. When a young lawyer in a big firm gave up his hefty salary to take a poorly paid post in the county prosecutor's office, Tom followed his every move, hoping the change in circumstances would lead to some insight about the human condition. When a developmentally disabled young man moved out of his mother's house and into his own apartment, Tom tagged along, eager to see where the adventure would lead.

Not all complications have resolutions, but all resolutions stem from complications. So Jon Franklin suggests finding your way into stories from the resolution end of the equation. And lots of resolutions, he points out, are as close as your nearest news source. "Most news stories are endings," he says, "without beginnings attached." A report on a traffic accident, for example, may conceal the heroic series of actions that led to the survival of a victim.

Franklin, a two-time Pulitzer winner, credits his ability to see the world in terms of story ingredients as the primary ingredient in his success. "I know what a story is . . . and equally important, I know what a story isn't. As a result, I can readily put my finger on a good yarn."

The savvy nonfiction storyteller soon realizes that good yarns are everywhere. A news story about a woman who survived ten days lost in the wilderness. The realization that you've finally put one of life's traumas behind you. A cop's quest for a killer. The mental stress neonatal nurses endure when their tiny patients die. An obsessed scientist. A washed-up quarterback. Just about any topic can yield a great story . . . so long as you know what you're looking for.

11

Story Narratives

Stories are like snowflakes in that they're all alike, but they're all different.
—Jon Franklin

Like any good craftsmen, skilled nonfiction narrative writers know their tools. Early in the process of launching a narrative, they cast cold eyes on their material and ask a fundamental question: "Just what sort of narrative are we talking about here, and what tools will I need to build it?"

They have a lot to choose from.

A story narrative comes closest to the protagonist-complication-resolution model that most of us have in mind when we talk about a "story." But there's considerable variety even within this basic category. Move beyond it, and you operate differently. Explanatory narratives often lack something as basic as a protagonist. In a narrative essay the narrator is the protagonist. A tick-tock is entirely reconstructive. A vignette is entirely observational.

All those forms offer rich possibilities for the nonfiction writer, and we'll get to each in its turn. But first things first. Let's talk about true *stories*, short and long.

SHORT STORY NARRATIVES

"The rich are different from us," Fitzgerald supposedly said. "Yes," Hemingway replied. "They have more money."

And short narratives are different from long narratives. They have fewer words.

That makes more difference than you might think because once you restrict the number of words, you limit the kind of story you can tell. The difference between a short and a long piece in nonfiction is the difference between the short story and the novel in fiction. A short piece of writing lacks the running room necessary to probe the complexities of character. So a general principle of fiction—that the novel explores character and the short story explores situation—also applies to nonfiction.

For that reason short nonfiction narratives focus on action. Stu Tomlinson's story about the cop who rescued a woman from a burning car, the example I used in chapter 1, had fewer than eight hundred words, nearly all of them devoted to the action line that began when the police officer saw the accident that created the situation. We learned nothing about the character of the victim, who didn't even speak until the final paragraph. And we didn't learn much more about Jason McGowan, the officer who saw the car crash, captured the driver who caused it, and struggled to put out a stubborn fire in the victim's car.

Short narrative writers also must confine themselves to one or two scenes. As a rule of thumb, I figure about five hundred words as a minimum for creating a scene and the action line it contains. Accordingly, Stu's eight-hundred-word burning-car story was essentially one scene, followed by a shorter episode in the hospital. A three-thousand-word magazine narrative might contain six scenes. A four-part newspaper series or substantial magazine cover story could hold thirty. A podcast can accommodate up to ten or so scenes an hour. A full-length book can hold a couple of hundred.

Short story narratives also have to start faster and end more abruptly, the narrative arc spiking up and falling precipitously. I urge writers to burst out of the blocks with immediate action. Stu began with "the pickup blew by . . ." He ended with a terse denouement, the hospital scene that gave the survivor a final word.

The arc, steep as it is, can include all the essential ingredients—exposition, rising action, crisis, climax, resolution/denouement. A short piece can have a theme, of course, but it will lack the depth and subtlety of longer, more literary narratives. Stu's action-packed adventure told us little more than that "decisive action saves lives."

Still, every true slice of life with a positive outcome says something about successful living. One of my favorites, a truly epic yarn dripping with guts and glory, popped out someplace I never would have thought to look, demonstrating that great narrative lurks all around us.

———————

David Stabler, the *Oregonian*'s classical music critic, attended the Oregon Symphony's Saturday night performance, and dutifully filed a review praising Canadian pianist Louis Lortie for his performance of Sergei Rachmaninoff's

Third Piano Concerto. That was no small achievement—the "Rach 3" is a dev-ilishly difficult blizzard of notes known as one of the toughest piano pieces in the classical repertoire. But Lortie was booked for a three-day run, and he had two performances to go.

Then, on Sunday evening the symphony's publicist called David during the performance. Lortie had injured his hand. He wasn't playing the Rach 3 that night, and he wouldn't be playing Monday either.

Hmmm. In story terms, a comet had just knocked a planet out of stable orbit, and David, who'd made the finals for a Pulitzer Prize with an earlier nar-rative, knew the game was afoot. He and his editor, Doug Perry, arrived in my office to plan the unfolding story. The narrative arc was far from complete, but Doug and I urged David to rough out a story draft anyway. The sooner you begin writing, the sooner your brain will begin processing the story.

Initially, David focused on the scramble to save the Sunday night perfor-mance. The draft he wrote the next day began this way:

> The phone call every orchestra manager dreads came ninety minutes
> before Sunday's Oregon Symphony concert. Louis Lortie, the star soloist
> of the evening, was in too much pain to play that night.
>
> What happened next was a race to save the concert, due to begin at
> 7:30 p.m.

That race made for a nice little drama, plenty to power a narrative feature for the cover of the lifestyle section. Thirty minutes before curtain, symphony conductor Carlos Kalmar huddled with the symphony president and the artistic director. The musicians gathering for the concert joined the conversation, a scene David reconstructed by interviewing the publicist and the principal par-ticipants.

> The musicians began suggesting alternatives, pieces they'd recently
> played: "The Flying Dutchman" Overture. The "1812" Overture, minus
> cannons. Beethoven's Fifth.
>
> The music had to be in the orchestra's library upstairs, which holds one
> hundred symphonic works, and it had to be substantial enough to fill the
> second half of the concert. Someone suggested asking the audience to vote
> on three or four pieces, but that idea went nowhere.
>
> When Tchaikovsky's Fourth Symphony came up, heads nodded. The
> musicians play the dark, turbulent piece fairly often, most recently in May
> with only minimal rehearsal. Standing in a group, they mentally played
> through their parts.

The symphony librarian gathered the scores and handed them out during intermission. Then the orchestra pulled off the impromptu performance by thundering through the Tchaikovsky and earning a standing ovation. The symphony president stationed himself to deal with patrons disgruntled because they'd been denied the Rach 3. Some expressed disappointment, but nobody asked for a refund.

David, Doug, and I worked our way through David's rough draft. It was short—about nine hundred words. David had laid it out as a chronology ("7:30 p.m. onstage" . . . "8 p.m. symphony office"), which emphasized the time pressure involved in salvaging the Sunday night performance. It did a good job of capturing the drama inherent in choosing a substitute piece of music and carrying off the improvised second half of the concert. But it closed with direct quotes from Lortie and an update on his condition, which kept the focus on the injured pianist and gave the story the flavor of a standard news feature, rather than a true narrative.

> "This is the last thing I wanted to happen to me," he said. "I'm the kind of person who goes through whatever. I considered playing with dropped notes, but it could have been a disaster. It was very difficult to choose. There's little time left, and you just follow your instinct."
>
> Lortie flew to Oakland, Calif., Monday to consult with specialists. "I'm really worried. I don't want to think about other concerts coming up."

But in paragraph eleven, about midway through the draft, was information with the potential to develop into a much larger drama. The symphony's artistic director, Charles Calmer, was anxious to satisfy patrons who'd come to the Sunday concert specifically to hear the Rach 3. Some had traveled long distances, and all were anxious to see a top musician tackle this notorious beast. Since Lortie canceled, Calmer had been on the phone, relentlessly dialing in an effort to find a substitute pianist for Monday's performance, the last in the three-concert series.

The significance of that emerged as Doug and I coaxed more information out of David. The paper was lucky to have such a knowledgeable music critic, one with three degrees in piano performance. David had himself "approached" the Rach 3, as he put it, attempting the score but never mastering it. His personal experience gave him special authority when talking about the music and special insight into what Calmer was trying to do. Only a handful of pianists could play the Rachmaninoff, stars who were usually booked a year or more in advance. So after the Sunday concert, David had remained in touch with

Calmer and the symphony publicist, following the search, which extended into Monday morning. David was dubious. He later recalled thinking, "Good luck finding someone who can play it *tonight*."

Calmer was more confident. And on Monday at 10 a.m., he scored. Yakov Kasman, a Russian pianist who'd won a silver medal in the Van Cliburn International Piano Competition, was teaching at the University of Alabama. He knew the Rach 3. He was available. And there was one seat left on the last plane leaving Birmingham with connections to Portland.

Here were the makings of a cliff-hanger drama with the elements of a wilderness survival story. Kasman had never been to Portland. He'd never met Carlos Kalmar, the symphony director. He'd never played the Rachmaninoff without a rehearsal, and he hadn't touched the piece for five months. An eight-hour flight would touch down in Portland at 7 p.m. With luck, he'd get to the concert hall a few minutes before curtain.

Before that Monday morning, I'd known nothing about the Rach 3. But as we talked, I grew more and more excited. If things worked out, David had a hell of a story on his hands, one that could easily grab a prominent slot in Wednesday's paper. He'd do the additional reporting he'd need to reconstruct the Kasman search, he'd attend the Monday night performance, and he'd spend Tuesday working with Doug and me to write the complete narrative.

After the first story conference, David did some additional reporting and made a second run through the story. He began the way he led his first draft, adding a bit of detail about the phone call, which the symphony director took at a restaurant near the concert hall. Then the story proceeded in narrative form, recounting the scramble to substitute Tchaikovsky's Fourth for the Rach 3. He didn't have his climax—the concert was still hours away. But all the pieces were in place:

> On Monday morning, Kasman jumped on a plane through Minneapolis but wasn't due to arrive until seven p.m., an hour before curtain. . . . Calmer planned to zip him from the airport straight to the hall, where Kasman would change into white tie and tails and briefly go over the music with Kalmar. Kasman would first touch the piano only minutes before his performance.

That evening David strolled into Portland's Schnitzer Concert Hall, an Italian rococo edifice that seats nearly 2,800. He settled into a seat in Row L, high in the balcony. And, purely by chance, David found himself next to Henry Welch, a Portlander who'd interrupted a Sacramento business trip to fly home for Sunday night's concert. The Rach 3 was Welch's favorite piece of classical music, and he'd groaned at the announcement that Lortie was hurt. When he'd heard about the Monday night replacement, he'd booked a seat for that concert, too.

Kasman's plane touched down on time. Calmer rushed him to the concert hall. Kasman went to the piano, where he had seven minutes to practice. Then he huddled with Carlos Kalmar, the symphony director, to go over tempos and transitions. At eight o'clock, Kalmar walked onstage to announce that the Rach 3 would go on. Welch clapped wildly. Kasman walked out from behind the curtain. "It was fabulous," David remembers. "Out walks this little Russian guy. He was not smiling. He looked as if he wanted to be somewhere else."

Kasman raised his hands to play and—astonishingly—absolutely nailed the entire thundering performance.

The next morning, David, Doug Perry, and I gathered in my office for our second conference. We walked through the entire narrative, talking about story arc and plot points. David wondered if he should even use the material on the scramble to save the Sunday night performance with the Tchaikovsky substitution. Wouldn't it be better, he asked, to focus entirely on the search for Monday night's Rach 3 soloist? We kicked it around. I argued that good narrative includes rising and falling tension, which the Tchaikovsky episode provided. And, because many of the Sunday night patrons were devoted fans who'd come specifically to hear the Rach 3, the episode would help set up the Monday performance by emphasizing the stakes riding on it. And besides, the Tchaikovsky performance offered some pretty good drama in its own right— eight new symphony players had never performed the Tchaikovsky with the Portland orchestra.

As we talked, I roughed out the narrative arc on a yellow legal pad. We came up with the plan duplicated in figure 7.

I urged David to develop the opening so that it functioned as a full-fledged scene that captured the atmosphere of the elegant restaurant where symphony president William Ryberg first heard that his star pianist was injured and couldn't play. When the fatal phone call arrived, I suggested, David should withhold its contents, heightening drama. We wrapped up the meeting, and David went off to write. When he came back with Version 3, his original opening had morphed into:

> At six p.m. Sunday, William Ryberg was sitting in the linen-tabled South Park restaurant, a block from the Arlene Schnitzer Concert Hall. Ryberg, the Oregon Symphony's president, and Seldy Cramer, who manages

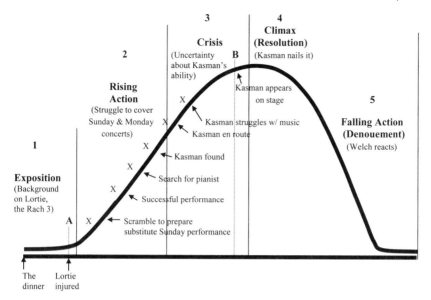

Figure 7. "Rescuing the Rach"

careers for international musicians, had just ordered seafood stew and Moroccan chicken when Cramer's phone rang.

Abruptly, without explanation, Cramer got up and left the restaurant.

The new version also introduced Henry Welch, stressing the sacrifices he'd made to attend the Sunday concert and his groaning disappointment when Lortie canceled and the symphony substituted Tchaikovsky's Fourth. Additional reporting revealed details that amplified the buildup for Kasman's risky performance. It pointed out that Kasman had never fully capitalized on his Van Cliburn showing by developing a top-flight concert career; so the Oregon performance would be a big opportunity for him. And it emphasized the size of the bet the symphony was making:

> Within minutes of hearing that Kasman had said yes, the Oregon Symphony's communications department sent e-mail messages to ten thousand symphony friends, made one thousand phone calls to Monday's ticket holders, and sent press releases to five radio stations, four TV stations, local newspapers and, of course, orchestra members.

David had a brief opportunity to interview Kasman after the performance, and he picked up details that brought the pianist's urgent trip across the country to life. Kasman had wolfed down chicken and pasta, his last meal for ten hours, while his wife frantically packed his bag. He had tried to work through the Rach 3 in his head during the long flight, but he remembered the music so poorly that he gave up in frustration.

Most important, Version 3 had an ending, and it was all that David, Doug, and I had been hoping for. Defying all expectations, Kasman had blasted through the entire performance with confidence and verve. The audience loved it.

Doug and I agreed that Version 3 had all the elements for broad reader appeal. We put it on the proposed schedule for the next day's paper, and I was confident that I could sell it at that afternoon's news meeting. All that remained was the final editing, followed by copyediting and design.

Doug and David gathered in my office. I sat at the computer, hands on the keyboard, and they pulled up chairs behind me. As is my habit, I read the copy aloud, and we discussed possible changes. The structure was solid. All that remained was fine-tuning the writing to maximize the drama and climactic resolution.

David still remembers one of those fine points. "Dreads" is a terrific kicker word, I said. It's one syllable, it has a strong consonant sound, and it has tremendous emotional content. Furthermore, it's about as close as you can get to "dead." So we have to figure out a way to end the first sentence with it. We fiddled with the words and came up with: "At six p.m. Sunday the phone rang with the news every symphony director dreads."

So it went through the copy. A tweak here, a bit of tightening there. I urged David to let his authority and voice come through. As a storyteller, he was more than a music critic here. He was an accomplished pianist in his own right. He knew the Rach 3. He could offer insight that would let naive readers like me understand how tough the damned thing actually was.

As the final edit proceeded, we added more background on the Rach 3, clarifying its diabolical reputation. We came up with the phrase "ogre of the musical world" to describe it. David mentioned that it had driven David Helfgott, the Australian prodigy who inspired the movie Shine, to madness. We talked more about its difficulty and added that "few of the world's pianists have large enough hands, or strong enough nerves, to take it on."

We worked at making better use of Henry Welch, the Rach 3 aficionado, especially in the conclusion. In Version 3, Welch appeared only once, to illustrate the following the Rach 3 has and the disappointment many fans felt when it was canceled Sunday. But in Version 4, Welch became a continuing character. We used him to set up Kasman's Monday performance, stressing the doubt that heightened the drama:

> At eight p.m., Welch, one of 2,354 expectant listeners, sat in Row L of the balcony, mopping his brow. His friend had called him at work that afternoon, saying the symphony had found a soloist. Welch was skeptical. He'd never heard of Kasman, and he knew the Rach. Nonetheless, he dashed home, showered, and changed.

Most importantly, Welch gave added cachet to the ending, embodying action that created an electrifying image for readers, one that resolved tension with the power of specificity.

> Kalmar raised his baton and the orchestra entered. Kasman, keeping his eyes fixed on the conductor, lowered his hands to the keys.
>   What followed defies explanation.
>   From the first notes, Kasman sailed through the music, playing the massive chords with voluptuous tone and even inserting a playful quip now and then. He missed a few notes at the top of some breakneck leaps, but nothing that disturbed the music's texture. Most extraordinary, his playing transcended the notes, difficult as they were, and took on the natural, assured quality of a storyteller enjoying his tale.
>   The final, thundering chords had him standing straight up off the bench. Welch rocketed out of his seat, shouting with joy. Around him, the audience erupted with cheers.

We sent the story off to the copy desk, which came up with a stellar headline: "A Round-the-Clock Race to Save the Rach." The designer combined the headline with mug shots of the symphony president and conductor on the Metro section news front, and a photo of Kasman at the piano on the jump page. The presses turned at midnight, and 350,000 copies headed for doorsteps, newsstands, and vending machines.[1]

On Tuesday the reaction rolled in. "What an incredible story you told this morning!" wrote one subscriber. "I was spellbound." Another called to say that, by David's crescendo conclusion, he was on the edge of his chair. It was, according to other readers, "a crackling story," "wonderfully written," "extraordinary." Praise rolled in from the newspaper's own staff, including the executive editor.

David, as is his way, calmly smiled and took it all in. Even more than Kasman, he projected "the natural, assured quality of a storyteller enjoying his tale."

LONG STORY NARRATIVES

The final version of David Stabler's ripping little yarn came in at just under 1,200 words, about standard for a newspaper feature, a two-page magazine spread, or a one-episode podcast. It would have worked as a broadcast or online news feature, too, and it had great multimedia possibilities. Because it was so short, it would focus almost exclusively on action in any medium, with scant attention devoted to character or scene. In David's version, we learned little about Yakov Kasman, other than the fact that he was gutsy enough to fly two-thirds of the way across the country and tackle a monstrously difficult piece of music, without practice.

The equation changes when you have room to spread your wings. Action will continue to play a central role, of course—we're talking about *story* narratives here, and it is action that creates the narrative arc. But expanded length allows a storyteller to paint vivid scenes and to develop character much more fully. Especially when the storyteller is someone with the talent of a Julie Sullivan.

Julie comes by her gift naturally, having grown up among Irish immigrant yarn-spinners. Her father and uncles, she remembers, tried to top one another with outrageous tales. "I grew up," she says, "listening to people tell stories *competitively*."

Born in Butte, she attended journalism school at the University of Montana, and worked at newspapers in Montana and Alaska before landing at the *Spokesman-Review* in Spokane, Washington. She knew little of narrative theory, but her instincts were to tell stories the Irish way, with good windups, climactic conclusions, and a focus on people. "You can't effectively write about people without narrative," she says. "There's no other way to capture what happens in a life."

In addition to her sense of story, she had a way with words, and the lyrical quality of her instinctual narrative attracted national attention. While she was in Spokane, she won the prestigious American Society of Newspaper Editors award for short feature writing.

She came to the *Oregonian* and plunged into work covering the upcoming census, a beat that led her to stories on immigrants abused by the incompetence of the Immigration and Naturalization Service. Rich Read joined the effort, which got me involved. Then my fellow managing editor, Amanda Bennett, assembled and led a team that included Julie, Rich, and some of the paper's best investigative reporters. The resulting series won the Pulitzer Gold Medal for Public Service, the highest prize in American journalism.

It also brought Julie close to the investigative team, which soon turned its attention to Central Oregon's Warm Springs Indian Reservation. Following a tip, the team turned up appalling statistics on the mortality rates among reservation children and young people. The I-team had plenty of firepower for documenting the fact that kids were dying at Warm Springs in numbers that dwarfed those elsewhere in the state. But it needed someone like Julie to tap the human side of the story, to illustrate the causes of this human disaster with a narrative that would let readers understand it in their bones.

Julie teamed up with Rob Finch, named two times as national Newspaper Photographer of the Year, and for four months the two of them repeatedly took to the highway, trekking for more than two hours over treacherous mountain roads to Warm Springs. But tribal society, ever suspicious of outsiders, shut them out. "It was horrible," Julie says, recalling the stone wall of hostility and indifference they met at every turn. Finally someone told them of an old man, living in a remote corner of the reservation, who had lost seven children to accidents, suicide, and murder. Julie and Rob drove to the hamlet of Simnasho, found Chesley Yahtin's house and knocked. He opened the door, saw the two of them, said "I don't talk to honkies," and slammed the door in their faces. Julie, who has a reputation for never coming back without a story, knocked again. Chesley Yahtin opened up once more, and Julie said, "Mr. Yahtin, I understand some of your children have died, and I want to talk to you about that."

What followed was a jaw-dropping trip to the inner sanctum of reservation life. Chesley Yahtin provided entrée to the Warm Springs courts, schools, social services agencies, jail, and, most importantly, his own family. He gave Julie all she'd hoped to find in the way of a central character, a narrative arc, and a window into the world that the *Oregonian* would eventually document in a series titled "A Place Where Children Die."

Once Julie realized she had the makings of a lengthy narrative, her editors directed her to me, launching a fulfilling partnership that would last until I retired from the newspaper. We began with long talks about what she'd discovered so far, trying to apply the universals of narrative theory to the specifics of the Yahtin family and the culture of Warm Springs. The story raised all the basic questions about characterization, scene-setting, structure, point of view, and theme.

Point of view was our first issue. Julie was smitten with Chesley Yahtin, and in many ways he seemed ideal for the central POV character. He'd been born when Warm Springs Indians still practiced many of their traditional ways, and then forced into the boarding schools that disrupted native culture and led to many of the problems that would eventually afflict the reservation. He was a warrior, a decorated Korean War medic, and he was a functional, hardworking wage earner who'd lost most of his children and was struggling to raise his grandchildren. He danced the old dances, and practiced many of the old ways. He was a "real Indian," as one White child said when he spotted Chesley. The main argument in his favor as the protagonist, from my point of view as editor, was that Julie really liked Chesley, and the old man was sure to emerge as a sympathetic character.

But as a protagonist, Chesley Yahtin suffered serious drawbacks. A good protagonist is, most of all, the captain of his fate. For a story to take a form that offers a valuable life lesson, the protagonist must engage the complication, grapple with it through a period of rising action, and ultimately resolve it through his own initiative. But in this story Chesley was much more the passive victim. He'd lost his children, and he struggled to cope with the grandchildren running wild in his own house. Nothing he did as Julie and Rob reported the story was likely to change that. Chesley might provide a flat action line for an explanatory narrative, but the odds were against him creating the arc of a true story narrative. That would require a character capable of significant change.

The weekend after Julie knocked on his door, Chesley Yahtin drove to see his daughter Dorothy in Portland, where she was enrolled in a residential treatment program for alcoholism. "She was," Julie remembers, "funny, big-hearted, generous, and a source of great quotes. She also was a loving mother who was a hopeless alcoholic. You were constantly torn between being delighted with her and wanting to kill her."

Dorothy, in other words, was no flat character. She had the depth and complexity Julie needed to capture a fully rounded human being. And Julie immediately recognized that Dorothy also epitomized the very problems that "Where Children Die" hoped to explain. Dorothy also carried the potential for change, if only she could kick the booze and reunite with her kids.

As Julie and I talked, I realized she already had the glimmerings of a strong theme that could not only anchor her narrative, but could also hold the entire series together. The problem at Warm Springs, she was beginning to conclude, was that the attempt to integrate Native Americans in the larger culture had wiped out the indigenous system of social control but had failed to replace it with anything else.

In the nineteenth century, the Warm Springs tribes had been forced off their ancestral lands, including the rich fishing grounds of the Columbia River, and moved onto the high desert land of the current reservation, which combined three tribes with different traditions and values. And in first half of the twentieth century, when Chesley Yahtin was coming of age, the White man's boarding schools tore kids like Chesley from their homes, suppressed their native languages, and destroyed a social structure based on multigenerational extended families. Chesley's generation never learned how to raise children the traditional way, gently teaching by example. In the old days, little discipline had been necessary because the kids had few temptations or alternatives. Unaware of any options, they modeled the responsible behavior of the adults they saw around them. But in the modern world, children raised without discipline amid the drugs, alcohol, and other temptations of modern culture ran amok.

Chesley's seven dead children embodied the disaster that resulted, as did the crippled survivors like Dorothy. They were the broken link in the chain of mid-Columbia Indian culture that had survived for millennia. If the Warm Springs tribes were to continue as an intact society, the chain would have to be repaired.

The title we would choose for Julie's narrative, "The Broken Chain," expressed that core concept. And the protagonist we chose reflected it as well. If anybody was to mend the chain, it would have to be Dorothy and the other members of her generation. The old men and women of Chesley's era were passing from the scene. Only what remained of the next generation—Dorothy's cohort—could salvage the children who'd been growing up without them. They had to step up.

Dorothy had a shot. She was sober for the first time in years, and she might just graduate from the alcohol-treatment program in Portland. If she did, she could possibly reclaim the kids who'd been taken away from her by the courts, the ones staying with Chesley in Simnasho. If she did that, she would have resolved her complication through her own actions. And Julie would have her narrative arc.

So we crossed our fingers and went with Dorothy. It was a risk. If she fell off the wagon, she'd probably lose her children for good, and we'd lose our chance for one of Jon Franklin's "constructive endings." We could still write a tragedy, a story about a complication defeating a protagonist. But what would one more Native American tragedy teach anybody? We wanted what Aristotle referred to as a comedy—a story about a protagonist defeating the complication.

So the story was Dorothy's. And it would have to begin with Dorothy. But where? Clearly, the rising action began with her trip to Portland and her enrollment in the rehabilitation program. What had preceded that? What ordeal had finally motivated Dorothy to try rising above her history of drunkenness and irresponsibility? Julie went back to Warm Springs and dug into Dorothy's recent past, interviewing tribal members who'd been with her when she hit bottom in the weeks before Julie and Rob entered the picture.

At first Julie's reporting was reconstructional. She interviewed witnesses who'd seen Dorothy hit her low point before she enrolled in alcohol treatment, and she gathered background on the Yahtin family. But then her reporting became increasingly observational. Julie stayed close to Chesley and Dorothy Yahtin, watching carefully and taking notes. Through it all, Julie enjoyed the luck of the Irish. After sixty days in treatment, Dorothy graduated from her alcohol rehabilitation program. She moved into transitional housing and counselors arranged for her son Cecil to join her. Dorothy started acting like a mother, nurturing Cecil as he adapted to his new world in Portland.

As a result of her success, Dorothy won temporary custody of her two older children, twelve and fourteen. She returned to the reservation, faced the tribal court, and cleared up six outstanding warrants for her arrest. She attended a tribal festival where she endured her dark night of the soul, an evening when she was sorely tempted to drink again, and she confronted her young daughter's drinking, a terrible echo of her own destructive past. That night, which Julie and Rob observed firsthand, would serve as the crisis segment for a beautifully developing narrative arc.

Dorothy returned to Portland with her daughter. The children thrived. The court awarded Dorothy full legal custody. Dorothy returned to the reservation on multiple visits, where she cared for her father and her oldest son. She had resumed her place as a link in the chain of Native American cultural life.

I asked Julie to prepare a theme statement. The process was new to her, and she didn't quite achieve the crisp subject–transitive verb–object form that I prefer. But what she came up with certainly captured the core idea that would guide her writing:

Theme: The most important people in children's lives are their parents. At Warm Springs, a generation of parents is missing.

Then she produced this scenic outline:

SCENE 1: Dorothy, an unmarried mother of five, hits bottom.
  — Crashes tribal chairman's party at Simnasho Longhouse.
  — Drives past her abandoned home and children.
  — Her father, the Medic, pulls her to safety—treatment in Portland.

SCENE 2: Alcohol orphans Dorothy's children.
— Her father, Chesley Q. Yahtin's isolated at home.
— Her young children get DWIs and into fights.
— Grandfather Yahtin is tired.
SCENE 3: "My name is Dorothy, and I'm an alcoholic."
— Graduates from NARA (alcohol treatment) with confessions and hope.
SCENE 4: Reunited
— Son Cecil reunites with newly sober Dorothy.
— Grandfather and boy distrust her from experience.
SCENE 5: Those left behind stumble.
— Son Cecil thrives while siblings at home are jailed.
— Grandfather suffers flashback en route to jail.
SCENE 6: Problems of missing generation begin a generation before.
— Chesley Yahtin forced into boarding school, loses language.
— Escapes to U.S. Army. Korean War medic.
— PTSD and alcohol destroy first marriage.
SCENE 7: Dorothy born into strong, sober second marriage.
— Family unravels when Dorothy's mother dies young of diabetes.
— Four brothers and one sister die violently.
SCENE 8: Dorothy becomes a pariah.
— Gives birth to cocaine-addicted baby, Amelio.
— Her father, the medic, and tribes save the baby.
— Dorothy runs from responsibility and the law.
SCENE 9: Sober now, Dorothy returns to make amends.
— Returns to Warm Springs, risking jail to face charges.
— Clears record.
— Regains temporary custody of her children.
SCENE 10: Returning to the reservation threatens sobriety.
— Annual reunion a catastrophe.
— Dishonors honored father.
— Dorothy flees to save herself.
SCENE 11: Dorothy is a mother for the first time.
— Children grow and change.
— Amelio thrives in foster care at Warm Springs.
— Dorothy gets full legal custody.
SCENE 12: Dorothy returns.
— Becomes safe, sober place, even on the reservation.

The outline produced a perfect narrative arc, which Julie and I sketched out to guide her writing (see fig. 8).

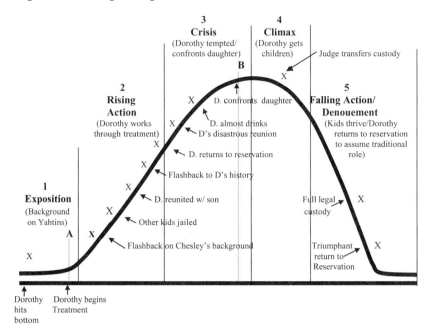

Figure 8. Mending the broken chain

With outline and narrative arc in hand, Julie began writing. And Rob profited from the careful prewriting work, too. The clear understanding of theme, the scenic outline, and the narrative arc guided his choices of images among the hundreds of exposures he'd made at Warm Springs and in Portland. The twenty spectacular photos that eventually appeared in the special section we devoted to the story showed all the key moments in Julie's narrative, from Dorothy's crisis night with her drinking friend on the reservation to her reunification with the kids.

Julie's first scene, a product of the careful reconstructive reporting she'd done, re-created the episode that launched the narrative arc:

Dorothy Yahtin spotted the glow of the Simnasho Longhouse, cars still in the parking lot, and limped toward the light. The rugged hills of the Warm Springs Reservation, flecked with sage, stretched toward the dark horizon.

Her hands were freezing in the late November chill. She remembers numbly opening the door and stumbling in.

The tribal chairman and his family, gathered for dinner on the 2002 Thanksgiving weekend, looked up.

Julie had tracked down a woman who had been in the longhouse that night, and who had taken Dorothy to her house, where she could sober up. The woman was a social worker, and to document the situation she'd taken a picture of Dorothy that gave Julie what she needed for the initial physical description so important to characterization. It captured Dorothy's image as she stumbled into the longhouse:

> Dorothy's long black hair hung around her battered face. A purple bruise, vivid in photos taken later, circled her swollen left eye. Her upper lip split over her sheepish smile. She smelled like warm beer.

The first section in any story needs a certain amount of exposition, and as the action line proceeded Julie slipped in background on the Yahtin family, giving readers the information they'd need to understand the complication. The 650-word episode ended with Chesley Yahtin arriving to pick Dorothy up from the house where she'd recovered from her binge and sending her off to Portland so that she could begin treatment for her alcoholism:

> Dorothy climbed into her dad's car, and he pulled onto U.S. 26. But instead of heading north to Simnasho, he turned southeast and drove to Madras, to the Greyhound bus station. He reached into his pockets and gave her every cent he had.
>
> Go to Portland, Dorothy, he said. Get into treatment. I cannot do this anymore.

By that point enough of the action line had been launched to provide breathing room for more expository digression. The story had readers on the hook, and Julie could safely begin a substantial background section on the Warm Springs tribes, the history of the reservation, and the Yahtins. That gave her a chance to write a fuller version of her theme statement, one that would allow readers to make sense of all that followed:

> Extended families have always shared child-rearing in Native American communities across the country. But parents such as Dorothy played a key role in that collective responsibility. Now, in the Yahtin family, like so many

on the reservation, the parents were missing. The chain that connected five hundred generations of mid-Columbia Indians had been broken.

She ended the section with a beautiful line that completed the central thought and foreshadowed the dramatic struggle that was to follow:

Children are precious, the tribal grandmothers taught. Gifts from the Creator. If you are careless with the children, the Creator will take them back.

The narrative continued on a track remarkably parallel to Julie's original outline. Scene 3 opened with Dorothy's bus arriving in Portland. She headed for Skid Road, plunged into an alcoholic binge, and ended up trying to kill herself by swallowing an entire bottle of Tylenol. After emergency medical care, she went through seven days of detox and began her treatment program. That marked Plot Point A—the protagonist's engagement with the complication. In this case, that meant Dorothy had begun the struggle to stay sober, to resume her role as mother, and to take her place as a link in the tribe's broken chain. Part 1 of the narrative arc—exposition—was over.

As it always does in the best stories, Part 2—rising action—had its ups and downs, as did the following section, the crisis. Remember the oscillating curve of rising action and crisis we discussed in the chapter on story structure? Dorothy's story fit the pattern (see figure 9).

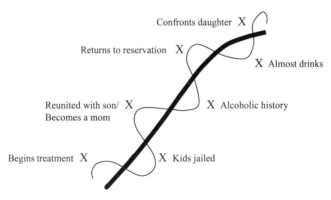

Figure 9. Dorothy Yahtin's roller-coaster ride to sobriety

The first down took place when two of Dorothy's children, twelve-year-old Chelsey and fourteen-year-old Sonny, had their own run-ins with alcohol and ended up in the reservation jail. As she did consistently throughout the narrative, Julie set the scene with sparse but compelling detail. Scene 6 opened with an establishing shot of the reservation:

> Spring unrolled in Warm Springs like a carpet, turning the cheat grass and bitterbrush a rich green.

Then she zeroed in on the jail, using a handful of details to capture the poignancy of young children locked in such a cold, stark environment:

> The two of them had a chance to get together in the jail's courtyard, a tiny concrete space surrounded by fifteen-foot cinder-block walls topped with concertina wire. Overhead, they could see a brilliant blue patch of Central Oregon sky, but nothing else.

But an up immediately followed. Dorothy stayed sober and her youngest, Cecil, joined her in Portland.

> Something was happening to Dorothy. She was going to parenting classes, counseling, and Alcoholics Anonymous twelve-step meetings. In late April, her behavior won her the right to rent an apartment on the second floor at the West Shelter, where she could stay as long as two years.
>
> For the first time in his life, in the spring of 2003, Cecil's mother was showing up. She was at school for Cecil's class play. She was at the corner when he got off the bus. She was at Lloyd Center when he skated for the first time, waiting for him at the edge of the ice.

That hopeful development provided a little more breathing space, and Julie seized it to drop into her second expository flashback, a downer historical overview of Dorothy's drug- and alcohol-addicted life.

After the flashback, Julie returned to the main action line, which was rising into another up. In Robert McKee's terms, the protagonist's "value charge" was taking a major swing in a positive direction. Rising action concluded as Dorothy returned to the reservation, settled her outstanding warrants, and won temporary custody of the kids.

Then the story moved into the crisis phase. That's when Dorothy and her children attended the tribal festival and Dorothy suffered that dark night of the soul, driving to buy booze with her friend, watching him drink, and almost falling back into the abyss of her own alcoholism. That's when she confronted her drinking twelve-year-old daughter, seeing her own life repeated before her eyes. It was what story theorists call the point of insight, the realization that changes the protagonist's understanding of the world and sets up the climax.

And the climax came, right on schedule. The tribal judge granted custody of the children to Dorothy, effectively mending the broken chain. The story moved into the falling-action phrase, the denouement that wrapped up the remaining loose ends. Dorothy returned to Portland and continued her new sober, responsible life. The court granted her full legal custody. She visited the reservation and assumed the nurturing role she'd long ago abandoned:

> Chesley had been performing Dorothy's duties for years. And no member of the tribe could finally rest and pass on to the next life until someone else came along to take his place.
>
> That weekend, Dorothy and Chesley cleaned Chesley's house. They swept his floors and did his dishes. They cooked for him. Then they went to see Chesley's best friend, a girl who lived in a remote home with an elderly grandmother. Dorothy and Chesley did that woman's dishes, too. They cleaned her house. Then they took Chesley's friend back to Simnasho to spend the evening with them.
>
> At midnight, Dorothy sat dozing in her father's chair. Around her, in the television glow, were the faces of her children, laughing and safe.
>
> And behind his bedroom door, grandfather slept.

With that, Julie had completed her narrative arc. Along the way, she'd crafted a complete story, one with an insightful theme, strong scenic construction, deep characterization, and a dramatic action line. She'd also contributed to an important investigative project—Julie's story and Rob's photos made up nearly three-quarters of the series' opening-day special section. In the other components of the project the I-team made a compelling case with facts and figures. But Dorothy Yahtin's narrative did what great storytelling does best, bringing the official documents to life in human terms. Story captured the experience and gave it meaning.[2]

12

Explanatory Narratives

Have the courage to digress.
—John McPhee

Rich Read walked into my office, sat down, and frowned. That, in itself, was unusual. Rich is a perpetually sunny guy, a world traveler who covered international business for the *Oregonian* with unflappable good cheer. Riots in Jakarta. Hair-raising escapes through mountain passes in Afghanistan. Endlessly delayed flights in one far-flung airport or another. Not to worry.

He's one savvy journalist, too. Rich ran the paper's Tokyo bureau for years. He's battled traffic in Bangkok, interviewed the Dalai Lama in Dharamsala, and penetrated the veil cloaking Pyongyang, the North Korean capital. He knows China like his neighborhood supermarket.

In fact, he'd just been in Thailand. The local currency, the baht, had collapsed, and the whole economy was falling with it. Rich walked past a Bangkok Mercedes dealership where cars sat on the lot—unbhat, you might say—despite markdown after markdown. The Thai economic bubble had burst, and the country's growing middle class had bailed out of the luxury-car market. Rich figured something big was afoot.

He headed back to our newsroom as a chain reaction of crises swept through the region's miracle economies. Singapore's currency collapsed, too. Indonesia was in turmoil. Even Japan, the region's economic colossus, was teetering. Our paper, like other news outlets, was publishing a steady dribble of dire reports, but they were impenetrable thickets of blather about distant dilemmas and cloudy consequences.

"Look," I vaguely remember Rich saying, "we've been running story after story on the Asian economic crisis and our readers don't have the slightest idea what's going on or why we should care." He had some ideas, he said, about how we might fix that.

He'd pitched a story to the business department without generating much enthusiasm. And senior editors, who already had one international project under way, were dubious about paying for another one. Rich's idea had been rejected twice before a last-ditch effort produced a change-of-heart. Approval in hand, he came to see me.

What he was thinking, Rich explained, is that we could follow some local product from its origin in the Pacific Northwest to its Asian destination. Along the way, we could talk about how trade ties Oregon to the rest of the Pacific Rim. Explain how changes in places such as Indonesia affect our local economy. Show readers how shifts in faraway markets upset things in little Northwest towns.

But what product? He considered several and finally landed on a doozy. It flowed to the Pacific Rim in vast quantities, where sales depended on the growing middle class, the group most threatened by the economic crash. Our region dominated its production. It was familiar, low-tech, nonthreatening, and easy to understand. If anything linked the Pacific Northwest to the Asian economic crisis, Rich said, it was the McDonald's frozen french fry.

He proposed tracking the route Northwest fries followed to McDonald's outlets in Asia, explaining how the trade system linked the Pacific Rim's economies as he went.

It struck me that he was talking about a classic explanatory narrative, the kind of structure the *New Yorker*'s John McPhee, one of my literary heroes, had used to teach readers about everything from geology to Alaska to basketball. I explained that to Rich, who was all ears. He'd never tried anything like one of McPhee's explainers.

McPhee used the structure for both magazine pieces and books. Book-length explanatory narratives are relatively common in science and medical writing. G. Wayne Miller's *King of Hearts*, which explores the origins of open-heart surgery, is an explanatory narrative. So is Michael Pollan's *Omnivore's Dilemma*. Documentarians use the structure, too, as do podcasters. At any point, the narrator can step into the ongoing narrative to supply explanatory exposition. The form is also perfect for an issue-oriented film documentary such as *Supersize Me* or broadcasts such as *Frontline* or *Nova*.

To make this approach work, I told Rich, you can't just follow a route; you have to track a person or a thing. An explanatory narrative requires close-to-the-ground specificity. Readers must visualize particular places at particular times. So if you're going to follow french fries, you have to track one particular batch of french fries. You have to follow the potatoes in one field on one farm, to the packing plant, to the ship, to the counter of the McDonald's where they're ultimately served.

To this day, that's the one part of a long conversation Rich remembers most vividly. He was a foreign correspondent, after all. He usually wrote analytical stories that covered sweeping subjects, big developments, and broad trends, weighty topics that sometimes engulfed millions of people across the entire Pacific Rim. Suddenly, this oddball editor was telling him to capture the universe in a grain of sand. Or, in this case, an economic tsunami in a french fry.

An hour or so after our first meeting, Rich and I met at the newsroom elevator and headed out for lunch. We strolled up the street to a Portland State University student hangout, picked up sandwiches in the cafeteria line, and sat down at a courtyard table.

Here's the idea, I said. What you want is a description that follows a series of actions. It's based on careful observation. Close to the ground. Lots of specific detail and movement. Ordinarily you'd be following a single person. But there's no reason you can't track an inanimate object instead. It could be a ship or a gun or a load of coal. But it must move, and in moving it will inevitably touch a series of characters. That brings the necessary humanity into the yarn. But it's the movement that matters. That creates the sequence of actions that establishes the narrative, and that's what gets you to places appropriate to explaining various aspects of your subject.

We munched on our sandwiches. Students came and went through the courtyard.

In this case, I told Rich, you'll be writing about french fries. That works—the fries will be headed out on a long journey through just the terrain you want to explore. But you won't be writing a story narrative. You have no protagonist struggling with a complication. The journey of the fries will simply serve as a spine that holds the piece together, that gives it shape. But it's a flat narrative line, A to Z, instead of an arc that takes a main character through rising action, a climax, and a resolution. Readers will want to follow it the way they want to follow any interesting narrative. But they're not gripped by dramatic tension, riveted to a sympathetic character's struggles to resolve some great challenge. Let's face it; they won't be desperate to find out what happens to a load of french fries. Something else must draw them along.

The attraction, I said, lies in a structural element unique to modern explanatory narrative. The writer follows an action line just as if he were writing a true story, one with a protagonist, a complication, and a resolution. Maybe, as was the case with one McPhee narrative, it's an Army Corps of Engineers officer riding a boat down the Atchafalaya River, inspecting Louisiana flood-control structures as he goes. But every once in a while, the writer stops the action, just pulls the curtain on the narrative. Then he goes off on a little exploration of the subject, an abstract explanation that gives depth and meaning to what the reader's been witnessing in the narrative. They're known in the trade as *digressions*, and they're the key to making an explanatory narrative work.

McPhee, I added, is famous for a sign he keeps posted over his desk. It says, *Have the courage to digress.*

Two structural elements drive the twin missions of an explanatory narrative. The action line creates its overall shape, moving the advancing narrative through time and space. It draws readers into the narrative by exploring new places, introducing new people, and creating mild dramatic tension, if only because the reader doesn't know what will happen next.

But digressions provide the actual explanation, placing the action line in some larger context. Action takes place on the lower rungs of the ladder of abstraction, where emotion rules. Explanation takes place farther up the ladder, where meaning holds sway.

In the purest print forms of explanatory narrative, which scrupulously separate the more abstract explanatory digressions from the more concrete action scenes, some sort of typographical device usually separates the sections. In manuscript, a star line, three asterisks centered and separated by about ten spaces—

★   ★   ★

—is the standard indicator, and such markers are known as "star-line breaks." In published work, a large capital letter at the beginning of a new section (a "drop cap"), a subhead, or a centered bullet—

—may serve the same function. In audio and video documentaries or in an explanatory podcast, a scene change usually signals a digression. The narrator may pop on-screen or into the audio track, signaling that an explanatory digression is beginning.

Whatever introduces it, a digression is a clear break from the leading edge of the ongoing action line, what Mark Kramer calls "the moving now." Here's a classic McPhee digression, taken from his tale about the Army Corps of Engineers and the effort to control Louisiana floods. The narrative, collected in McPhee's *Control of Nature*, grinds to a halt—literally—when the *Mississippi*, the riverboat carrying McPhee and his army hosts, hits a sand bar:

> then, with a profound structural shudder, the *Mississippi* is captured by the Atchafalaya. The mid-American flagship of the U.S. Army Corps of Engineers has run aground.

Then McPhee has the courage to digress, leaving us hanging at this intriguing point in the action line so that he can explore the history of flood control in the Mississippi Delta:

> After going on line, in 1963, the control structures at Old River had to wait ten years to prove what they could do. The 1950s and 1960s were secure in the Mississippi Valley. In human terms, a generation passed with no disastrous floods.

One secret to successful digression is to preserve dramatic tension by bailing out of the action line at just the right moment. If the writer creates a cliff-hanger by pausing when something hangs in the balance, the reader will usually hang around to see what happens when the narrative resumes. Or, as Mark Kramer puts it: "It's frequently best to digress in the middle of the action, not between actions, because then we remember well and we're happier to come back."

McPhee left us stuck on a sandbar. David Grann, another *New Yorker* contributor, put us in the hands of an obsessed New Zealander who's determined to catch a live giant squid and keep it in captivity. His scheme? Head out to sea in a small open boat and fish for baby giant squid, the beast's paralarvae. Grann met him to join the expedition:

> For months, he had been carefully working out our destination, studying squid migration patterns as well as satellite readings of water currents and temperatures. His plan was to go south, where he had found the paralarvae before. At the last minute, however, he changed his mind. "We're going north," he said. As we got back in his truck, he added, "I should warn you, there's a bit of a cyclone coming our way."

A cyclone in an open boat, eh? Guess I'll hang around for that one. The situation carries what Mark Kramer, with admirable academic detachment, calls "high emotional valence." And, he adds, "the higher the emotional valence, the longer the digression."

So I'll indulge David Grann while he educates me about the history of sea monsters and explains how the giant squid may be responsible for much of it.

> For as long as sailors have been going out to sea, they have been returning with stories of monsters. The Bible speaks of "a dragon that is in the sea"; the Roman encyclopedia "Naturalis Historia" tells of an enormous "polyp."

Conversely, a pause that occurs at a less dramatic moment calls for a shorter, less intrusive digression. McPhee did a series of *New Yorker* stories on freight haulers such as barges and trains. One segment in the series, "A Fleet of One," followed a long-haul trucker as he crossed the United States carrying a load of hazardous materials. The travel was largely uneventful, with only an occasional steep hill and a few bad drivers to enliven the action. McPhee kept his digressions short, weaving them into the action line instead of breaking them out as sections separated typographically.

> As we began to roll for the Pacific Northwest, he said, "We're weighing 79,720, so we'll have to plug our brains in to see where we're going to fuel." In this trade, if you were "grossed out," you were flirting with the weight limit. In weigh stations, they could "make you get legal"—keep you right there until you discharged enough cargo to not be overweight.
>
> "Grain haulers, they may know a farmer who will take it, but this corrosive stuff is something else," Ainsworth said. His twin saddle tanks, one on either side of the tractor, could hold three hundred gallons, and "a full belly of fuel," at seven pounds a gallon, would weigh twenty-one hundred pounds. We never had anything like a full belly. Constantly he had to calculate, and cut it fine.

The clever toggling of action and explanation makes a well-crafted explanatory narrative enormously compelling. A master can draw us into subjects that would ordinarily blow by us with nary a glance. I've read three John McPhee books on geology, a subject that's never kept me awake at night. And, Lord help me, I once read eight thousand words on sagebrush.

A large part of that appeal lies in the underlying structure of a piece, the framework that holds the scenes, action line, and characters visible to readers. Because that invisible structure—not the more obvious elements of the writing—drives and directs the narrative, Jon Franklin refers to it as "the ghost in the machine."

All accomplished narrative writers—whether of explanatory or other forms of the genre—give structure its due. Most struggle with an outline of some sort before they begin writing. McPhee says outlining is essential to his process. "Going through all that creates the form and the shape of the thing," he says. "It also relieves the writer, once you know the structure, to concentrate each day on one thing. You know right where it fits."

Because an explanatory narrative progresses steadily through successive, top-to-bottom sections of scenic action and explanatory digression, it assumes a structure that Michael Roberts, longtime writing coach at the *Arizona Republic*, likens to a layer cake. Sketching out the structure, which is something I do with every narrative I edit, produces something that looks like this:

Outline for an Explanatory Narrative
Narrative Opening Scene
Digression 1
Narrative Scene 2
Digression 2
Narrative Scene 3
Digression 3
Narrative Scene 4
Digression 4
Narrative Scene 5
Digression 5
Narrative Scene 6
Digression 6
Narrative Closing Scene

Rich Read was set to bake a very tall cake. Following a load of potatoes from a Pacific Northwest farm to Asia would require a lengthy action line. And he'd need quite a few expository digressions to explain something as complicated as the Asian economic crisis. He had a lot of reporting to do.

After our lunch meeting, Rich went looking for his personal batch of french fries. He knew the business was a big player in the Pacific Northwest—$2 billion in annual revenues—and that it accounted for a significant slice of the region's exports, including shipments to the Pacific Rim. But he didn't know much more than that.

He called the J. R. Simplot Company in Boise. As you'd expect from a huge Idaho agribusiness, Simplot was heavy into potatoes. It was, in fact, the world's leading supplier of the McDonald's french fries that fast-food aficionados stuffed into their mouths from Jakarta to Miami to Moscow.

On that first call, Rich hit pay dirt, launching a remarkable string of luck that would accompany his entire narrative. The Simplot PR man in Boise was an old reporter, and he immediately grasped Rich's scheme. He called the big Simplot processing plant in Hermiston, Oregon, and arranged a visit for Rich and a photographer, Kathryn Scott Osler. The two of them climbed into a company car and headed up the Columbia Gorge for a five-hour grind to the land of giant circle-pivot farms.

From the air, the entire region is evidence for the cultists who think crop circles are created by little green men. But aliens have little to do with circle-pivot agriculture in the Columbia Basin. Water from the big river powers huge irrigators that propel themselves relentlessly around anchors in the center of the fields, creating the lush crop circles that dapple the arid landscape.

The Simplot plant, rising in the wide-open spaces of the Columbia Plateau, was an agri-tech marvel of motion and smells. Machines peeled an avalanche of russet potatoes and launched them into banks of french knives, the cutting blades that gave the french fry its name. The sliced spuds popped into the vegetable oil that permeated the plant with a heavy, hot-grease smell for partial cooking before flash freezing and packing in large cardboard boxes. Each box carried a bar code.

The whole scene was, Rich recalls, a visual feast, perfect for narrative scene-setting. He turned to the assistant manager guiding his tour and told him he was particularly interested in french fries headed to Indonesia, the country hammered hardest by the Asian economic crisis.

The lucky streak held: "Well," said the Simplot man, "that's where this bunch is headed." He was quite sure, he added, because a Muslim holy man had just been out to certify the plant's conversion to halal standards, the Islamic equivalent of kosher. The certification assured Muslim consumers that the fries contained no animal fats barred by the religion's dietary laws. And the plant's main Muslim customer was Indonesia.

Rich looked at Kathryn. Kathryn looked at Rich. A simultaneous realization struck them both. "These are *our* potatoes," Rich remembers thinking. "We're in the moment. This is part of the narrative right here!"

"So where did you get these potatoes?" Rich asked.

———————

In some ways, reporting tactics for an explanatory piece echo reporting tactics for any narrative. To get the scenic detail, on the one hand, and the larger thematic meaning, on the other, narrative writers must range farther up and down the ladder of abstraction than typical journalists. To explore the bottom rungs of the ladder, they interview and observe for revealing detail—a Muslim holy man conducting a halal inspection. To climb higher, they look for ways their specific examples fit into larger patterns—the french fry, for example, as a stand-in for growing Pacific Rim trade.

Because nonfiction narrative writers need detail they're unlikely to get any other way, they rely more on observation—as opposed to interviewing and document research—than conventional reporters do. They plunge into their subjects, leaving their old realities behind. Like ethnologists, they quietly watch and listen, practicing fly-on-the-wall techniques for getting at nuances that would be otherwise inaccessible.

But the explanatory narrative layers another reporting level onto narrative reporting. The digressions flow from another angle of approach, a slant created by the explanatory journalist's driving curiosity about how things work. Cynthia Gorney says the key is asking the right questions, "tuning the brain so that everything around you is a source for stories." You must constantly interrogate your story, she explains. To find a good explainer, take a couple of steps back from the case at hand, asking "Why does this matter? Why here? Why now?"[1]

She advises that would-be explanatory journalists look beyond conventional sources, talking to janitors as well as administrators, home-care aides as well as doctors. She suggests haunting internet bulletin boards and chat rooms, reading specialty journals related to the topic, hanging around "backstage" in places where relevant things take place. And she offers a list of questions designed to bare the mechanisms that turn our world:

How do they *do* that?
Where does that *come* from; where does that *go?*
Who *is* that guy?

How did this get to be such a *mess?*
What's it *like* to be him or her?

———————

The assistant manager led Rich Read and Kathryn Scott Osler into a basement room. A woman hunched over a computer. Rich repeated his question. Who, he wanted to know, had grown the spuds the packers were using to create the day's batch of french fries?

As it often does these days, modern technology made the narrative writer's job easier. That bar code on each box of fries allowed the packer to track each shipment from grower to eater. Rich realized that his editor's improbable assignment—actually following one batch of potatoes through the whole system—was within reach.

The woman punched some keys. That day's potatoes, she said, had come from a big agribusiness operation, a mom-and-pop supplier, and a Hutterite farm.

And who, Rich asked, were the Hutterites?

Once again, Lady Luck had smiled. The Hutterites were an Anabaptist sect similar to the Amish—with a notable exception. They embraced modern technology to run some of the country's most efficient, profitable farms. But, although they used GPS systems to guide state-of-the-art tractors through their fields, they still dressed traditionally and lived communally. They dripped journalistic color, and they'd be a boffo launch pad for the series.

Rich scribbled down the name of the Hutterite farm manager. But when he called, the manager's reserve cooled the hot trail. The Hutterite was friendly, but—despite broad hints—he seemed puzzled by Rich's crazy proposal. He said nothing about coming out to the farm. He would, however, agree to a cup of coffee in Moses Lake, a few minutes from the farm but five hours from Portland. OK, said Rich, thinking that it was a long drive for a cup of coffee.

It wasn't likely to stop at that. A good reporter gets access, and Rich is a great reporter. Over that Moses Lake coffee, he casually asked the farmer what he and his brethren did in the winter. Why, they worked in the woodshop. And what a woodshop! With the farm's profits they'd filled it with factory-quality power tools, which they used for making beautiful furniture. Rich brightened. He's been woodworking all his life. He pounced on the point of common interest, talking tools, techniques, and projects. Before the lathe could stop spinning, Kathryn and he were following the Hutterite to the farm—to see the woodshop.

They entered the Hutterite world softly. Rich talked wood and kept his pen in his pocket. Kathryn kept her cameras holstered. The manager relaxed. The conversation warmed. "Say," Rich said, "Do you suppose we might see the farm, too?"

As the farm tour began, a Hutterite woman appeared in a barn door, wearing a bonnet and traditional dress and framed in perfect light. Still, Kathryn held fire, careful not to spook her subjects. Soon she was sitting on the woman's side of the communal dining hall, soaking up the female perspective on Hutterite life. Over on the men's side, Rich chatted about woodworking, farming, and international trade. "Once you've eaten with somebody," Rich said later, "and you haven't made a total fool of yourself, then you're okay."

He soon had an invitation back to the farm, where he talked his way into the cab of a combine. Over the next few hours, his host, trapped in an enclosed space with an inquisitive reporter, loosened up and told Rich everything he needed to know about circle-pivot potato farming in the Columbia Basin. As Rich explored the savvy business practices of Hutterite farmers, who were well aware of their ties to the Asian economy and the dangers posed by currency collapses in far-off lands, he collected the arresting image he'd use to begin his tale:

> At the start of the french fry trail, strong Hutterite women in long dresses sliced seed potatoes and tipped their bonnets to tradition, dusting modern farm machinery with goose wings.

Rich and Kathryn had set out to explain a complex phenomenon that affected half the planet. And they aimed to track an action line that stretched across the Pacific Ocean. Early on, Rich and I realized that we were talking about a whole series of stories and many thousands of words.

Even though most explanatory narratives don't need the space the french fry saga ultimately consumed, all demand some length. The scene-digression-scene structure simply cannot be compressed past a certain point. I generally figure on print scenes averaging about five hundred words, which translates to twelve column inches in a newspaper. A digression can be any length, but probably should average about the same length as the scenes that contain the action. If the writer simply weaves the digressions into the narrative, rather than breaking them out as separate sections, the ratio should remain about the same—one word of digression for every word of action. That's an extremely rough approximation, of course, but it's useful to thinking about structure during the earlier stages of the writing process.

Any story needs a beginning, a middle, and an end. And creating a layer cake means you need a digression between the beginning and the middle and another digression between the middle and the end. That's the minimum, it seems to me, for a true explanatory narrative. It's a form I call the 3+2 explainer—a structure containing three narrative scenes separated by two digressions. In outline, it looks like this:

A 3+2 Explainer
Narrative 1: Introduce the lead character and pose the explanatory question.
Digression 1: Provide the necessary background and overall context.
Narrative 2: Follow the lead character through the main body of the action line.
Digression 2: Complete the explanation.
Narrative 3: Bring the action line to a logical stopping place.

I'm tempted to say that mastering the form doesn't require brain surgery, but at the Oregonian we did, in fact, use the 3+2 to explore a new form of pediatric brain surgery. You can use the 3+2 to tackle just about anything. Steve Beaven, a feature writer for the Oregonian, used it on highly diverse topics, always with great success.

He picked up one of his first 3+2 subjects when he was working the police beat, which is where he discovered "scanner heads," the hobbyists who spend their days and nights listening to police and fire dispatch messages on scanner radios.

I can't imagine why anybody would voluntarily listen to a scanner. I've served my own time on the police beat, and the duty often requires that you monitor a scanner at your desk. For me, few annoyances compare to the constant buzz and babble a scanner creates as it automatically bounces from channel to channel, picking up shards of chatter about minor accidents and crimes. But legions of scanner fans feel otherwise. They have their own associations, blogs, and national magazines. They often dash out to the fires and crime scenes they hear about on their scanners, and they're well known to the cops and firefighters they meet there.

Steve Beaven seized on that pattern to create his narrative line. He ran into his key source, a seventy-eight-year-old scanner head named Joe McCarthy, at—surprise!—a house fire. The fire was a humdinger, involving an exciting rescue and a fatality. So Steve's observations of Joe at the fire gave him all he needed for his second narrative segment. Later, he visited Joe at home, interviewing while he observed his subject living with scanner babble as a constant backdrop.

Steve started his tale this way:

A house fire in southeast Portland. Heavy flames shooting from a second-floor window. Someone trapped inside. Joe McCarthy, sitting in front of his television, turned off the forensics show . . . and grabbed the scanner squawking on his dining-room table.

Then Steve worked his way through the classic 3+2 structure:

The Scanner Heads Outline
Narrative 1: Joe, at home, hears scanner report on house fire.
Digression 1: An overview of scanner radios and scanner heads.
Narrative 2: Joe witnesses the house fire, including a dramatic rescue.
Digression 2: Scanner head psychology, as illustrated by several local hobbyists.
Narrative 3: Joe back home, listening to his scanner and talking about his passion.

———————

Like the Simplot packing plant, the Hutterites kept good records. At the farm, Rich Read zeroed in on Circle 6, the exact plot of ground that produced the Indonesia-bound spuds. With the packing-plant scene already in his pocket, he had his first two narrative scenes safely in hand. Next—tracking the frozen french fries into some Asian stomachs.

The fries chilled in a Hermiston warehouse while Rich chilled back in Portland. Then the phone rang. "Our fries," said the Simplot PR man, are on the move.

Once again Rich made the long drive to Hermiston. Outside the potato-packing plant, he met Randy Thueson and watched as warehouse workers loaded twenty tons of frozen french fries into the trucker's tractor-trailer rig. Rich climbed in the cab, and the two of them headed west, hauling 113,000 servings of Hutterite fries toward the Port of Tacoma.

More luck. Thueson was a Vietnam vet who once lobbed rockets into North Vietnam from an American warship. The connection gave Rich a natural entrée into digressions on the modern history of Southeast Asia, the warlike economic destruction wrought by something like the currency crisis, and the mechanics of Pacific Rim trade. The constantly moving action line greased the explanatory skids. After summarizing the political situation in Indonesia, for example, Rich quickly returned to the lumbering truck: "Thueson downshifted, attuned so precisely to the engine that he never touched the clutch, his left hand steering into a crucial turnoff."

Rich and Randy pulled into the port, and a crane operator snagged the containers of frozen fries, raised them high overhead, and dropped them into a Danish freighter bound for Yokohama. Rich went aboard, chatted with the German captain, and met a Texas couple who'd booked passage. They promised to report back on details of the trip, and they eventually provided Rich with bits of color—such as the orcas the outbound ship passed on its way out of Puget Sound and the huge sea turtle it surprised in the South China Sea—that would brighten the narrative.

Randy Thueson was just one of several colorful characters readers met along the french fry trail. Like many of the human beings who appear in explanatory narratives, Randy was a bit player, rather than a protagonist. He was, in other words, a means to an end—getting the french fries to port—rather than an end in himself. Still, character plays a key role in an explanatory narrative. Interesting characters help draw readers through the narrative. And the walking, talking human beings that populate most explanatory narratives are the vehicles the writer uses to explore the subject at hand. The characters, through their words and actions, do the explaining.

As with most characterization, the writer emphasizes just a few key personality traits and bits of personal history. For a broadcast documentary, a voice-over or on-screen commentary can fill in background while video pictures the character.

For a multipart podcast such as Serial, the central figure, Adnan Syed, was a character puzzle. Figuring out who he really was promised to explain whether or not he committed the crime. Narrator Sarah Koenig's slowly unfolding quest to unravel Syed's character was a key source of the dramatic tension that drove the narrative

In the case of a newspaper or magazine story, still photographs help bring key characters to life, and the text fills in important background. Kathryn Scott Osler's photos pictured all the key characters in Rich Read's french fry story. So Rich described Randy Thueson only briefly as "a wiry man with a trim brown mustache and frizzy gray hair," mentioned his Vietnam experience, and observed his skills as a driver. More importantly, Thueson provided informed commentary on subjects important to Rich's story. He talked about once meeting J. R. Simplot, the potato king who worked with Ray Kroc to develop the frozen french fry as a McDonald's staple. He commented insightfully on the US system of interstate highways, which kept America competitive with cheaper, more compact economic powers. Then he delivered his load and disappeared from the story.

Some explanatory narratives call for more developed characters. A Steve Beaven 3+2 explainer on Lou Gilbert, "the greatest salesman who ever lived," focused on Lou himself. The old man's personality and style played a central role in the explainer's theme, which explored the ways retail salesmanship has changed over the decades. So Steve spent much more time and space rounding out Lou's character, tapping most of the standard literary tools for bringing human beings to life on the page. He worked a physical description into the text early. (Lou was "seventy-eight, with a hearing aid, a balding head, and a body like a bowling ball.") Certain aspects of his clothes and other belongings— what Tom Wolfe calls "status indicators"—told readers something about his social class, income, and general place in society. Because they were so central to his role as a salesman, Steve faithfully reproduced multiple examples of Lou's speech and mannerisms, two always-useful tools for developing character. And Steve devoted an entire digression to Lou's personal history, which went a long way toward revealing what motivated his sales techniques. Tracy Kidder, you will remember, devoted an entire book to exploring the character of Paul Farmer, the humanitarian doctor who serves the poorest of the poor in Haiti.

Rich and Kathryn rejoined the fries in Hong Kong, where the freighter carrying them was delayed by broken equipment. They bluffed their way into a security area by walking through gates with an Australian repairman. High on the ship's mast Rich held an umbrella over the repairman to protect him from the monsoon rain as he worked. Then Rich and Kathryn caught up with the captain and crew.

Meanwhile, in Indonesia, the economic crisis was well on its way to destroying the country's young middle class, the driver for the country's new prosperity and—coincidentally—the prime market for McDonald's french fries. The country appeared to be headed for full-scale rebellion, with rioters in the streets.

Before leaving Hong Kong, Rich called Hermiston to check in on plans for the fries. Because of the Indonesian civil unrest, the shippers had diverted the Hutterite load to Singapore. As planned, Rich and Kathryn then winged their way to Vietnam, where they squeezed in another story on a Nike contract factory, another Pacific Northwest connection to the region. Then they headed into a remote Chinese agricultural zone where J. R. Simplot was outsourcing some potato production to farmers who still relied on horse-drawn carts and stored their harvests in caves. The idea was to more cheaply serve Asian french fry markets. The effect was severe competition for high-tech American producers such as the Hutterites.

Tracking the humble french fry, as Rich was continually discovering, unlocked more and more examples of globalization's unification of economies across the Pacific Rim and beyond. The actions of a small-time dirt farmer in a far-off Chinese village affected the driver of an air-conditioned combine in the Columbia Basin. And the Asian economic crisis, as readers would learn, had plenty to do with daily life in the *Oregonian*'s circulation area.

Rich and Kathryn followed the french fry trail to Singapore, where the spuds from Circle 6 were finally nearing their destination. Part of the cargo ended up at a McDonald's on bustling Orchard Road. Rich and Kathryn checked the cardboard boxes in the fridge. Yep. There was the telltale barcode. These were *their* fries.

The Enver family stepped up to the counter and ordered a batch. "After narrowly escaping economic and political meltdown and traveling halfway across the globe," Rich noted, "the cooked fries had seven minutes—according to McDonald's rules—to cross the counter."

The fries arrived. The family's Eurasian kids dug in. Kathryn snapped a picture.

The core purpose of an explanatory narrative—duh!—is explanation. The action line exists because it's an effective way to show how something works. Some story elements inevitably appear when you describe action. The characters you introduce along the way face problems they must resolve. And scenes, one of the key ingredients in any more complete story, also play a critical role in explanatory narrative.

But all the elements of a true story narrative seldom figure in the layer-cake approach to a challenging subject. A french fry is not a protagonist. And even explanatory narratives that focus primarily on human beings often cycle through a whole cast of characters, rather than following one individual who spearheads the narrative line.

Shorter explanatory narratives may stick with a principal character. But even those usually don't pursue a full story structure. We meet the scanner head or the greatest salesman who ever lived not to follow them through a narrative arc, complete with point of insight and climax, but to share a few brief episodes that serve as windows into their worlds.

But nothing says you can't use an explanatory structure to tell a true story—one that encompasses a complication, change, character development, and resolution. Rich Read did just that in the first big project he tackled after "The French Fry Connection." Because he hoped to explain global economic themes *and* tell a complete story in the literary sense, this effort was even more challenging.

Rich met Keiichi Takahashi during the days when Japan, then securely astride the Pacific Rim like an economic colossus, was building factories throughout the United States, including Oregon. Takahashi, who managed an Oregon plant for the giant Japanese corporation NEC, turned out to be a rare breed. A former student revolutionary and the son of an artist, he showed in-dividuality and candor rare in Japanese men. He thrived in the States, relishing the American way of life. But the conflicts between his less fettered style and Japanese tradition clearly caused strain. Rich, who'd spent years observing Jap-anese culture firsthand, watched with growing interest.

Eventually, Japan's economy faltered. Takahashi closed the Oregon plant and returned to Japan, where he struggled with NEC's hidebound hierarchy and fought a losing battle to keep a failing domestic factory afloat. Then he took a job managing NEC's efforts to outsource manufacturing and to survive the rising competition with growing economic powers such as China, Korea, and Taiwan. Rich kept in touch with Takahashi, noting how the executive's career responded to the oceanic currents rearranging the Pacific Rim economy. Rich and I scheduled a weekly meeting at a local coffee shop, where we chat-ted about Takahashi for months, gradually seeing the emerging outlines of a sweeping story.

It eventually appeared as "Racing the World," a three-part series that told Takahashi's story while it explored the larger economic issues. The first episode began as Takahashi arrived to take control of the Oregon factory, an event that Rich immediately put in his explanatory context.

> During the next decade, Takahashi would grapple with the decimation of American and Japanese manufacturing, the explosion of offshore outsourcing, and the rise of China. Ultimately, lost jobs would unleash powerful political forces in both Japan and the United States.

The human dimension of the story unfolded across the same decade. Takahashi was less bound to traditional Japanese values because of his family background, his student experiences, and his time in the United States. When the world changed around him, he suffered a kind of cultural crisis of faith. As NEC factories closed and colleagues lost jobs that once would have been guaranteed for life, Takahashi felt his old allegiance to his company fade. As Rich put it, "The loss of loyalty, unthinkable three decades before, was liberating." Takahashi emerged at the end of the series a new man, much more like his counterparts in Europe and America. He no longer worked slavishly long hours. He spent time with his family. He played golf and savored good food. His eventual fate in NEC seemed clear—the company would downsize, and Takahashi would take an early retirement. The traditional economic order was gone, and so was the traditional Japanese executive.

The explanatory narrative that tells a more complete story can have tremendous popular appeal. Richard Preston's *The Hot Zone* hit the best-seller lists, inspired movies, and triggered a nationwide obsession with deadly viruses. Preston, a former John McPhee student, specializes in science writing. Starting with a single case of Ebola in Africa, Preston created a three-part structure that shifted points of view as it built toward the outbreak of an Ebola-like disease that wiped out a colony of macaque monkeys in Reston, Virginia. More deadly even than COVID-19, Ebola kills most human beings it infects, and the incident dripped high drama.

Unlike Rich Read, Preston didn't follow a single character through the entire story arc. But the history of Ebola, the story of the army biologists who deal with deadly pathogens such as Ebola, and the battle to contain the outbreak in Virginia provided plenty of arc for a narrative that held readers through a fascinating tour of modern virology, the natural history of the filoviruses, and the potentially deadly consequences of human tampering with the world's ecological systems. The storytelling strategy paid off by producing a real nail-biter, a ripping good read that also offered the kind of biological lessons that most of us could never get in any other way—and that unfortunately hadn't been absorbed by key policy makers when a deadly coronavirus did emerge in 2020.

———————————

Their pursuit of the lowly french fry would lead Rich and Kathryn to one more stop—the riot-torn city where the fries had originally headed. The situation in Jakarta would vividly illustrate the street-level effects of the hard-to-grasp abstraction—the Asian economic crisis—they'd set out to document.

They found rioters in the streets and the city in flames. The warehouse manager responsible for keeping McDonald's french fries safely frozen fretted that the warehouse generators would run out of fuel. He desperately searched for a driver crazy enough to pilot a gasoline tanker through the flaming neighborhoods. In the end, he saved the fries, but five hundred human beings died in the streets that day, and the spreading unrest toppled the government.

For Indonesians, the crisis had reached tragic proportions. But for Rich and Kathryn, their incredible run of luck along the entire french fry trail had continued. Rich had terrific action scenes to power the narrative and provide takeoff points for digressions on the way the french fry trade depended on the middle class and why the middle class was, in turn, critical to the rise of Asian economies. Kathryn had powerful photos of angry Indonesians in the streets.

"When something as prosaic as a french fry can reach far-flung Indonesian islands," Rich would write, "consider how far dollars, yen, and Euros can go. When merchants risk their lives to save a stash of potatoes, consider how readily global economic forces can topple governments and build or destroy nations and regions."

Back in Portland, Kathryn edited her photos, and Rich worked out his structure, crafting a detailed outline that tracked each narrative segment and digression. Then he settled down to write, eventually producing more than ten thousand words, 285 column inches of newspaper copy that the paper would display in a four-day series. The *Oregonian*'s artists enhanced Rich's text with graphics keyed to the action and explanation. A global map tracked progress of the Circle 6 fries across the Pacific. Other maps showed the specific places the french fry trail traversed. One timeline traced the progress of the potatoes. Another outlined the developing economic crisis. Kathryn's photos spanned a bridge of images stretching from Hutterite women working on the farm to Chinese kids downing french fries in Singapore.[2]

The series generated tremendous response. "I normally skip over articles like this," wrote one woman, "because they're so boring." But, she confessed, she'd found herself scrambling to find Day 1 after she stumbled across Day 2. Then she plunged into the rest of the series.

Other comments testified to the explanatory narrative's seductive powers, its ability to bring nonexperts to a subject, to interest them in it, and to draw them into a new level of understanding. The series, wrote one, "made people who weren't aware of business understand what this is all about." Another noted that "ordinarily, I wouldn't read a business story," and then added, "This is fantastic." A third reader wrote to say that "nothing else has helped me see the scope of the Asian economic crisis."

Over the years, reactions like that have made me a huge fan of the explanatory form. Action really does explain process. Which is why I chose to write this chapter, which aimed at explaining the process of creating an explanatory narrative, by building it around the action line Rich and Kathryn created when they reported "The French Fry Connection." This is, in other words, an explanatory narrative that explains explanatory narrative.

Rich's series blitzed its way through the awards circuit, including first place in a prestigious national business-writing competition. Then word leaked from the secretive Pulitzer Prize judging process. "The French Fry Connection" was a finalist in the explanatory-journalism category.

On the day of the official Pulitzer announcements, the *Oregonian*'s staff gathered in The Well, site of the daily news meetings. The Associated Press wire feed scrolled up a large screen, displaying minute-by-minute bulletins on the category winners. Explanatory journalism rolled into view. Rich Read had won the *Oregonian* its first Pulitzer in forty-two years. The staff cheered. Reporters and editors hugged. Champagne bottles popped. The publisher passed out bonus checks.

The following month, Rich and the paper's top editors gathered in New York for the awards ceremony. Grinning, Rich rose from the *Oregonian*'s table in the rotunda of Columbia University's Low Library and trooped onstage to accept a certificate and another check from the university president. Coincidentally, John McPhee, there to receive a special lifetime achievement award for his pioneering work in explanatory narrative, followed Rich to the stage. As the ceremony ended, Rich and I made our way to McPhee's table. Thanks, we said. We stole the whole plan for "The French Fry Connection" from you. In his own shy way, McPhee smiled.

That night, the newspaper's owner took the entire crew out to dinner at Le Cirque, then New York's toniest restaurant. Movie stars and media celebrities chatted at neighboring tables. More champagne flowed. Elegant salads arrived, presaging a dinner that promised a cutting-edge culinary experience. Then the head chef arrived with a gleaming silver chafing dish. He leaned over the table and ceremoniously lifted the lid. He grinned, peering through the steam that rose from a heaping mound of french fries.

13

Other Narratives

A narrative is a chronology with meaning.
—Jon Franklin

At its most basic level, a narrative simply describes a sequence of actions. It doesn't need a point of insight, a climax, or a complication. It can result from observational or reconstructive reporting. It might be book length, or it might unfold in just a few lines.

It helps to understand the options. If you think story narrative exhausts the possibilities, for example, you'll inevitably run into material that fails to fit. You know it's good stuff, rich in emotion or suspense, or just plain human quirkiness. But it lacks a protagonist. Or it fails to create any dramatic tension. It may unfold in one act, with no scene changes whatsoever.

More than once I've counseled frustrated writers who've been struggling to fit square narrative material into a round narrative hole. Usually it's someone fairly new to the game, someone who thinks of "narrative" as synonymous with "story." Something inside tells them that what they've collected is worth something, but what? Often they're on the verge of discarding the whole misbegotten enterprise when a simple suggestion opens up possibilities they hadn't imagined.

I've already mentioned a couple possibilities. I introduced the "tick-tock" in chapter 6. The tale of the ill-fated Oregon fishing boat *Taki-Tooo* was a story narrative, but it was entirely reconstructed from Coast Guard records and interviews with survivors, relying on none of the immersion reporting typical of some story narratives. Like Erik Larson's *The Devil in the White City*, it was a highly detailed, you-are-there work of history.

Gay Talese's "Mr. Bad News," first published in *Esquire* during the heyday of New Journalism, demonstrated a narrative alternative to the simple catalogs of accomplishments that sometimes pass for profiles.[1] Like other narrative profiles, Talese's portrait of *New York Times* obituary writer Alden Whitman gives readers a chance to see subjects in action, moving through their own worlds. It begins with Whitman rising on a typical morning in his New York apartment. He makes himself some tea. He scans the papers for news of ailing celebrities who may soon need an obituary. He takes the train downtown and enters the newsroom, ready to write. It's a simple, brief action line. But through it all, Talese digresses in the manner of an explanatory narrative so that he can discuss obituary writing as an art form.

But mastering the story narrative, the explanatory narrative, the tick-tock, and the narrative profile still won't give you a narrative for every situation. Let's say you see something intriguing on a downtown street corner. Well, maybe you can write a stand-alone vignette that fits nicely into a newspaper travel section, on the back page of a specialty magazine, or in your personal blog. Or perhaps something happened to you yesterday and produced a powerful emotional response. Maybe that has the makings of a one-thousand-word personal essay.

The possibilities aren't quite endless, but they're broader than many writers suspect. The important thing is that you stay open-minded. If you have something that will entertain your friends over a drink, you probably have the makings of a narrative that will sell somewhere. It's just a matter of finding the form that fits.

VIGNETTES

A vignette is a single scene, standing alone. So the chapter devoted to scenic construction offers guidelines that also apply to writing vignettes.

Like all scenes, a vignette includes an action line running through a geographical place and lacks the complete arc of a story narrative. Vignettes have no complication, crisis, or resolution. They may not have a protagonist, although they often feature a POV character or two.

Vignettes differ from ordinary scenes in one important way: Because they stand alone, vignettes must work harder to offer a slice of life that's rich in theme, that reveals some important secret to good living.

Walt Harrington, the former *Washington Post* writer who's become a guru of modern narrative nonfiction, calls vignettes "journalistic haiku," a phrase that captures the form's reality-based content, limited length, and evocative ability to tap larger truths. For the same reasons, reporters and editors also refer to vignettes as "tone poems." Whatever you call them, they have a natural market in newspapers, magazines, and even television. Charles Kuralt of CBS News was a master of the form. They're also ideal for first-person online media such a such as blogs or personal websites.

Vignettes cover the gamut of human experience. Earl Swift of the *Virginian-Pilot* described Valentine's Day in divorce court, where a series of couples testified to the perils of love gone wrong. Angela Pancrazio, my favorite writer-photographer double threat, worked with me on a series of vignettes on everything from the man who reset a tower clock every spring and fall to a religious zealot who dragged a huge cross around downtown streets. The *Oregonian's* Katy Muldoon snagged one of the best vignettes published during my years at the paper on the fly, too—quite literally.

This gem fell into Katy's hands, as great vignettes often do, under perfectly ordinary circumstances. She found herself stuck at an airport gate, her plane interminably delayed. Most of us know what happens then. The sullen passengers slump in their seats. They grumble, increasingly irritable. The most agitated argue with the ticket agents. The only sane strategy, of course, is to make the best of a situation beyond any passenger's control. When Katy saw some of her fellow victims doing just that, she also saw the opportunity that led to this:

> At Gate 66, the collective groan mumbles, then rumbles, then builds to an invective-riddled roar in a scant few seconds.
>
> A pilot has called in sick. The San Francisco-to-Boston flight will depart late. Really late. Maybe three hours. Maybe six.
>
> What?
>
> What!
>
> Passengers stomp and whine and sigh and, resigned to the misery, wander off to eat up time over taste-free sandwiches and $7.59 beers.
>
> Well, most do.
>
> But not the middle-aged, blue-blazered man with the guitar, who started his trip earlier on this morning in Portland, headed to Boston via San Francisco.
>
> And not the gray-haired guy with the harmonica, who announces to anyone in earshot that he had the option of catching an earlier flight, but opted for this one . . . this insultingly late one. . . . arrrgh!
>
> No. They stay put at Gate 66, where the guitar case acts as a conversation starter and one thing leads to another and wouldn't you

know it, but they play plenty of the same songs, guitar guy and harmonica man do.

"Your Cheatin' Heart." "Folsom Prison." "Rollin' in My Sweet Baby's Arms." All the standards for music men of a certain age.

They take out their instruments and warm up their voices, and a third fellow sitting nearby says into his Bluetooth phone, "Yeah, I'm at the airport and there's a sing-along going on." And harmonica man says to anyone in earshot, "Have any requests . . . besides, 'Shut up!'?"

Just as he laughs at his own joke a little old lady with a bright white perm hollers out from Gate 64, "On Top of Old Smokey!"

The guitar strums and the harmonica whines, and travelers who as a general rule avoid eye contact glance at each other and smile.

But not skinny Ms. Tight Pants, Ms. Snakeskin Flats, Ms. Louis Vuitton bag, who asks loudly in her imperious New York accent to anyone in earshot: "Are they horrible? They're HORRible.

"Oh, my God. Oh, my God.

"Horrible. Horrible.

"Oh. My. God.

"They think they're good?

"They think they're good.

"Oh, my God. Horrible."

And guitar guy and harmonica man and a dozen or more sing-along passengers move on to "Irene Goodnight," and when it ends, applause erupts all the way from Gate 66 to Gate 64.

And Ms. Tight Pants, Snakeskin Flats, Louis Vuitton bag New Yorker says, to anyone in earshot: "Oh. My. God."

Around her, passengers cringe.

Her voice could grate cheese.

Notice a few things about the piece. It's extremely short—just over four hundred words. It's strong on voice, the author's wry personality coming through in constructions such as "What? What!" It's a single scene that takes place in a single locale. It's not a story, in the strictest sense of the word, because nobody changes, nobody has a point of insight, and nobody resolves a complication. No, it's just a slice of life that reveals something universal. But Katy's vignette ran on the cover of the Sunday travel section, and I'd bet my next canceled flight that for many readers it highlighted that gusher of verbiage. It probably made them a little more patient, too. Who'd want to end up like Ms. Tight Pants?

BOOKEND NARRATIVES

On the shelf to my right sit a couple of marble bookends, a gift that resulted from a food-writing workshop. They're massive things, and they easily support the entire shelf's collection of hard-backed reference books. Which makes a decent metaphor for the structure of a bookend narrative. . . . To write one, you bracket a stretch of expository material with two pieces of more engaging scenic action, opening and closing with narrative that has the power to hold the longer, duller content in the center.

I still remember a long-ago example from what is now the *Tampa Bay Times*, which grabbed my attention during one of my periodic teaching visits to the Poynter Institute, the midcareer school for journalists. Some mysterious malady was afflicting pelicans, the iconic bird of the St. Pete waterfront. The reporter included a great deal of expository information—background on pelicans, interviews with experts, statistics, theories about the problem. But he chose to open on a fishing boat, bobbing on Tampa Bay while the captain waved a mackerel baitfish before a hovering flock of pelicans that rose and fell, twisted and turned in response to every movement of the bait. "I call it the pelican symphony," said the captain.

Once the writer had snagged readers with that enticing bit of narrative, he moved into the duller expository material. After he'd waded through that, he completed the bookend strategy by closing with a final scene on the fishing boat.

The bookend vastly expands the possibilities of using narrative for serious trend, issue, and policy stories. You could, conceivably, write a report on a sewer-bond election by opening with Ms. Grundy confronting her flooded basement and closing with Ms. Grundy sobbing on her couch. You could cover a legislative debate about physician-assisted suicide with John Doe, a terminal-cancer patient, contemplating the barbiturates he'd stashed in his medicine cabinet. And so on.

One of the most compelling examples I've seen was a C. J. Chivers story that launched an irresistible narrative on page one of the *New York Times*. Chivers, who provided some of the bravest and best frontline coverage of the war in Iraq, opened with the shooting of a marine radio operator:

> The bullet passed through Lance Cpl. Juan Valdez-Castillo as his Marine patrol moved down a muddy urban lane. It was a single shot. The lance corporal fell against a wall, tried to stand, and fell again.
>
> His squad leader, Sgt. Jesse E. Leach, faced where the shot had come

from, raised his rifle and grenade launcher, and quickly stepped between the sniper and the bloodied marine. He walked backward, scanning, ready to fire.

The narrative continued for two more paragraphs, detailing the efforts to save the young marine and to confront the invisible threat. The next paragraph constituted what's called a "turn," a sudden climb on the ladder of abstraction to address the macrocosm that the opening represented:

> This sequence on Tuesday here in Anbar Province captured in a matter of seconds an expanding threat in the war in Iraq. In recent months, military officers and enlisted marines say, the insurgents have been using snipers more frequently and with greater effect, disrupting the military's operations and fueling a climate of frustration and quiet rage.

With insistent New York Times thoroughness, four full columns then detailed the new insurgent tactic and American efforts to counter it. Chivers reported on a military conference aimed at addressing the threat. He included statistics on sniper casualties. He detailed field tactics designed to thwart would-be snipers. He talked about the sniper focus on radio operators, who linked infantry squads with air and artillery support. And finally, in the last four paragraphs, he returned to the narrative:

> After Lance Corporal Valdez-Castillo was shot and evacuated, a sweat-soaked, bloodied Sergeant Leach led his team through the rest of the wire. When the marines re-entered the wire, an angry debriefing began. . . .
>
> Little was said about how to kill the sniper; the marines did not know where he was. They passed cigarettes and smoked them in the sun, and fumed.
>
> "I'll carry the radio next time," said Lance Cpl. Peter Sprague. "I don't have any kids."

THE PERSONAL ESSAY

The first master of the personal essay, the sixteenth-century Frenchman Michel de Montaigne, argued that the hubris of writing about himself was justified by the fact that his personal experiences offered lessons for the rest of humanity. To teach those lessons, of course, you must first re-create your own experience so that others can share in it. One way to do that is to write a little narrative.

Montaigne, described by Phillip Lopate as perhaps "the greatest essayist who ever lived," typically opened a piece with a little slice of his own life. In "Of a Monstrous Child," for example, he began by noting that the day before he'd seen a deformed boy. He then recalled other deformities he'd encountered in life. But because God was responsible for all things, Montaigne argued, nothing was a deformity in his eye. Therefore, "nothing is anything but according to nature." Men who believed otherwise, he concluded, were ignoring the grand scheme of things.[2]

Therein lies the form for one of the most adaptable and useful varieties of modern narrative. At shorter lengths—one thousand words is standard—the personal essay is a staple of op-ed and magazine writing, a five-minute read that populates everything from community newspapers to personal blogs to service magazines to quality national publications. They often occupy a "Last Word" position on a magazine's final page, where they serve as a sign-off for the entire issue. I once sold one to a national fly-fishing magazine.

The contents are infinitely varied, but the basic structure contains common elements. All personal essays follow Montaigne's lead and include a narrative, a turn, and a conclusion. They're inductive, in other words, moving from the particular (a deformed child), then rising on the ladder of abstraction (arguing that everything born of nature is part of God's plan), and concluding with some cosmic truth. (Ignorance moves humans to judge rare natural events as unnatural.)

The one-thousand-word convention has a practical basis. The length, which is about five double-spaced pages of typescript, combines with one large photo or illustration and a title to fill a single magazine page. You can tackle a thousand words from many directions, but I like a simple, straightforward structure that I use in my own writing and teach to narrative-essay novices. It looks like figure 10.

I usually turn to the personal essay when I've been emotionally affected by something I've experienced, without quite knowing why. The fly-fishing essay came about after I found myself deep in the woods, in tears, at a memorial to some stranger's golden retriever. I puzzled about my odd reaction—I'm not given to tears over strange dogs—and finally decided to write the narrative as a way of discovering my own feelings. The result seemed worth sharing with a larger audience.

I followed my basic one-thousand-word structure closely. And when Gabrielle Glaser, an experienced feature writer new to the essay form, walked into my office at the *Oregonian* and told me about an unusual experience, I suggested it to her.

She'd been walking through a neighborhood retail district when an obese

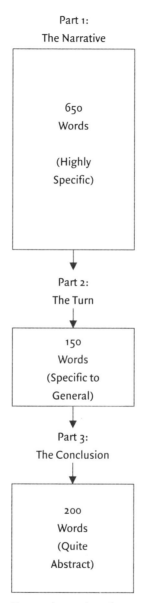

Figure 10. The one-thousand-word personal essay

woman riding a mobility scooter tumbled off the curb. That set a series of events in motion, events that led to some unusual actions on Gabrielle's part, and left her wondering what it all meant. The first step, I said, was to write the narrative segment. Gabrielle began this way:

> "Don't call 9-1-1," the woman wheezed. "Don't call 9-1-1." Her scooter had caught an edge on the curb, and she lay crumpled in the Northwest Twenty-Third Avenue gutter, her oxygen tubes dangling. A group gathered quickly. We were able-bodied; surely we could pick the obese woman back up.
>
> But no one really knew how to get started. "I'm so big," she said. "I'm sorry." The arm of the mobility scooter was trapped under her, poking into her back, and there weren't enough of us to budge it.

A tall, short-haired man named Dave stepped forward, and calmly organized the bystanders. Gabrielle recruited two men from a passing Mustang to help, and—with Dave's direction—the group got the woman back on her scooter. Dave cleaned her wounds. The woman begged him not to call an ambulance, apparently worried about the cost. He assured her that he wouldn't, that everything was under control, and that "I've been in a lot of situations worse than this."

Two bystanders escorted the woman to her doctor's office. Gabrielle, who helped with the rescue and cleanup, pegged Dave as a military type, and on impulse she invited him for a drink. He talked vaguely about his experiences, implying that he'd seen combat in the Middle East. When she described it, the episode caused skepticism:

> My husband knows the macho world of the military well and had questions about Dave's claims. My sister wondered why I'd taken him out for a beer. People I told the story to wondered why we hadn't called 9-1-1.

So what do you conclude from all this? I asked Gabrielle. Why were you willing to throw caution aside and sit down for a drink with a perfect stranger? What does the whole episode reveal about the human condition?

We kicked it around. Gradually, a theme emerged, one that Gabrielle approached via a turn that sprouted from the question about why nobody called 911.

> But we didn't need to. I watched Dave command a group of strangers, including a guy with tattoos down to his fingertips. I saw him direct the

guys in the Mustang. I saw him soothe the woman when she looked at him, ashamed.

I bought him a beer because I wanted to know more. How does a guy just home from Baghdad—if indeed he was just home from Baghdad—cope in a world where the rules are different? That's the first thing we usually think about returned veterans. We focus on war's toll, the physical and psychological scars it leaves on soldiers.

But this man, who had led me to believe he was the kind of veteran who saw plenty of action, had just coped very well with this world. And that got me to thinking. Not about the usual negatives that go with sending young men off to war. But about the skills Dave brought to the miniature crisis on Northwest Twenty-Third and Flanders.

Maybe sending men out into a dangerous world where they have to be brave, decisive, and resourceful pays some dividends for society, Gabrielle concluded, benefits that we ignore in the heat of debate about other consequences of war. And, as a native Oregonian, from pioneer stock, Gabrielle thought she recognized what those benefits might be. She wrapped them up in a neat 160-word conclusion:

> There, on Twenty-Third, most bystanders immediately thought about calling 9-1-1. Instead of just handling the challenges that life doles out to us, we summon specialists. We hand off the tasks we can't (or don't want) to do ourselves—including, almost, untoppling a poor sick woman from her motor scooter.
>
> Maybe some of these men returning from hostile worlds bring something home other than post-traumatic stress syndrome. Something that used to be typical of us all. Something that was ingrained, part of being American.
>
> "I wasn't thinking," Dave said. "I just did."
>
> He drained his beer. He laughed, and the veins on his neck popped out.
>
> "I have to keep reminding myself," he said. "You guys are all just civvies."

The essay ran in the next Sunday opinion section. I suspect that tens of thousands read it and that not a few spent time talking about leadership, urban life, and personal responsibility. I'm confident that, for many of them, Gabrielle's essay produced a "crossover." The ultimate payoff for a personal essay is when readers follow the writer from the specific to the general, then cross over to a new ladder of abstraction and descend it to the specifics of their own lives. Maybe some of Gabrielle's readers thought about how their own military experience changed the way they operate in civilian society. Maybe others thought about occasions when they shifted responsibility to some paid expert, rather than taking it themselves. Maybe some of those resolved to show more initiative in the future.

If you don't like my suggested structure for a short personal essay, you have plenty of options. You can break the narrative into pieces, inserting intermediate conclusions along the way. You can minimize the narrative and expand the more abstract discussion of the subject. Or you can let the narrative dominate while the cosmic conclusion emerges from subtle literary cues. That's what E. B. White, America's answer to Montaigne, did in his 2,800-word masterpiece "Once More to the Lake."

White's essay, first published in *Harper's* and republished dozens of times since, took readers to the lake where White had spent a large chunk of his boyhood:

> One summer, along about 1904, my father rented a camp on a lake in Maine and took us all there for the month of August. We all got ringworm from some kittens and had to rub Pond's Extract on our arms and legs night and morning, and my father rolled over in a canoe with all his clothes on; but outside of that the vacation was a success and from then on none of us ever thought there was any place in the world like that lake in Maine. We returned summer after summer—always on August first for one month.

In his adulthood, White returns with his son, and that visit makes up most of the narrative. It's a nostalgic and eerie experience for White, who notes the inexorable changes that have altered the lake (the country lanes that once included a third rut where horses walked while pulling wagons have been reduced to two ruts), the way his son slips into White's old role as the boy visiting the lake (dragonflies land on the boy's fishing pole, just as they once did White's), and a sense of the process that inevitably replaces one generation with the next:

> I began to sustain the illusion that he was I, and therefore, by simple transposition, that I was my father. This sensation persisted, kept cropping up all the time we were there. It was not an entirely new feeling, but in this setting it grew much stronger. I seemed to be living a dual

existence. I would be in the middle of some simple act, I would be picking up a bait box or laying down a table fork, or I would be saying something, and suddenly it would be not I but my father who was saying the words or making the gesture. It gave me a creepy sensation.

The narrative continues, father and son fishing, exploring, watching a thunderstorm. White grows more unsettled, stricken with the feeling that his own time is ending just as his son is coming into flower. Unlike the standard model, the narrative runs right to the final paragraph, where White describes his son readying himself for a dip in the lake and then concludes with a stunner of an O. Henry ending:

> He pulled his dripping trunks from the line where they had hung all through the shower, and wrung them out. Languidly, and with no thought of going in, I watched him, his hard little body, skinny and bare, saw him wince slightly as he pulled up around his vitals the small, soggy, icy garment. As he buckled the swollen belt suddenly my groin felt the chill of death.

COLUMNS

Newspaper, magazine, online, and audio columns usually run about eight hundred words. Most are think pieces, commenting on some recent event and including standard report-writing devices such as statistics and direct quotations. But eight hundred words provide plenty of room for a little narrative. And, in fact, some of the most successful columns attract loyal readers with storytelling skills, rather than table-pounding opinion. Mike Royko, a syndicated *Chicago Tribune* columnist who for years was one of the country's most popular, often took a storytelling tack, frequently featuring his mythical alter ego, Slats Grobnik.

Margie Boule, who spent years as a columnist at my newspaper, didn't employ a fictional character, but she did rely heavily on narrative. She wrote for the lifestyle section, and she wrote about everyday subjects that don't carry the gravitas of the news sections. Her high standing in readership surveys puzzled some of her hard-news colleagues, who had a tough time understanding the success of what they regarded as lightweight subjects. They just didn't understand the appeal of a good little story. The one I grabbed and stuck in my narrative files was, as Margie put it, "a tale of two Katherines, two blue ribbons, and six perfect chocolate-chip cookies."

It seems that forty-five years ago Katherine Carella took a home-economics class from Kathryn Fritz Finnicum. The lessons stuck, and "it was Kathryn Fritz Finnicum's voice that Katherine Carella heard as she rolled out pie dough or chopped nuts for brownies or added buttermilk to mashed potatoes."

As part of her teaching, Mrs. Finnicum had formed a 4-H Club and guided her students as they baked entries for the county fair. When ten-year-old Katherine Carella won a blue ribbon for a loaf of nut bread, it was one of the highlights of her childhood. She often thought of that blue ribbon over the years, and after her husband retired she entered another county-fair competition.

> Katherine decided to prepare brownies, snickerdoodles, pound cake, oatmeal-raisin cookies, and chocolate-chip cookies.
>
> She read through cookbooks, pored over family recipes. And she tracked down Kathryn Fritz Finnicum's phone number through friends, and called for advice.

Margie's tale was pretty much pure narrative at this point. But some powerful themes were beginning to emerge: The long-lasting impact of a caring teacher, the importance of childhood achievements to shaping character, the way skills of home and hearth link the generations.

Katherine Carella spent a hot afternoon baking in her kitchen, and she delivered the results to judges at the fair. Her husband caught her enthusiasm, and he entered some of the vegetables he'd started raising when he retired. After the judging, they went to the fair to see how they'd done. Mr. Carella won second- and third-place ribbons for his green beans and cherry tomatoes. But Mrs. Carella did even better:

> "And then I saw the blue ribbon on my chocolate-chip cookies. I thought, 'Yes! Yes! Yes! I did it! I can still do it!'"
>
> In her excitement, Katherine Carella called her old mentor.
>
> "She was like a little kid, just elated," says Kathryn Finnicum. "I told her, 'It makes me smile too, kiddo.'"

Then, having spun the yarn, Margie ended the narrative and let the sweet little lessons of life emerge in the kind of abstract conclusion typical of a personal essay:

> Since then Kathryn's been thinking about the years she spent teaching the 4-H girls. "You don't know what you've put into kids' minds until the years pass," she says. "I'm glad Katherine shared this with me. I'll tell you, it's very rewarding. It made me feel like I did some right things in this world."

After the fair closed, Katherine picked up the family prize money: $7.50. Angelo, the banker, noted they'd spent $160 on ingredients. "He said, 'We'll have to talk to our accountant about how we report this to the IRS,'" Katherine laughs.

But she has no doubt it was a good investment. "There were many prizes in addition to the ribbons," Katherine says. Angelo has new pride in his beans and tomatoes. Katherine's childhood teacher, Kathryn Fritz Finnicum, "learned she had instilled in a child the love of learning and accomplishment that endured over time. And I was able to tell a teacher, 'Thank you.'"

FIRST-PERSON NARRATIVE ISSUE ESSAYS

An essay, it's been said, is a way of "taking an idea for a walk." In the case of narrative issue essays, the metaphor's literally true. The essay writer's legwork carries her from source to source, exploring issues, poking and probing, looking for information that will help expand the idea. Such quests are a magazine mainstay, and serious publications such as *Harper's* and the *New Yorker* feature first-person essays that explore issues in narrative form. *Atlantic* senior correspondent James Fallows regularly contributes such essays to his magazine. They can be long—fifteen thousand words or more. And they can cover an issue in impressive depth. For one of his most renowned *Atlantic* pieces, "The Fifty-First State," Fallows spent months interviewing dozens of sources about the pending invasion of Iraq. The resulting essay led readers from one source to another as Fallows forged his argument—that the United States would certainly defeat Saddam Hussein's armies but would then find itself bogged down in the war's aftermath, caught between the sectarian factions that Saddam had controlled with an iron fist. The prediction, of course, proved tragically prescient.

Michael Pollan has used the form for both magazines and books. You can use narrative, he argues, not only to explore places but also to explore systems. *The Omnivore's Dilemma*, his best-selling examination of the American food-production system, is a case in point. *Dilemma* grew out of shorter magazine work, including a *New York Times Magazine* piece, "An Animal's Place."

The article begins with a quiet little narrative action line, launching Pollan's quest by rubbing two contradictory ideas together.

The first time I opened Peter Singer's *Animal Liberation*, I was dining alone at The Palm, trying to enjoy a rib-eye steak cooked medium-rare. If this sounds like a good recipe for cognitive dissonance (if not indigestion), that was sort of the idea. Preposterous as it might seem to supporters of animal rights, what I was doing was tantamount to reading *Uncle Tom's Cabin* on a plantation in the Deep South in 1852.

From that apt launching point, Pollan plunges into the animal-rights literature with a special focus on the issue of meat eating and the American food-production system. His fourth paragraph is a "nut graf," a *Wall Street Journal*–style summary of why the issue's important:

> That animal liberation is the logical next step in the forward march of moral progress is no longer the fringe idea it was back in 1975. A growing and increasingly influential movement of philosophers, ethicists, law professors, and activists are convinced that the great moral struggle of our time will be for the rights of animals.

Singer's book, Pollan admits, "succeeded in throwing me on the defensive." And, from that point on, he takes us along on a first-person journey of discovery. In the next paragraph he mentions Germany, which has passed a law granting animals a constitutional right to respect and dignity. He confronts the arguments of Singer, a Princeton philosophy professor, one by one. He surveys the opinions of other animal-rights activists, and deals with them in turn, much as James Fallows might take us through a series of interviews. He takes readers to factory farms, where chickens and pigs live short, brutally restricted lives in service to maximum food production. He concedes that animals feel pain, that some are thinking beings, and that subjecting wild animals to brutal deaths so that we can wear their furs seems particularly unnecessary. The more he explores, the more he appears on the verge of putting his rib-eye steak aside and turning vegan.

Then, by way of contrast, Pollan takes us along on a trip to Polyface Farm:

> But before you swear off meat entirely, let me describe a very different sort of animal farm. It is typical of nothing, and yet its very existence puts the whole moral question of animal agriculture in a different light. Polyface Farm occupies 550 acres of rolling grassland and forest in the Shenandoah Valley of Virginia. Here, Joel Salatin and his family raise six different food animals—cattle, pigs, chickens, rabbits, turkeys, and sheep—in an intricate dance of symbiosis designed to allow each species, in Salatin's words, "to fully express its physiological distinctiveness."

At Polyface Farm pigs churn compost, and contented cows graze pastures before chickens move in to harvest insect larvae out of the cow pies, spreading the manure and eliminating parasites. All is in balance. To be sure, the animals die to feed people, but in the meantime they live full lives that allow them to express their basic nature. And, according to Pollan's argument, they then die humanely so that we can express ours.

Finally, Pollan turns the tables and attacks the vegans. Eating animals is part of our own animal nature, he argues. Besides, if everybody was vegan even more animals—field mice and birds, for example—would die under the wheels and blades of the machines used to raise row crops. Furthermore:

> A deep Puritan streak pervades animal-rights activists, an abiding discomfort not only with our animality, but with the animals' animality, too. However it may appear to us, predation is not a matter of morality or politics; it, also, is a matter of symbiosis. Hard as the wolf may be on the deer he eats, the herd depends on him for its well-being; without predators to cull the herd, deer overrun their habitat and starve.

And so, Pollan proceeds as he takes us along on his personal journey. Some of it moves through physical space—the restaurant where it begins and the farm where he makes his case for a new kind of agriculture. But most of it is through the mental space of arguments and counterarguments. He has indeed taken an idea—the notion that meat eating is evil—for a walk. After his nine-thousand-word stroll, he finds the idea wanting, but he has achieved a new level of understanding. The American factory farm is evil. But that doesn't mean that meat eating is, too. There's a third way, and that will become the narrative that drives his *Omnivore's Dilemma*, a phenomenal best seller that introduced hundreds of thousands of readers to Pollan's thinking.

And, once again, it was the effective use of narrative that opened the door.

DOCUMENTARY FILM

No book on narrative nonfiction can ignore documentary film. But this book will come close.

Why?

In part because I've built *Storycraft* on my personal, in-the-trenches experience, the firsthand knowledge that comes from writing, editing, and coaching narrative nonfiction. And I simply don't have that experience with film or video. The technical dimensions of filmmaking, by themselves, require years of study—and practice—to thoroughly understand. I won't pretend to have that expertise.

For those interested specifically in documentary film narrative structure, good sources include Robert McKee's *Story*, Christopher Vogler's *The Writer's Journey*, and Syd Field's *Screenplay*, three volumes of valuable story theory that I have cited and discussed elsewhere in this book. John Truby's *The Anatomy of Story* also has a fine reputation in the field. (Truby's written scripts for films such as *Sleepless in Seattle* and *Shrek*.)

And Ken Burns, who long ago established himself as a true genius in documentary storytelling, offers a complete online master class in documentary film. Guest lecturers in his series include the likes of Werner Herzog, Ron Howard, and Annie Leibovitz.

Not that the fundamentals of story theory, the kind of basics that *Storycraft* does cover, aren't relevant to documentary film. One of the themes that emerge from all the recent books on screenwriting is the importance of story theory to that craft. This emphasis echoes the recent surge of discoveries by neuroscientists about how central the brain's story apparatus is to the way we see the world.

And, like the brain scientists, we are all increasingly aware that the same principles apply to storytelling in just about any form, be it nonfiction or fiction. As I noted in the first paragraph of chapter 1, my aha moment came at an Ira Glass presentation, when I realized that he used the same theory for constructing episodes of *This American Life* that we used for building narrative nonfiction stories at my magazine. I put that belief to the test after I retired from full-time work in the news business and wrote my first novel. I certainly struggled with the new form. But with a lot of help from my fiction-writing friends, I ultimately finished a manuscript, found a publisher willing to take a chance on a first-timer, and released *Skookum Summer* to good reviews. A best seller it wasn't, but for me it was absolute proof that the same story theory applies to a magazine narrative, a novel, or a film, be it a drama or a documentary.

PODCASTING

"Who knows what evil lurks in the hearts of men? The Shadow knows!" (Cue maniacal laughter and eerie music.) And with that introduction, children all across the land shuddered in front of huge console radios bristling with vacuum tubes, anticipating another thrilling yarn narrated by the deep-in-an-empty-barrel voice of Orson Welles.

In the late 1930s, virtually every American knew the Shadow. For decades the melodramatic crime-fighting character—each episode closed with "As you sow evil, so shall you reap evil!"—populated the pages of pulp fiction, comic books, and feature films. The character's enduring popularity was a testament to the power of radio drama in the medium's golden age.

Narrative found a place in radio almost from the beginning. Broadcasters found ways to immerse listeners in powerfully intimate imaginary spaces, and local stations were already experimenting with short broadcast plays in the early 1920s. A French drama set aboard a sinking ship proved realistic enough when originally scheduled to air in 1924 that the French government, fearing listeners would mistake it for an actual SOS, refused to allow its broadcast. (It finally appeared on the airwaves in 1937.) The following year, Orson Wells panicked a huge American audience by conning them into believing a Martian invasion was underway in New Jersey. Lest anybody still doubted it, the Mercury Theatre's broadcast of "The War of the Worlds" firmly established the power of radio.

Lighter fare, such as situation comedies like *Fibber McGee and Molly* ran for decades before television finally killed them off. *Amos 'n' Andy* aired from 1928 to 1960, its huge audience (at times up to half of the network total) captivated by innovative microphone work that engaged listeners in a believable imaginary space. Its broad, racist stereotypes perpetuated by White actors playing ignorant, gullible Black characters ultimately brought widespread condemnation. (The NAACP characterized it as "a gross libel of the Negro and distortion of the truth.") After a brief TV run with Black actors it, too, died.

Now new technology has yanked audio drama out of the grave. Podcasting combines the intimacy and engagement of old-time radio with the on-demand convenience of internet streaming. And the podcast, as it turns out, is an excellent vehicle for modern techniques of narrative nonfiction. Its similarity to other contemporary forms, such as the extended personal issue essay, makes me comfortable enough with the form to consult with beginning podcasters, and it's so new that, unlike documentary film, it hasn't generated a large library devoted to applying story theory to the form.

Not that podcasting isn't a fundamentally new medium. For one thing, its length is infinitely flexible. Unlike a conventional radio program, a podcast can run five minutes or—as a series of episodes—fifty hours. And the podcast is ideally suited to first-person narration with the natural intimacy of the medium expressed in the authentic voice of the narrator. That, in turn, enhances the personal touch the narrator brings to a podcast.

That intimacy seems to be at the heart of the podcast's appeal. It's a mood that capitalizes on one of radio's core traits. More than one podcast analysis mentions Franklin D. Roosevelt's "Fireside Chats" as a prime example of the warmth and inclusion that well-performed audio can create.

"When the host is speaking right into the listener's ears," writes Siobhan McHugh, "the intimacy ratchets up even more. But podcasting turns those qualities up to 11, for two reasons: People usually listen privately, often through headphones; and it's an opt-in medium. That sets up the perfect conditions for intimacy."

I usually listen to podcasts in my car, barreling along the freeway with my black lab riding shotgun. That's an intimate space, too, and a good podcast narrative makes the miles fly by.

For all those reasons, podcasting has exploded in the past decade. One survey of Apple podcast offerings came up with an astounding half a million individual selections. They cover the waterfront, with everything from conventional radio programs—*On the Media* or, say, *Car Talk*—available for streaming to arcane discussions of subjects such as pet birds or Peruvian food. Like the specialized magazine, think of a subject and you'll probably find a podcast devoted to it.

Most of that multitude take the form of topically organized programs. Some, however, are true narratives, built out of scenes, operating near the bottom of the abstraction ladder at least some of the time, and following sequences that may—or may not—trace a narrative arc. As I indicated earlier, *This American Life*, the public broadcasting weekly show that first aired in 1995 and quickly established Ira Glass as a fixture in American storytelling, follows the principles of story theory religiously in an innovative nonfiction format. And Sarah Koenig, a former producer at the program, ventured out into a much more expansive podcast format with *Serial*, an instant classic that has won a huge audience—a world record 340 million downloads by the end of 2018—along with every major award in American broadcasting.

Serial's season 1, first broadcast in 2014, ran a dozen episodes in an informal first-person format that took listeners along as Koenig explored the 1999 murder of Hae Min Lee, a Maryland high school student, and the arrest—and eventual conviction—of Adnan Syed, a classmate, for the crime.

Sarah Koenig's opening lines sets the tone for all that follows.

For the last year I've spent every working day trying to find out where one high school kid was for an hour after school one day in 1999. Or if you want to get technical about it—and apparently I do—where a high school kid was for twenty-one minutes after school one day in 1999. This search sometimes feels undignified on my part. I've had to ask about teenagers' sex lives—where, how often, with whom?—about notes they passed in class, about their drug habits, their relationships with their parents, and I'm not a detective, or a private investigator. I'm not even a crime reporter. But, yes, every day this year, I've tried to figure out the alibi of a seventeen-year-old boy.

Music—a hallmark of the form pioneered by *This American Life*—plays in the background, helping set the mood the way it does in a theatrical film. Koenig's personal reactions to her reporting experience are front and center, helping draw listeners into her quest. The language is informal, conversational. (The high schooler is a "kid," not a student.) And Koenig emphasizes her lack of qualification for investigating the case, putting herself on the amateur level of her listeners. Everything about Koenig's approach—which by 2020 had already produced two additional seasons with a fourth in the works—is calculated to make the podcast a shared experience in which the audience will participate.

Of course, all of that "contrived informality," as Siobhan McHugh called it, and self-deprecating humility is largely a con job. Cynthia Gorney, the wonderful narrative nonfiction writer whose work I've cited multiple times, decided to give podcasting a whirl and discovered that the technical expertise required was alone a significant barrier to a casual fling with the new medium:

> Reporting a podcast story was deeply different from the reporting I'm accustomed to: There are *things*. You can't interview without them, and they have buttons and sliders and multiple cords that must fit into multiple plugs before you can get to work. They have gauges you have to keep checking while you're simultaneously making sure the clock doesn't bong or a passing garbage truck doesn't grind its gears in the middle of an interviewee's excellent remark. And the blinking red light! Oh God, the blinking red light. I still have dreams about it.

Cynthia Gorney created her first podcast for *99% Invisible*. Roman Mars produces the show, which is partially funded by Kickstarter campaigns that raise hundreds of thousands of dollars per season. And in 2014 Mars founded Radiotopia, a collective of two dozen independent podcasts with titles such as *The Truth, Strangers*, and *Theory of Everything*. Together, the collective's shows are downloaded more than 19 million times a month.

Those numbers help explain why newspapers, once a secure home for quality narrative nonfiction, have moved into podcasting in a big way. Nikole Hannah-Jones hosted 1619, a *New York Times* serial podcast that paralleled the newspaper's print series produced on the four hundredth anniversary of American slavery. And the *Los Angeles Times* had a major hit with *Dirty John*, a serial that took the form of a story narrative as it tracked the ill-fated romance between a naive interior designer and a cad who set out to seduce her and set off an ultimately fatal chain of suspenseful events. *Times* reporter Christopher Goffard, the narrator, quickly returned to the podcasting format with *Detective Trapp*, a true-crime drama of the sort that seems ideally suited to the format.

Experiments with true-crime podcasting aren't limited to American newspapers. The *Age* and *Sydney Morning Herald* produced *The Last Voyage of the Pong Su*, a ten-episode drama on the attempt of a North Korean crew aboard a North Korean ship to smuggle 150 kilos of heroin into Australia.

Once big, respectable newspapers were involved in podcasting, it was no surprise that big, respectable awards programs jumped in, too. The Peabody Awards recognized *Serial* in 2015 and *S-Town*, another hugely popular spin-off from *This American Life*, in 2018. In 2019 the board of the Pulitzer Prizes announced a new award "For a distinguished example of audio journalism that serves the public interest, characterized by revelatory reporting and illuminating storytelling." The new award lumps together all audio journalism, everything from newscasts to investigative stories to audio documentaries. But surely narrative nonfiction will occupy a prominent place among the winners, as it does for other broad categories such as feature writing.

What more proof do we need that, in the world of nonfiction storytelling, podcasting has arrived?

14

Ethics

Either something happened, or it didn't.
—Ted Conover

My fundamental principles are simple enough: Be honest, get it right, keep everything transparent. Don't fudge, ever, even if a tiny departure from reality produces a huge payoff in drama, clarity, or style.

Easy to say. Far tougher to execute. The ethics of narrative range from pure blacks and whites to the most subtle shades of gray. I've never worked on a major narrative project that didn't raise ethical questions, some excruciatingly difficult.

Let's say you decide to follow a big merger as it goes down. The principals of two giant power companies, one of them operating in your town, agree to let you in if you'll keep mum until the deal is done. You're already facing ethical question number one: Do you gag yourself even if you witness something that may damage the interests of your readers?

If you agree, the path ahead gets even murkier. The CEOs of both companies meet secretly in a distant city. The room is empty except for you and the two bosses. When you write, do you reveal your presence or opt for the greater drama of describing the two executives bargaining nose to nose by themselves?

Then you decide you'd like to get some motion and scenic pizzazz into an action line that, so far, is mostly confined to phone calls and conference rooms. You suggest that one of the key execs visit the turbine room at a hydroelectric dam, talking about the business as she walks by the roaring dynamos. It's a perfect scene—big, noisy, active, and emblematic of what the company does. It even gets the boss in contact with some of the folks who actually make electricity. But is it kosher to alter reality by suggesting the visit?

As the project proceeds, you find yourself getting closer to one of the execs. She's warm and likable, and she takes a shine to you, too. You share drinks after a long day, and she starts talking more like a friend than a source. She spills some juicy background information. Can you use it as is? Or do you have to warn her that you might use it and give her a chance to take it off the record? And what about the way you'll portray her in your finished article? If you write something that reflects badly on her or her company, will you be betraying your friendship?

So it goes. If you call one of your sources back to explain an earlier conversation, can you blend those clarifying comments into the first dialogue? If you ask another what she was thinking when she made an important decision, do you include that unverifiable internal monologue in your narrative? If three execs have three different versions of a meeting—and they will—whose version will you choose? What do you do if the deal falls through and your sources ask you to pull the plug on the whole narrative?

And that's just a narrative on a business deal. Think about the ethical pitfalls in a story about a physician-assisted suicide. Or an adoption gone bad. Or a prominent public figure involved in an illicit affair with an employee.

THE CHALLENGE

Writing nonfiction narrative is like viewing a distant butterfly on an old black-and-white TV. Reality may exist out there, but capturing it with an imperfect recording device fuzzes the outlines, dims the colors, and neglects everything that takes place outside one narrow field of view. When we write, Walt Harrington says, "We learn that the complicated worlds we enter are next to impossible to re-create in words."

Every attempt to do so alters reality in some respect, and every alteration represents an ethical choice. Consider the previous paragraph's quotation from Walt Harrington. As it happens, I heard the quote myself, when Walt delivered the keynote for a 2004 National Writer's Workshop session in St. Louis. As Walt spoke, I jotted what he said down, word for word, in my notebook. I'm a trained journalist, I have a good shorthand system, I was paying close attention, and I'm confident that the quote's absolutely accurate.

But what if I'd missed the conference and reconstructed the quote by interviewing folks who attended? Hundreds packed that ballroom, and I could reach almost all of them via the registration list. But if I interview them, I'll discover that some don't even remember the line, and others don't remember it well enough to repeat it accurately. Even fewer will have written it down. Of those who did, fewer still will have it absolutely right. Maybe somebody even wrote, "We learn that complicated worlds are possible to re-create in words."

Any reconstructed narrative, even an account by a reliable eyewitness, is an approximation of what really happened, and some postmodernist types interpret that to mean no external reality exists. For purely practical reasons, I can't buy that argument. The most important purpose of nonfiction narrative is to help us cope with a challenging world. The closer we come to portraying that world accurately, the more helpful our stories will be. No, we'll never get it absolutely right, and we'll never find an absolute consensus on much of anything. But the only ethical approach is to get as close as possible.

We can move that rickety old black-and-white camera closer to the butterfly. We can add a voiceover that describes the colors. We can bring on experts, Ken Burns style, to explain the butterfly's biology and importance. We can point the camera in different directions, showing context and process. We can research the butterfly's past and speculate about its future. We can, in other words, do a thorough, honest job of reporting and writing. Which is to say, we can apply the same standards that guide Walt Harrington:

> When I write that the spring water is fifty-one degrees, I have measured it with a thermometer. When I write that on a visit to the White House, I sipped La Crema Reserve Chardonnay and ate smoked salmon mousse, I have checked old White House records through the Bush presidential library. When I write that a series of mountains in the Kentucky countryside rises seven hundred, eight hundred, and nine hundred feet, I have checked those elevations on soil conservation maps. When I write that I remember my father and I, as a boy, riding in the car one night singing "The Red River Valley," as we drove through the dip in Ashland Road just past Virgil Gray's house, I have relied on my memory of that night and the song but checked with my father to learn that it was Virgil Gray who lived in the house. Then I drove two hours to visit Ashland Road to make sure there really was a dip in the road just past Virgil's home.

BREAKING FAITH

In 1980 Janet Cooke admitted that she'd invented a child heroin addict for "Jimmy's World," her Pulitzer Prize–winning *Washington Post* story. Cooke left the paper in disgrace, and the *Post*'s humiliated editors gave the Pulitzer back. Things went downhill from there. In 1998 Stephen Glass was exposed for inventing sources and making up at least part of twenty-seven stories he wrote for the *New Republic*. In the same year, *Boston Globe* metro columnist Patricia Smith resigned from the paper after admitting she'd made up people and quotations. Fellow *Globe* columnist Mike Barnicle then resigned in the face of charges that he'd plagiarized some columns and made up others. In 2001 Michael Finkel combined several characters and created a composite for the *New York Times Magazine*. In 2003, the *New York Times* revealed that Jayson Blair stole some passages in a feature story and invented others. In 2004, *USA Today* editors concluded that star foreign correspondent Jack Kelley "fabricated substantial portions of at least eight major stories, lifted nearly two dozen quotes or other material from competing publications, lied in speeches he gave for the newspaper, and conspired to mislead those investigating his work."[1]

In 2011, the public learned that reporters for the *News of the World*, Rupert Murdoch's raunchy British tabloid, routinely listened in on private cellphone conversations by pop-culture celebrities, members of the royal family, a murdered schoolgirl, and the families of dead soldiers. The hacking scandal brought down the tabloid and several prominent executives in Murdoch's organization. In 2014, *Rolling Stone* published "A Rape on Campus," a poorly sourced story that provoked intense push-back. Ultimately the magazine retracted the report, issued an apology, and settled a major libel suit. In 2018 *New York Times* editors reprimanded a young reporter and yanked her off her beat after they learned she was having an affair with a government source.[2]

Some of those scandals were especially damaging because they originated at news media that ranked as among the world's most respected. As the daily parade of corrections testifies, even the *New York Times* doesn't get everything right. But something labeled nonfiction should at least represent a stab at reality. "Truth may be many things," as Walt Harrington also said in St. Louis, "but it is not nothing at all."

It is certainly not a "composite character," the refuge of nonfiction scoundrels such as Janet Cooke and Michael Finkel. Both argued that they'd combined real sources encountered during actual reporting and created composites that reflected a real-world truth. Gail Sheehy, the best-selling author of pop-psychology books such as *Passages*, once invented a prostitute named "Redpants," presented her as an actual hooker, and defended herself by arguing that a line identifying the woman as a composite was dropped during editing. Whatever. I hold with John McPhee. "Where I came from," he said, "a composite character was a fiction."[3]

THE ETHICS OF MEMOIR

After *Angela's Ashes* was published in 1996, Frank McCourt's tale of growing up in an impoverished Irish family quickly soared to best-seller status, earned critical acclaim, and won a Pulitzer Prize. As the book rolled toward sales of more than 5 million, only a few voices questioned how McCourt could remember exact dialogue from his early childhood. Aggrieved citizens of Limerick, the Irish city where much of McCourt's action takes place, did step forward to point out dozens of errors in his description of the city. McCourt counted his profits and moved onto a twenty-four-acre estate.

Nobody claimed McCourt's memoir was invented from the ground up, but much of his dialogue was obviously invented and he clearly didn't apply Walt Harrington's standards to verify historical accuracy. Still, McCourt won his Pulitzer for *nonfiction*. Did it deserve the label?

Many of my journalistic colleagues would take issue with McCourt's prize. Many writers who teach and practice creative nonfiction would have a hard time understanding their objections. And that ethical divide shows itself most clearly in the practice of memoir.

Journalism texts lay down unambiguous law on accuracy. Quote exactly. Spell names correctly. Get the smallest details absolutely right.

Creative nonfiction textbooks differ widely on their standards of accuracy, sometimes within the same text. In *Writing True: The Art and Craft of Creative Nonfiction*, Sondra Perl and Mimi Schwartz started out with the kind of distinction someone like me, Jon Franklin, or Walt Harrington can salute. Creative nonfiction, said the authors, depends on:

> An allegiance to veracity, drawing on fact to write truthfully about the real world—and drawing on memory and imagination to show us this world in full color. If you are changing or inventing facts to make a better story, you are writing fiction. If you are using existing facts to write the story of your experience, you are writing creative nonfiction.

Perl and Schwartz opened the subject of memoir and illustrated with a passage written by Alice Walker, quoting directly from a conversation that allegedly took place when she was twelve. Then their standards of accuracy grew increasingly flexible:

> Creative nonfiction writers, intent on being creative *and* truthful, walk a thin line that other writers do not. Journalists and scholars, with their allegiance to fact, tend to avoid the ambiguities of memory and imagination. Fiction

writers with their allegiance to story have no qualms about inventing interesting worlds. But creative nonfiction writers, with their intent to write good stories that are true, must grapple with the boundary between ethical and artistic clarity. Too much reportage and we cross into scholarship or journalism. Too much imagination and we cross into fiction.

And then Perl and Schwartz carved out a middle ground that I find troubling. "If we stick only to hard, verifiable facts," they write, "our past is as skeletal as line drawings in a coloring book. We must color them in." And "coloring them in" includes letting "imagination fill in details we only vaguely remember."

Given the vagaries of human memory, that concession is, to me, a license to write fiction and label it fact. I suspect Perl and Schwartz would disagree, arguing, perhaps, that "coloring in" is a way to get at "emotional truth."

The idea of "emotional truth" often pops up during discussions of accuracy in the context of creative nonfiction. Maybe you can't get every detail right, goes the argument, but you can capture a larger meaning that's essentially truthful. The argument is common enough in the world of academic nonfiction, but it's hardly universal. "Go to a writers' conference on creative nonfiction," Perl and Schwartz say, "and two terms—emotional truth and factual truth—create a storm of controversy."

The issue came to a head after the 2003 publication of James Frey's *A Million Little Pieces*, a cliché-ridden memoir that supposedly recounted Frey's struggles with alcoholism and addiction. In 2006 the book earned an endorsement from Oprah Winfrey and sold 3 million copies. Then the Smoking Gun, a truth-squading Web site, exposed it as a fraud.

At first Frey's publisher, Doubleday, trotted out the idea of "emotional truth." "Recent accusations . . . notwithstanding," read a news release, "the power of the overall reading experience is such that the book remains a deeply inspiring and redemptive story for millions of readers." Frey himself took refuge in the same argument, telling Larry King that he "stands by the book as the essential truth of my life." Oprah herself defended the book as valuable regardless of the factual details.

But *A Million Little Pieces* contained virtually no truth, emotional or otherwise. Frey eventually admitted he'd written it as a novel that was rejected by seventeen publishers before Doubleday's Nan Talese said she'd publish it if he recast it as a memoir. Frey and Talese had reached the bottom of an ethical slippery slope, where the only difference between a novel and memoir, it appeared, was that a memoir sold better.

The Smoking Gun's expose sparked a national uproar. Oprah, feeling the heat, retreated from her earlier defense and invited Frey back onto her show, where she savaged him because he had "betrayed millions of readers." Random House, Doubleday's parent company, offered a refund to any reader who felt deceived.

But equally suspect memoirs just keep popping out of the muck at the bottom of the slippery slope. Margaret Seltzer won rave *New York Times* and *Los Angeles Times* reviews for a memoir titled *Love and Consequences: A Memoir of Hope and Survival*. The book appeared under the byline of Margaret B. Jones, and—as it turns out—that was just the beginning of the deception. As Jeff Baker, the book-review editor at my newspaper, pointed out, Ms. Jones/Seltzer is White, not Native American as she claimed. She grew up in an affluent suburb, Sherman Oaks, California, not in a South Central Los Angeles foster home. She did not graduate from the University of Oregon, although she did attend the school as an ethnic-studies major. And, as Jeff pointed out, she never had been "a drug-dealing, crack-cocaine-cooking member of the Bloods street gang."

David Sedaris takes a slightly more defensible approach to memoir, readily admitting that much of what he writes is fiction. As Sarah Lyall reported in the *New York Times*:

> Mr. Sedaris has always said that he exaggerates for effect, particularly in dialogue; an author's note in the new book describes the stories as "realish." He also maintains that in the sort of essays he writes, reality is a subjective, slippery concept, particularly as no two people have the same recollection of the same event. "Memoir is the last place you'd expect to find the truth," he said.

Well, maybe not the last place. American movies have long blurred the line between truth and fiction, and nobody expects literal truth from Hollywood, even when films such as Oliver Stone's *JFK*, *W.*, or *Escobar* present twisted history as though it were fact. Even documentaries, an increasingly popular category that leads viewers to expect honest reporting, is often loose with facts. Robinson Devor, whose *Zoo* is supposedly a documentary about bestiality, concedes that his films aren't true in the conventional sense of the word. "I have always said that we're trying to get to the spirit of the events, not to do a 'Sixty Minutes'–style expose," he says. He, too, resorts to an emotional-truth argument to justify his deception. If someone depicted in *Zoo* sees the film, he admits, "They might say, 'That's not how it was.' And I would ask, 'Have I been true to your words and your spirit?'"[4]

This postmodernist view of reality even extends to radio news, according to Philip Gerard, who wrote an essay describing his experience working for a moving company that destroyed a woman's belongings. When she finished crying, the woman said, "It's not right to cry over things" and gave him a copy of William Styron's *Sophie's Choice*. According to the story, Gerard submitted the piece to an *All Things Considered* producer. She liked it a lot but thought the Holocaust context of *Sophie's Choice* was pretty heavy to drop into a piece about losing material things. Couldn't it be, she asked, a different book?

A different book! Why do I find that so offensive? Is it because *All Things Considered* is one of the country's leading news programs, which ought to guarantee a reasonable allegiance to facts? Maybe. But when I calm down and think about it, I come back to the core belief that *anything* presented as nonfiction ought to guarantee a committed allegiance to facts.

It's equally outrageous that John Berendt's *Midnight in the Garden of Good and Evil* squatted on the *New York Times* nonfiction best-seller list for 216 weeks, even though—when questioned about some of his facts—Berendt admitted, "This is not hard-nosed reporting, because clearly I made it up."[5]

As *Midnight* demonstrated, "nonfiction" labels on books don't guarantee a commitment to absolute accuracy. Walt Harrington says that a prominent book editor told him that his fussy precision was "too journalistic," that he "wasn't being just a journalist now, but an author." Another told him he had no problem changing the age at which something happened to a character from forty to twenty if it improved the narrative.

That appalled Walt, and it appalls me. We both come out of journalism, after all. And, as "Hiroshima" author John Hersey once said, "The legend on the journalist's license should read, 'None of this was made up.'"

SPECULATION

The minute you start reporting, you'll discover how many assumptions—some right, some wrong—you make during an ordinary day. New reporters almost always learn hard lessons from a series of embarrassing mistakes. When I was editing *Northwest Magazine*, I assigned a young freelancer to a story on lottery winners. He interviewed a woman who'd collected a big payout and asked her what she did first after getting the news. She told him she'd taken the family out to Burger King. He spiced it up a little bit in the writing, reporting that she'd taken her tribe to Burger King for Whoppers, the chain's signature burger.

Whoa! The woman was a vegetarian who chose Burger King for its salad selection. In high dudgeon, she called me to complain that the writer had damaged her reputation. She settled down eventually, and I thanked the magazine muses that she hadn't filed a libel suit.

Some assumptions are reasonable, I suppose, and an honest writer might make them for the sake of good storytelling. Richard Preston did so frequently in *The Hot Zone*, his riveting account of an Ebola virus outbreak. But when he was reconstructing scenes based on reasonable assumptions, Preston let readers in on any leaps of faith by sprinkling his copy with tip-off words such as "probably," "perhaps," and "maybe."

> In the afternoon, it would have rained, as it usually does on Mount Elgon, and so Monet and his friend would have stayed in their tent, and perhaps they made love while a thunderstorm hammered the canvas. It grew dark; the rain tapered off. They built a fire and cooked a meal. It was New Year's Eve. Perhaps they celebrated, drinking champagne.

By the time Preston did his reporting, Monet was dead of an Ebola-like virus, an unfortunate fact that seriously limited the prospects for an interview. So if Preston hoped to write a full-fledged narrative, complete with vivid scenic description, some speculation was inevitable. He traveled the route Monet took and filled in the blanks with passages such as the champagne-drinking episode. Fair enough. When I read *The Hot Zone*, I knew exactly what Preston was doing.

Erik Larson faced a similar challenge. The witnesses of the original events depicted in *Devil in the White City* are all dead, too, although over a century has passed since the Chicago World's Fair and Father Time, not Ebola, was the killer.

Like a more traditional historian, Larson used footnotes to document his sources, a tactic that avoids the clutter caused by attributions such as "he probably thought" or "as he recalled in his memoir." Footnotes do occasionally appear with popular narrative, and even newspapers experimented with them after the ethical scandals of the nineties. The *Wall Street Journal* footnoted its reconstruction of the September 11, 2001, terrorist attack in such detail that some critics scoffed at the technique as overkill.

Footnotes notwithstanding, Larson's scarce in-text attribution bothered me, and I often paused in the narrative to ask how he could possibly know some of the things he described. At one point he wrote that a woman walked into an upstairs room. "The day was hot. Flies rested on the windowsill. Outside, another train rumbled through the intersection." I suppose you could check the day's temperature in contemporary sources. You could even uncover the frequency of trains moving through an intersection. But how, I wondered, would you know about flies on the windowsill, and how would you know that a train rumbled through the intersection at that exact moment? Those don't strike me as the kind of details anyone would record, and Larson's footnotes are silent on the matter.

Larson is hardly cavalier about such issues. His author's note reveals his major sources, including trial transcripts, memoirs, and newspaper accounts that included excerpts from primary sources such as letters and telegrams. The dogged, exhaustive nature of the research is impressive. Still, Larson often goes beyond the facts in hand. At one point he describes the nocturnal activities of his serial killer:

> At night, after the first-floor stores had closed and Julia and Pearl and the building's other tenants were asleep, he sometimes would descend to the basement, careful to lock the door behind him, and there to ignite the flames of his kiln and marvel at its extraordinary heat.

In his footnotes, Larson concedes this is speculation based on the fact that "Holmes was known to pace at midnight, suggesting he was not a restful sleeper. Psychopaths need stimulation. The kiln would have been an irresistible attraction. Admiring it and igniting its flames would have reinforced his sense of power and control over the occupants above." Hmmm. All that may be true. But stretching those facts to create an actual scene is a bit much for me.

As an editor, I might have suggested that Larson write, "From what we know about psychopaths, it's easy to imagine Holmes descending to the basement, carefully locking the door behind him, and igniting the kiln to marvel at its extraordinary heat." It's clunkier, to be sure. But it makes me less uneasy.

Good-faith narrative writers can disagree about how much speculation you can use to flesh out a skeletal action line. But for me the bottom line is that readers should know exactly where you learned what you claim to know. I'm not alone. Contest judges often insist on that kind of transparency, and the Pulitzer board once rejected a worthy finalist because the writer failed to make the source of her information clear. In 2003 the American Society of Newspaper Editors underscored the concern by issuing by a special statement on attribution when it announced its annual writing awards:

> Our judges have been concerned in recent years about stories, particularly in narrative writing, where attribution was missing. Fortunately, we have found that the finest writers have no difficulty working attribution into

their work; but we have been troubled to have to reject some otherwise fine writing for lack of proper sourcing.

SHOWING YOUR CARDS

I might quibble with Erik Larson about particulars, but the essay on methods he included in *Devil* meets my basic test of transparency. Readers can see what he did and make up their own minds about his standards of accuracy, evidence, and fairness. I'm a fan of such notes, and most of the narrative projects I've edited carried a similar message. Here's my editor's note for Tom Hallman's Pulitzer winner:

> To report "The Boy behind the Mask," Tom Hallman Jr. spent hundreds of hours, for more than ten months, poring over medical records, reading Lightner family journals, hanging out at the Lightner house, attending school with Sam, interviewing Sam's friends, and twice traveling across the country with the family. He saw virtually every important development with his own eyes and heard every key conversation with his own ears.
>
> As a result, relatively few scenes in "The Boy behind the Mask" are reconstructed, and those are the result of careful interviews with participants. Each such scene contains attributions to the memories of the participants.
>
> No dialogue appears within quotation marks unless Hallman heard a conversation himself.

An author's note also gives the writer a chance to reveal any departures from absolute truth. Lauren Kessler's *Dancing with Rose* grew out of Lauren's experience as an aide in an Alzheimer's care facility, where she showed up for regular shifts to care for patients. But Lauren, who headed the University of Oregon's program in narrative nonfiction, was no ordinary aide, and her reporting strategy raised obvious privacy concerns. Lauren explained how she dealt with them in this author's note:

> This is a work of nonfiction. Maplewood is a real place, but that is not its real name. The people in this book—the residents of Maplewood, their families, the institutional caregivers, and the administrators—are real people. I've changed some of the names to ensure privacy, but in only one small instance (a hometown) have I knowingly changed any facts of details about their lives. The events and incidents chronicled in the book happened. Those few I did not directly witness I reconstructed based

on the interviews with those who were present. All of the conversations recorded in the book took place. I heard them (and participated in many of them) and wrote them down in my reporter's notebook at the time or soon thereafter.

IMMERSION

In a way, an immersion reporter is a house guest, invited into private spaces with the tacit understanding that household rules apply. A good guest is polite and nonjudgmental. He follows his host's lead, disrupting the household routine as little as possible. He does his best to help out, easing the burdens of having a stranger around.

Nobody's more polite, nonjudgmental, and helpful than Rich Read, which accounts for a lot of his success as a Pulitzer-winning immersion reporter. His reputation no doubt helped get him invited along when a medical team headed for Sri Lanka after the 2004 tsunami. Once there, the team found whole villages swept away, fishing fleets destroyed, and grief-stricken parents who'd lost their children. At one point, an overwhelmed team member turned to Rich. Could he help out with the simple task of sorting some pills? No, said Rich. I can't.

At first blush that seems like a rude breach of a guest's unspoken compact with his host. And yet, it's a perfect illustration of the weird conflicts that immersion reporting often poses. The medical team's job was to save Sri Lankan lives. Rich's job was to document their work without altering reality via his own involvement, a mission he explained to team members before leaving for Sri Lanka.

Experienced reporters disagree about how detached they need to be. Bob Steele, the Poynter Institute's ethics specialist, visited my newsroom and convened a group of reporters, editors, and photographers to discuss the issue. "Sometimes I think we use our distance by saying we can't get involved," one of the participating journalists said. "But sometimes that stops us from getting down to those deeper layers." That, she added, distorts reality in its own way. Several other participants said they wouldn't hesitate to sort pills in a disaster zone. "We want it our way," an editor said, "but we're not willing to do it the other's way." He turned to Rich Read. "What if you needed medical care?" he asked. "Would you want them to leave you dying by the side of the road?"

After listening to the debate Steele weighed in on the ethics of immersion. "Different folks have different duties," he said. "The journalist's duty is unique and essential." And, he concluded, that duty includes four ethical mandates: 1) Speak the truth. 2) Remain independent. 3) Minimize harm. 4) Be accountable.

Do the same rules apply when you write in first person? When you're playing a part in your own narrative, anything that happens to you can be a legitimate part of the story. When Robin Cody was reporting *Voyage of a Summer Sun*, his first-person account of a canoe trip down the Columbia River, he certainly wouldn't have hesitated to rescue a drowning swimmer. In fact, such an episode would have been a grand narrative opportunity.

And does Bob Steele's injunction to "speak the truth" mean revealing everything about who you are and what you're up to? For *Newjack*, Ted Conover went undercover and applied for a job as a prison guard. For nearly a year, he showed up for work every day at Sing Sing, and the other guards—not to mention the prisoners—had no idea he was taking notes for a book. More recently, Conover did something similar when he took a job in a meatpacking plant for a *Harper's Magazine* story. Conover justified his deceptions by noting that they were last resorts. He'd tried to get conventional access for both stories but was turned down. The importance of the two subjects justified, in his mind, the deception he employed to get access.

He nonetheless has limits on deception, and he listed several in a Nieman Storyboard Q&A by Katia Savchuk after publication of his guidebook *Immersion: A Writer's Guide to Going Deep*:

> Don't actively lie. Don't make up a false backstory to explain why you're there or to get a job. I think you can avoid it in practically every case by not answering questions or saying you don't want to talk about it. Some people will say you're being deceptive simply by putting on a prison guard uniform or federal meat inspector uniform. To a degree, they're right. On the other hand, I'm not pretending to do the job—I'm actually doing it.
>
> I think you should never surreptitiously enter a therapeutic space, like a twelve-step group. And you should never enter into an intimate relationship with someone while doing this. You should not do things that would strike the normal you as unethical, because it's not like you get a pass on ethical behavior just because you're undercover.

Other narrative writers decide differently. Mary Roach once thought about going undercover as a surgeon so that she could attend a $500-per-person plastic-surgery clinic, cadaver head provided. She decided to stay up front about her role as a reporter, which strikes me as the sound ethical choice. Most newsrooms ban anonymous reporting unless it's at an event available to anybody. And, truth be known, most of us don't qualify for anything involving a cadaver head.

BETRAYAL

In 1979 Jeffrey MacDonald, an army doctor accused of murdering his pregnant wife and two daughters, invited Joe McGinniss, a narrative journalist who'd written the enormously popular *The Selling of the President*, to write about his case. Clearly, MacDonald and his lawyers expected favorable treatment. But after McGinniss immersed himself in the story, he concluded that MacDonald was, in fact, guilty, a pathological narcissist who killed his family for warped psychological reasons. *Fatal Vision*, his book on the case, condemned MacDonald in terms even more damning than the court's, which convicted the doctor in 1979. MacDonald eventually sued McGinniss for fraud. The case ended with a hung jury, and McGinniss settled out of court for $325,000.

The story didn't stop there. In 1989 Janet Malcolm led off a two-part series in the *New Yorker* with this incendiary line: "Every journalist who is not too stupid or too full of himself to notice what is going on knows that what he does is morally indefensible." Her prime example? Joe McGinniss.

Malcolm's thesis, later released in book form as *The Journalist and the Murderer*, was that the kind of relationships narrative reporters forged with sources were a form of seduction that often led to betrayal.

A wail of protest erupted in the journalistic mainstream. "Not us!" cried the wounded scribes. "We're the good guys."

Well, maybe. But the fact is that inherent contradictions color relationships between journalists and their sources, contradictions that narrative nonfiction writing often magnifies. I thought then—and I think now—that Malcolm had a point.

The problem is that writers and sources often bring conflicting expectations to a narrative project. Sources bring everyday social norms to the relationship, presupposing sympathy and loyalty. But for a reporter, sources are means to ends. "People forget you're there to work," Ted Conover says. "They think of you as a friend."

So what can you do to ease the conflict and head off the sense of betrayal? Explain the ground rules going in, says Bob Steele. Describe your role as a writer and how it might differ from what sources expect. "I'm a big believer," he says, "in ethical front-end decision making."

When Rich Read approached Keiichi Takahashi about a long-term reporting project on the Japanese businessman's career, Rich wrote a note outlining all the reasons Takahashi might not want to cooperate. Takahashi wrote back, arguing the opposite, which gave Rich pretty much carte blanche. Both men made their expectations clear, and they ended the project on good terms.

I joined the two of them for a well-lubricated dinner the next time Takahashi came to the United States.

Inara Verzemnieks, another reporter I've worked with on several narrative projects, takes a similar tack. She insists on having "a very direct conversation" early on. "There have been times," she says, "when I've almost tried to talk people out of doing stories."

On a long project, that direct conversation bears revisiting. Sensitive writers engage sources in their process. "Here's what I'm thinking about . . ." "I know you think X, but I'm interpreting what she said as Y." "Ultimately, I'm the one who has to tell this story, and we're just going to have to agree to disagree on that one."

But does transparency extend to sharing your unpublished manuscript with your source? Responsible writers disagree, in part because "prepublication review" was long considered a newsroom no-no. Showing a source an unpublished story was itself considered an ethical violation, a way of surrendering control to sources and tainting the reporter's independence. Mary Roach still subscribes to that principle. She'll read quotations back to sources to make sure she has them straight, and she'll double-check facts with sources, if necessary. But she won't let a source read an entire manuscript. "If they have a chance to change things," she explains, "they will."

I dunno. I've often let sources read all or part of my manuscripts, an exercise that I always precede with the proviso that I'm totally open to correcting errors but that my interpretations remain my own. If you've been transparent all the way through the process, the manuscript shouldn't hold any huge surprises. And a source review helps you ensure that you have everything exactly right. I bought David Stabler a cup of coffee so that he could review my account of "A Round-the-Clock Race to Save the Rach," the tale of Sergei Rachmaninoff's Third Piano Concerto that I told in chapter 11. I'm glad I did. I'd misspelled "Sergei."

IMAGINARY PATTERNS

One of the earliest brain-research findings relevant to storytelling ethics is also among the most chilling. In 1944 Fritz Heider and Marianne Simmel showed their experimental subjects a film of shapes moving around a screen. As Elizabeth Hellmuth Margulis reported, the participants "tended to view the shapes as interacting animate beings with agency, independent of instructions. To make sense of the apparently abstract geometric shapes and their movements, people inferred a narrative."

It's not much of leap to Lisa Cron's conclusion that "your brain doesn't like anything that appears random, and it will struggle mightily to impose order—whether it's actually there or not."

The phenomena is so well-established that it even has a name. Cron notes that "'pareidolia' is the tendency to see shapes when they're not actually there. "Like the Man in the Moon, or the Virgin Mary in a potato, or a dinosaur in a cloud."

Other commentators see the human weakness for conspiracy theories—no matter how outlandish—as a product of the same brain wiring. These days such theories reign at the highest levels of government, a sad case of pattern recognition run amok.

It shows up in narrative nonfiction, too, and I've seen examples of it in the work of friends and acquaintances. Nothing sparks the search for patterns like the need to find a story out there in the chaotic bloom and buzz of messy reality. The unfortunate result can be a narrative built on a shaky foundation of upside-down logic. "It doesn't make sense that this murder happened as a result of some random crime. Therefore, it must be the result of a conspiracy, deep corruption among those who must have something to hide."

Yeah . . . maybe. And, in the absence of hard evidence, maybe not. Maybe Lee Harvey Oswald did act entirely alone, as unlikely as that may be. Or maybe the prisoner you're hoping to exonerate with a dramatic podcast really did commit murder. Maybe your brain is telling you that something's there when shapes are just randomly moving around a screen.

Responsible nonfiction storytellers will always pause, step back, and ask themselves: "What do we really have that leads us to conclude that this, in provable fact, is what happened?" Above all, keep an open mind, and never make a claim you can't prove beyond a reasonable doubt. Your credibility is at stake, as are the reputations of both institutions and human beings.

STORY STRUCTURE AND STYLE

An old newsroom gag refers to stories that are "too good to check." The phrase is tongue in cheek, of course, and it's usually used just as a reporter, with a sigh, picks up the phone to double-check a good story. But, like all gags, it turns on a grain of truth. A good story *is* a temptation. When we take off in pursuit of one, we run the risk of ignoring evidence that might contradict it, either because we don't want to spoil it or because we simply don't think of possibilities outside the story template. "In pursuit of a story," Lauren Kessler admits, "even virtuous nonfiction writers are tempted by the dark side."[6]

A complete story calls for a protagonist. So the dark side credits one character with more responsibility for resolving a complication than she deserves. A complete story calls for a climax. So the dark side invests a minor incident with more significance than it deserves. A complete story calls for resolution. So the temptation is to wrap up loose ends more neatly than is ever the case in real life.

James Frey fell prey to all those temptations. When what started as a novel morphed into a memoir, Frey just couldn't let go of the story elements that a novelist has at his disposal, without concern about anything that actually happened. "I wanted the stories in the book to ebb and flow," Frey explained, "to have dramatic arcs, to have the tension that all great stories require."[7]

I've certainly felt the same temptations. When Sam Lightner's surgery failed to give him a normal face, Tom Hallman and I felt palpable disappointment, and—I'm ashamed to admit—not just because the outcome was such a disappointment to Sam himself. The surgery's failure meant failure of our narrative arc: We'd envisioned a complication created by the pressure on Sam to look like everybody else and an inciting incident created by Sam's high school enrollment, which upped the conformity pressure. Tom had witnessed the scene where Sam himself, in true protagonist style, made the decision to have the risky surgery. And the story had then followed a beautiful curve of rising action that led naturally to a successful surgery.

Downplaying or ignoring the surgical failure wasn't an option. Unlike James Frey, Tom and I were too steeped in newsroom culture to cook the books. Besides, Ben Brink's photos of Sam after the surgery told the whole story. As H. G. Bissinger, author of *Friday Night Lights*, put it, "If you're trying to get it right, you really do suffer with the facts you have."

The only ethical resolution was to abandon a year's work on the story or to find a new narrative arc. Tom kept reporting. And *his* point of insight came when he saw Sam telling an administrator who offered to let him bypass a long high school registration line that "this is where I belong." By persevering, Tom had uncovered an even more authentic story. Sam was coming to terms with his situation and moving on, which is the way most successful adults deal with real-world challenges.

If you want the whole nine yards of story and your material just doesn't provide it, a truly ethical reporter will face facts and correctly label his work as fiction. David Simon, the *Baltimore Sun* police reporter who wrote the nonfiction narratives *Homicide* and *The Corner*, went that route when he created *The Wire*, his stunningly effective fictional portrait of Baltimore crime, corruption, and decay. Simon's decision is the nonfiction writer's ethical version of fishing or cutting bait. You can write a nonfiction book or produce a documentary. You can write a novel or produce a feature film. But you can't secretly mix fiction's reliance on imagination with nonfiction forms, no matter the temptation.

CRAFT

In even the most scrupulous work of nonfiction you *will* make mistakes. In this book I've checked every fact I had the slightest doubt about. But I have no doubt that some things are still wrong. No human being can get a hundred thousand words absolutely accurate. The real route to responsible nonfiction is not absolute accuracy but good faith. You work hard at your craft and do your best to get everything right. You check and double-check. And you never deliberately falsify anything, large or small.

The devil never quits suggesting a fib or two. "We're all aware of the temptations posed by the little lies of daily storytelling," Lauren Kessler says. "The fish that grows in the telling, the clever retort that we think of ten minutes too late."[8]

I'm even antsy about slight modifications to direct quotations. I used a line from Norman Sims as an epigraph for the chapter on voice and style. In *The Literary Journalists*, Norm wrote, "Voice brings the authors into our world." I plunked that down under "Chapter 4" and thought about how much better it would be if it read: "Voice brings authors into our world." I dropped "the," which as far as I could see had absolutely no impact on Norm's meaning. But the change ate at me. I put "the" back in. I took it out again. Ultimately, I decided that I couldn't make the change honestly and put "the" back. Silly me. All that fuss over something so trivial.

I'm probably overdoing it. Many perfectly ethical nonfiction writers wouldn't hesitate to make a minor change to a quotation, provided it didn't affect meaning. David Hayes, a well-regarded Canadian feature writer, readily admits that "I've edited dialogue a bit my entire career." The hemming and hawing, the stumbles and false starts that typify speech add nothing, goes the argument, and eliminating them allows the intended meaning to come through. Hayes says he'd want somebody to edit the dross out of his comments, a point he makes with the observation that "if only, well, it doesn't usually happen, thank God, but if only once somebody didn't edit, you know, my dialogue a bit, at least, I mean if they didn't fix what I say and leave some of it out, I'd be pretty unhappy, it would sound pretty bad. On paper, I mean."[9]

Editing out meaningless meandering is one thing. Putting quotation marks around questionable dialogue is something else, and ethical nonfiction writers recognize the distinction. For *The Devil in the White City*, Erik Larson noted that "anything between quotation marks comes from a letter, memoir, or other written document."

Neither can you seek out sources you know will make your point and ignore those who will muddy your theme, a practice known as "casting." And you can't give the impression that you witnessed something you reconstructed. Rick Bragg, a Pulitzer-winning *New York Times* feature writer, ended his career at the newspaper after filing a first-person feature story datelined "Apalachicola, Fla."[10] The piece dripped with vivid description. An oysterman's boat "idles along," "gently intruding on the white egrets that slip like paper airplanes just overhead." In fact, Bragg had visited Apalachicola only briefly, "toe-touching" to justify the dateline on the printed story. He saw none of the oysterman's actions, which were reported by a stringer. Bragg didn't lie outright, but he did deceive. The *Times* suspended him for two weeks, the furor kept growing, and Bragg eventually submitted his resignation. Nobody was more outraged by the deception than several of his colleagues. "We do our own reporting here," said Alex Berenson, a business reporter. "At least most of us do."[11]

ETHICAL HABITS OF MIND

Although virtually every narrative nonfiction project involves ethical issues, no two pose precisely the same questions. Writing about the real world is just too complex, too nuanced, and too filled with unpredictable humanity to reduce any situation to an ethical formula. The only workable route to ethical behavior is working through a process that weighs competing interests, asks key questions, and considers all the practical alternatives. Ethical nonfiction is a journey, not a destination.

The journey begins when a story idea takes shape, and the first questions should measure the idea against its ethical implications. Can you get access to key sources honestly? How much can you observe directly, and how much will you need to reconstruct? If you do reconstruct, how likely are you to find reliable witnesses and supporting documentation? What about your own prejudices? Will your theme emerge from your reporting, or will you impose it on the facts, describing the world not as it is, but as you want it to be?

The questions continue through the reporting. Am I using diverse, representative sources, or am I trying to make a case by casting? How do my sources know what they know? Have I double-checked eyewitness accounts against documentary evidence? Do my sources have conflicts of interest? Do I?

And so it goes, right down to the final editing. Can you vouch for the verbatim accuracy of anything inside quotation marks? Can you back up every generalization with hard evidence, or should you ratchet your claims down a notch or two? Do the attributions make the sources clear, keep the chronology straight, and reveal when you're speculating? Are you sure she ate a Whopper?

Much of the process boils down to what's known as "prosecutorial editing," a habit of mind that questions everything with the same tough intensity that a district attorney brings to bear on a criminal defendant. In my newsroom we tried to make it a regular part of the reporting, writing, and editing process, something that characterized the thinking of writers and editors alike.

After we won the Pulitzer Gold Medal for Public Service and the Pulitzer Prize for Feature Writing in 2001, an editor at *Columbia Journalism Review* (CJR) asked Amanda Bennett and me to write about the two projects. The article we produced focused on the prosecutorial process that kept both of them wedded to high ethical and reporting standards. We wrote it as a play in six acts, each act a scene that illustrated reporting and ethical standards such as "Quote Only What You Know Firsthand," "Report Only What You See," and "Choose the Story You Can Verify."

Amanda led the team that won the gold medal for its investigation of the US Immigration and Naturalization Service. Rich Read and Julie Sullivan spent more than a year reporting abuses at the local INS office. Then investigative reporters Kim Christensen and Brent Walth joined them as they took the story national, documenting widespread examples of institutional racism, incompetence, and corruption. As Rich's editor, I participated in team meetings and had a chance to watch great prosecutorial editing at work.

Amanda often played the DA. At one point, she gathered the team in a conference room and wielded a Magic Marker at the whiteboard, running the group through its paces. What did they hope to prove? "Corruption," said one reporter. "Secret prisons," said another. "Bungling," said a third. All right, Amanda responded, what would it take to prove each of them? She'd list each item of suggested evidence, and the team fanned out across the country to gather it.

The group set explicit standards for evidence and balance. Everything they published would come from primary sources, they would avoid material from interest groups, they would use opinion from across the political spectrum, and they would find at least three examples—from diverse sources and regions—to buttress every point.

When the project moved into its writing phase, Amanda assembled the group again, playing the DA as she challenged each conclusion. She described the process in our CJR article:

"You've picked isolated incidents and strung them together," charged Bennett, role-playing a critic. Walth began ticking off the statistics that proved that each anecdote was representative of many others.

"You're sensationalizing a few kids' stories," she continued, referring to a piece on children in jail. Sullivan recounted many other examples that didn't make the story cut.

"You're playing into the hands of political partisans," she said; Read began citing evidence gathered from both political parties, as well as from non-political sources.

In the meantime, I was working with Tom Hallman on "The Boy behind the Mask," that year's Pulitzer winner for features. For the CJR article, I described the way Tom reconstructed Sam Lightner's hospital dialogue from the boy's handwritten questions and the way we recast the story's theme to fit the changing arc of the story. I described the way Tom went through the complete seventeen-thousand-word manuscript marking everything he'd heard or witnessed himself with a yellow highlighter, demonstrating that more than 80 percent of the story stemmed from firsthand reporting. And I showed how the prosecutorial attitude worked during the editing:

> At one point in his draft, Hallman described other patients staring at Sam in a hospital waiting room. "They all looked at Sam, and seemed to feel that whatever the problem was that brought them here, it couldn't be worse than the boy with the face."
>
> But Hart's markup cautioned Hallman to "be careful of statements such as 'seemed to feel.' We don't want anybody accusing us of mind-reading."
>
> Hallman went back to his notes and rewrote the scene: "Sam found a seat and flipped through a stack of magazines. He caught the eye of a woman sitting across from him. She turned away. Sam saw her whisper something to a woman sitting next to her before both turned back to stare."

My own thinking about ethics has changed completely since the days when I taught a course on the subject at the University of Oregon. For the class, students worked their way through a series of ethics case studies and wrote their own personal ethics code, which they presented in a term paper. Later, after I went to work for the Oregonian, I created a database containing a dozen or more newspaper, broadcast, magazine, and news-organization ethics codes so that we could consult them when we faced ethical questions. But, in truth, I never found any of the codes especially helpful, and I haven't used one in years. It's the questions you ask, not the answers you give, that determine how ethically you operate.

Several good lists of key questions have appeared in the last decade or so. And, although none does more than skim the surface of all the issues you might face for even one narrative piece, I still find them useful. I'm partial to the list assembled at the Poynter Institute by Bob Steele and Chip Scanlan.[12]

> **Questions for Nonfiction Storytellers**
> By *Chip Scanlan and Bob Steele*
>
> 1. How do I know that what I have presented really happened the way I say it did?
> 2. Is it true? According to whom?
> 3. Do I not only have the facts right, but also the right facts?
> 4. How complete is my reconstruction? Is it based on one source, two, or several? Have I tested it against the memory of other participants?
> 5. Have I sought independent verification from documentary sources, such as historical accounts or public records? For example, my source describes a "dark and stormy night." Did I call the National Weather Service and get the weather report for that date?
> 6. Do I have a high level of confidence in my sources? Could I have been fooled by an unreliable source with a faulty memory or an ax to grind?
> 7. Is my purpose legitimate? Am I trying to convey the reality of an event for my readers or simply trying to entertain or impress people with my writing ability?
> 8. Does lack of attribution—a hallmark of reconstruction—diminish credibility? Does a reconstruction need an editor's note to help readers understand how the story was reported and sourced?
> 9. Am I willing and able to fully disclose and explain my method to my editor? To my readers?

My thinking about the *purpose* of nonfiction narrative ethics has changed, too. As a young reporter, ethics were a way of securing the cooperation of news sources, ensuring fairness, winning credibility with readers, and avoiding libel suits. Those remain worthwhile goals, of course. But as my career shifted from news reporting to nonfiction storytelling I found additional principles and motives.

Everything I've learned about story reinforces my belief that only a commitment to truth and decency unbridles the full power of storytelling. The long history of nonfiction narrative tells me that it plays a fundamental and central role in the way we cope with our world. The discoveries about the way story works as an organizing principle in the human brain tell me that we find meaning in the cause-and-effect flow of narrative. And my expanding appreciation of the multitude of narrative forms tells me that the nonfiction story is an enormously flexible tool capable of dealing with just about any challenge facing any writer. Nonfiction stories may lack perfect protagonists, clear climaxes, and precise points of insight. But they still can trump even the best fiction if only the audience *believes*.

Tom Wolfe long ago pointed out that readers respond so readily to artful nonfiction for exactly that reason. "And all the while," he wrote, "quite beyond matters of technique, it enjoys an advantage so obvious, so built-in, one almost forgets what a power it has: the simple fact that the reader knows *all this actually happened*."

We turn to nonfiction narrative to understand our world. We feel its power when we sense that it reveals the secrets of successful living by showing us how our fellow human beings master the challenges we all share. And that insight may be the writer's most valuable contribution, the mission that justifies all toil and frustration and turmoil that come with an honest effort to find the patterns that define our common experience.

Ultimately, the best reason for ethical reporting and writing is the power of truth.

Acknowledgments

Special thanks go to Paul Schellinger, my original editor, who recognized the potential of *Storycraft* and provided the guidance that made it a reality. To Mark Reschke, my copy editor for both editions, whose sharp eyes saved me from many an embarrassment. And to Mary Laur, who believed in the book from the beginning and took Paul's place as editor of the second edition after he left UCP. To Cynthia Gorney, Miles Harvey, and Norman Sims, the conscientious reviewers who improved the book with dozens of valuable suggestions. To Sandy Rowe, the former editor of the *Oregonian*, and the paper's other top editors who provided me and the writers who worked with me a haven where nonfiction narrative could thrive. And to Karen Albaugh, whose unflagging support kept hope alive on the darkest days.

Notes

PREFACE

1 Rich Read and Julie Sullivan's stories were part of continuing *Oregonian* coverage of the US Immigration and Naturalization Service that ran from April through December of 2000. Other references to articles published in the *Oregonian* are fully cited in the bibliography.

CHAPTER ONE

1 Ira Glass spoke on December 1, 2001, at the Nieman Conference on Narrative Journalism in Cambridge, MA.
2 Gould and Pinker discuss story archetypes and the universality of story in various places. For an example from Gould, see his "Jim Bowie's Letter & Bill Buckner's Legs." Pinker addresses such issues in *The Language Instinct* (1994) and *How the Mind Works* (2009).
3 For a discussion of how narrative forms of newspaper stories perform against other structures, see Debra Gersh, "Inverted Pyramid Turned Upside Down," and the Readership Institute's *Impact Study*, produced by Northwestern University's Media Management Center in 2000 and available through the Readership Institute at Northwestern. For the results of a study on how students grasp narrative structure relative to other forms, see Carole Feldman, "Youths' Writing Skills Fail to Impress."
4 Michael Price, "World's Oldest Hunting Scene."
5 Gottschall, *Storytelling Animal.*
6 Carey, "This Is Your Life (and How You Tell It)."
7 D'Cruz, Douglas, and Serry, "Narrative Storytelling."
8 McKee is quoted by Janet Burroway in *Writing Fiction: A Guide to Narrative Craft*, 3.
9 Pinker, "Toward a Consilient Study of Literature."
10 Plot definitions are from Burroway, *Writing Fiction*, and from Macauley and Lanning, *Technique in Fiction.*
11 You can read the complete story at www.press.uchicago.edu/books/hart.
12 Conover is quoted in Boynton, *The New New Journalism*, 11.
13 Talese made his comments at the 2001 Nieman Conference on Narrative Journalism.
14 To read Tom's complete story, go to www.press.uchicago.edu/books/hart.

CHAPTER TWO

1 Ephron made her comment at the 2001 Nieman Narrative Conference.
2 From a Chip Scanlan interview in *Nieman Storyboard*, November 29, 2019.
3 Rhodes is quoted in Sims, *The Literary Journalists.*
4 Tom French made this comment on WriterL, a narrative nonfiction listserv that was operated by Jon and Lynn Franklin. It is used with permission.

5 Mary Roach made the comment at "Putting the Non Back in Nonfiction," a University of Oregon School of Journalism seminar held in Portland, OR, on February 9, 2007.

6 Jim Collins made this comment at the 2001 Nieman Conference on Narrative Journalism. The Spring 2002 issue of *Nieman Reports* contains excerpts from the Collins presentation and many others.

7 To read Mark's completed story, visit www.press.uchicago.edu/books/hart.

8 References to the Dickens formula are ubiquitous. One is in the *Encyclopedia of World Biography* (1994).

9 Ted Conover made the comment at "Putting the Non Back in Nonfiction," a University of Oregon School of Journalism seminar.

10 C. O. Brink's translation of Horace is one of the standards and is listed in the bibliography.

CHAPTER THREE

1 Bates, Hallman, and O'Keefe, "Return of the River," A1.

CHAPTER FOUR

1 Lapham is quoted in Cheney, *Writing Creative Nonfiction*.

2 Davidson is quoted in Sims, *The Literary Journalists*.

3 Conover is quoted in Radostitz, "On Being a Tour Guide."

4 Kidder, "Facts and the Nonfiction Writer," 14.

5 Dillard's "Encounters with Chinese Writers" is quoted in Cheney, *Writing Creative Nonfiction*, 80.

6 Plimpton is quoted in Cheney, *Writing Creative Nonfiction*, 19.

7 Both McPhee quotations are from "Travels in Georgia," as reprinted in Sims, *The Literary Journalists*, 39.

8 Sims, *The Literary Journalists*, 40.

9 The Mary Roach quotations are from at "Putting the Non Back in Nonfiction," a University of Oregon School of Journalism seminar.

CHAPTER FIVE

1 Forster is quoted in Macauley and Lanning, *Technique in Fiction*, 87.

2 Wilkerson made the comment at the 2001 Nieman Conference on Narrative Journalism.

3 Stein, "Branded by Love."

4 Kaufman, "Learning Not to Go to School."

5 Tomlinson, "John Lee Hooker."

CHAPTER SIX

1 Quoted in Lisa Cron, *Wired for Story*.

2 Quoted in Cron.

3 Chekhov first made the comment in an 1889 letter to a friend, but repeated variants

throughout his life. The origins of the quotation are traced in Rayfield, *Anton Chekhov: A Life*.

CHAPTER SEVEN

1 In chapter 4 of *Wordcraft*, titled "Force," you'll learn about intransitive verbs, passive voice, expletives, and other threats to vigorous, forceful writing. Chapter 5, "Brevity," explains how redundancy, unnecessary auxiliary verbs, and tics such as our tendency to describe the beginnings of actions, rather than the actions themselves, deflate potentially strong, engaging narrative.
2 Emphasis added.
3 In *Wired*, Lisa Cron quotes Bransford, whom she describes as a "literary blogger extraordinaire."
4 Tom French talked about pace at the 2002 Nieman Conference on Narrative Journalism, held November 8–10 in Cambridge, MA, and his talk is summarized in the Spring 2002 issue of *Nieman Reports*.
5 French discussed "A Gown for Lindsay Rose" at the 2007 Nieman Narrative Conference.

CHAPTER EIGHT

1 Harvey, "Tom Wolfe's Revenge."

CHAPTER NINE

1 Pinker is quoted in Cron, *Hardwired for Story*.
2 Nora Ephron's comment is from the 2001 Nieman Conference on Narrative Journalism.
3 Cather, *O Pioneers!*
4 Franklin said this at the 2001 Nieman Conference on Narrative Journalism.

CHAPTER TEN

1 Holmes is quoted in *Nieman Reports*, Spring 2002, 20.
2 Cynthia Gorney provided the list of immersion-reporting techniques and made this comment during a 2006 workshop at the *Oregonian*.
3 From Plimpton, "The Story behind a Nonfiction Novel."
4 From Kramer and Call, *Telling True Stories*.
5 Boynton, *The New New Journalists*, 54.
6 Boynton, 16.
7 Dash, Conover, and Cramer are quoted by Robert Boynton in *The New New Journalists*.
8 Mary Roach was speaking at "Putting the Non Back in Nonfiction," a University of Oregon School of Journalism seminar.
9 Tom French was speaking at the 2001 Nieman Conference on Narrative Journalism.
10 Cynthia Gorney described her reporting methods in the interview that introduced her winning entry in the American Society of Newspaper Editors annual writing competi-

tion. The interview, along with Gorney's winning stories, was published in the Modern Media Institute's *Best Newspaper Writing 1980*.

11 Plimpton, "The Story behind a Nonfiction Novel."

12 Roach was speaking at "Putting the Non Back in Nonfiction," a University of Oregon School of Journalism seminar.

13 Fuson is quoted in Stepp's "I'll Be Brief."

CHAPTER ELEVEN

1 For David's complete story, visit www.press.uchicago.edu/books/hart.

2 To read Julie's complete story, visit www.press.uchicago.edu/books/hart.

CHAPTER TWELVE

1 Cynthia Gorney talked about reporting explanatory narratives during a 2006 workshop at the *Oregonian*.

2 To read the complete series, visit www.press.uchicago.edu/books/hart.

CHAPTER THIRTEEN

1 "Mr. Bad News" is reprinted in Talese's anthology, *Fame and Obscurity*.

2 "Of a Monstrous Child" is reprinted in Lopate's *Art of the Personal Essay*.

CHAPTER FOURTEEN

1 Morrison, "Ex–*USA Today* Reporter Faked Major Stories."

2 Eustachewich, "NY Times Reassigns Reporter in Leak Scandal."

3 McPhee is quoted in Sims, *The Literary Journalists*, 15.

4 Quoted in Levy, "Give It to Me Straight, Doc," D11.

5 Quoted by Harrington in "The Writer's Choice."

6 "Putting the Non Back in Nonfiction," a University of Oregon School of Journalism seminar.

7 Wyatt, "Frey Says Falsehoods Improved His Tale."

8 "Putting the Non Back in Nonfiction," a University of Oregon School of Journalism seminar.

9 David Hayes made his comment on WriterL, a now defunct listserv for narrative nonfiction writers.

10 "An Oyster and a Way of Life, Both at Risk," *New York Times*, June 15, 2002.

11 Berenson is quoted in Kurtz, "Rick Bragg Quits at *New York Times*."

12 The list comes from Chip Scanlan's column on the Poynter Institute Web site: http://www.poynter.org/content/content_view.asp?id=9506.

Bibliography

Aldama, Frederick Luis. "The Science of Storytelling: Perspectives from Cognitive Science, Neuroscience, and the Humanities." *Projections: The Journal of Movies and Mind* 9 (June 1, 2015).

Altmann, Jennifer Greenstein, "Assembling the Written Word: McPhee Reveals How the Pieces Go Together." *Princeton Weekly Bulletin*, April 7, 2007.

Aristotle. *The Poetics*. London and New York: Penguin, 1996.

Arrowsmith, Charles. "Daniel Mendelsohn: 'Ecstasy and Terror' Spans the Greeks to 'Game of Thrones.'" *Washington Post*, October 17, 2019. Reprinted in the *Oregonian*, December 15, 2019.

Baker, Jeff. "'Memoir' More about Lies and Consequences." *Oregonian*, March 5, 2008.

Banaszynski, Jacqui. "Listen Up!" *Nieman Storyboard*, December 8, 2019. https://nieman storyboard.org/storyboard-category/digital-storytelling/.

Bates, Doug, Tom Hallman Jr., and Mark O'Keefe. "Return of the River." *Oregonian*, February 11, 1996.

Beaven, Stephen. "Lou Gilbert Says Lou Gilbert Is the Greatest Salesman Who Ever Lived." *Oregonian*, December 28, 2003.

Beaven, Stephen. *We Will Rise: A True Story of Tragedy and Resurrection in the American Heartland*. New York: Little A, 2020.

Bernton, Hal. "Distant Water." *Oregonian*, April 12–14, 1998.

Berry, Deborah Barfield, and Kelley Benham French. "1619: Searching for Answers: The Long Road Home." *USA Today*, August 21, 2019.

Binder, Doug. "Help from Above." *Oregonian*, February 14, 2002.

Bingham, Larry. "Nothing to Do but Climb." *Oregonian*, October 23, 2004.

Bissinger, H. G. *Friday Night Lights*. Cambridge, MA: Da Capo Press, 2000.

Blundell, Bill. *The Art and Craft of Feature Writing*. New York: New American Library, 1988.

Blundell, Bill. "The Life of the Cowboy: Drudgery and Danger." *Wall Street Journal*, June 10, 1981. Reprinted in American Society of Newspaper Editors, *Best Newspaper Writing 1982*. St. Petersburg, FL: Modern Media Institute, 1982.

Boo, Katherine. *Behind the Beautiful Forevers: Life, Death and Hope in a Mumbai Undercity*. New York: Random House, 2012.

Bottomly, Therese. "News Is Vital, but Its Delivery Evolves." *Oregonian*, January 5, 2020.

Boule, Margie. "A Teacher's Long-Lasting Lessons Yield Blue-Ribbon Results." *Oregonian*, September 12, 2004.

Boulenger, Véronique, Olaf Hauk, and Friedemann Pulvermüller. "Grasping Ideas with the Motor System: Semantic Somatotopy in Idiom Comprehension." *Cerebral Cortex* 19 (August 2009): 1905–14.

Boyd, Brian. *On the Origin of Stories: Evolution, Cognition, and Fiction*. Cambridge, MA: Harvard University Press, 2009.

Boynton, Robert S. *The New New Journalism*. New York: Vintage Books, 2005.

Brink, C. O. *Horace on Poetry*. Cambridge: Cambridge University Press, 1971.

Burroway, Janet, with Elizabeth Stuckey-French and Ned Stuckey-French. *Writing Fiction: A Guide to Narrative Craft*. 10th edition. Chicago: University of Chicago Press, 2019.

Campbell, James. *The Final Frontiersman*. New York: Atria Books, 2004.

Carey, Benedict. "This Is Your Life (and How You Tell It)." *New York Times*, May 22, 2007.

Carroll, Joseph. "An Evolutionary Paradigm for Literary Study." *Style* 42, nos. 2–3 (Summer–Fall 2008): 103–35.

Cather, Willa. *O Pioneers!* New York: Vintage Classics, 1992. First published in 1913.

Cheney, Theodore A. Rees. *Writing Creative Nonfiction*. Cincinnati: Writer's Digest Books, 1987.

Chivers, C. J. "Sniper Attacks Adding to Peril of U.S. Troops." *New York Times*, November 4, 2006.

Clark, Roy Peter. *Murder Your Darlings*. New York: Little Brown, 2020.

Cody, Robin. "Cutting It Close." In *Another Way the River Has: Taut True Tales from the Northwest*. Corvallis: Oregon State University Press, 2010.

Cody, Robin. *Voyage of a Summer Sun*. New York: Alfred A. Knopf, 1995.

Cole, Michelle, and Katy Muldoon. "Swimming for Life in an Angry Sea." *Oregonian*, June 12, 2003.

Connors, Joanna. "Beyond Rape: A Survivor's Journey." *Cleveland Plain Dealer*, May 4, 2008.

Conover, Ted. *Coyotes: A Journey through the Secret World of America's Illegal Aliens*. New York: Vintage Books, 1987.

Conover, Ted. *Immersion: A Writer's Guide to Going Deep*. Chicago: University of Chicago Press, 2016.

Conover, Ted. *Newjack: Guarding Sing Sing*. New York: Random House, 2000.

Conover, Ted. *Rolling Nowhere: Riding the Rails with American's Hoboes*. New York: Viking, 1984.

Conover, Ted. *The Routes of Man: How Roads Are Changing the World and the Way We Live Today*. New York: Alfred A. Knopf, 2010.

Conover, Ted. *Whiteout: Lost in Aspen*. New York: Random House, 1991.

Cron, Lisa. *Wired for Story: The Writer's Guide to Using Brain Science to Hook Readers from the Very First Sentence*. Berkeley, CA: Ten Speed Press, 2012.

Curtis, Wayne. "In Twain's Wake." *Atlantic*, November 2007.

Dakota Spotlight. Podcast hosted by James Wolner. https://dakotaspotlight.com/.

D'Cruz, Kate, Jacinta Douglas, and Tanya Serry. "Narrative Storytelling as Both an Advocacy Tool and a Therapeutic Process: Perspectives of Adult Storytellers with Acquired Brain Injury." *Neuropsychological Rehabilitation*, March 1, 2019. https://www.tandfonline.com/doi/abs/10.1080/09602011.2019.1586733.

DeSilva, Bruce. "Endings." *Nieman Reports*, Spring 2002.

Didion, Joan. *Slouching towards Bethlehem*. New York: Farrar, Straus, Giroux, 1968.

D'Orso, Michael. *Eagle Blue*. New York: Bloomsbury, 2006.

Drake, Donald. "The Disease Detectives." *Philadelphia Inquirer*, January 9, 1983.

Dzikie, M., K. Oatley, S. Zoeterman, and J. B. Peterson, "On Being Moved by Art: How Reading Fiction Transforms the Self." *Creativity Research Journal* 21, no. 1 (2009): 24–29.

Egri, Lajos. *The Art of Dramatic Writing*. Boston: Writer, Inc., 1960.

Ellis, Barnes. "A Ride through Hell." *Oregonian*, July 14, 1991.

Engel, Susan. *The Stories Children Tell: Making Sense of the Narratives of Childhood*. New York: Freeman, 1995.

Ephron, Nora. *Wallflower at the Orgy*. New York: Viking, 1970.

Eustachewich, Lia. "NY Times Reassigns Reporter in Leak Scandal." *New York Post*, July 3, 2018.

Fallows, James. "The Fifty-First State." *Atlantic*, November 2002. Reprinted in *The American Idea: The Best of the Atlantic Monthly*, edited by Robert Vare. New York: Doubleday, 2007.

Feldman, Carole. "Youths' Writing Skills Fail to Impress." *Oregonian*, June 8, 1994.

Fink, Sheri. *Five Days at Memorial: Life and Death in a Storm-Ravaged Hospital*. New York: Crown Publishers, 2013.

Finkel, David. "The Wiz." *Washington Post Magazine*, June 13, 1993.

Fitzgerald, F. Scott. *The Great Gatsby*. Cambridge and New York: Cambridge University Press, 1971.

Foster, J. Todd, and Jonathan Brinkman. "The Green Wall." *Oregonian*, March 29, 1998.

Franklin, Jon. *Writing for Story*. New York: Mentor/New American Library, 1986.

French, Thomas. "Angels & Demons." *St. Petersburg Times*, October 26–November 9, 1997.

French, Thomas. "A Gown for Lindsay Rose." *St. Petersburg Times*, February 28, 2003.

French, Thomas. "Serial Narratives." *Nieman Reports*, Spring 2002.

French, Thomas. "South of Heaven." *St. Petersburg Times*, May 12–15, May 19–21, 1991.

Gardner, John. *The Art of Fiction: Notes on Craft for Young Writers*. New York: Alfred A. Knopf, 1984.

Gawande, Atul. *Being Mortal: Medicine and What Matters in the End*. New York: Metropolitan Books, 2014.

Gawande, Atul. *Complications: A Surgeon's Notes on an Imperfect Science*. London: Picador, 2002.

Gawande, Atul. "How Childbirth Went Industrial." *New Yorker*, October 9, 2006.

Gerard, Philip. *Creative Nonfiction: Researching and Crafting Stories of Real Life*. Long Grove, IL: Waveland Press, 1996.

Gersh, Debra. "Inverted Pyramid Turned Upside Down." *Editor & Publisher*, May 1, 1993.

Glaser, Gabrielle. "I Witness." *Oregonian*, May 13, 2007.

Goldsmith, Jack. "Jimmy Hoffa, My Stepfather, and Me." *Atlantic Monthly*, November 2019.

Gorney, Cynthia. "Chicken Soup Nation." *New Yorker*, October 6, 2003.

Gorney, Cynthia. "Mic Drop? A Veteran Longform Writer Trades Notebook for

Headphones, Text for Sound." *Nieman Storyboard*, October 18, 2018. https://nieman storyboard.org/stories/mic-drop-a-veteran-print-reporter-puts-down-her-notebook -and-puts-on-headphones/.

Gottschall, Jonathan. *The Storytelling Animal: How Stories Make Us Human*. Boston: Houghton Mifflin Harcourt, 2012.

Gould, Stephen Jay. "Jim Bowie's Letter & Bill Buckner's Legs." *Natural History*, May 2000.

Grann, David. *Killers of the Flower Moon: The Osage Murders and the Birth of the FBI*. New York: Doubleday, 2017.

Grann, David. *The Lost City of Z: A Tale of Deadly Obsession in the Amazon*. New York: Doubleday, 2009.

Grann, David. "The Squid Hunter." *New Yorker*, May 24, 2004.

Hall, Stephen S. "Journey to the Center of My Mind." *New York Times Magazine*, June 6, 1999.

Hallman, Tom, Jr. "The Boy behind the Mask." *Oregonian*, October 1–4, 2000.

Hallman, Tom, Jr. "Collision Course." *Northwest Magazine*, October 9, 1983.

Hallman, Tom, Jr. "The Education of Richard Miller." *Oregonian*, September 13, 1998.

Hallman, Tom, Jr. "Fighting for Life on Level Three." *Oregonian*, September 21–24, 2003.

Hallman, Tom, Jr. "A Life Lost . . . and Found." *Oregonian*, December 20, 1998.

Hammett, Dashiell. *Red Harvest*. New York: Alfred A. Knopf, 1929.

Harr, Jonathan. *A Civil Action*. New York: Vintage Books, 1995.

Harrington, Walt. *The Everlasting Stream: A True Story of Rabbits, Guns, Friendship, and Family*. Boston: Atlantic Monthly Press, 2007.

Harrington, Walt. *Intimate Journalism: The Art and Craft of Reporting Everyday Life*. Thousand Oaks, CA: Sage Publications, 1997.

Harrington, Walt. "The Journalistic Haiku." A paper presented to the Canadian Association of Journalists national convention, Vancouver, BC, May 7–9, 2004.

Harrington, Walt. "The Writer's Choice." *River Teeth*, Fall 2008/Spring 2009, 495–507.

Harrison, Jim. *Off to the Side*. New York: Atlantic Monthly Press, 2002.

Hart, Jack. *The Information Empire: A History of the Los Angeles Times and the Times Mirror Corporation*. Lanham, MD: University Press of America, 1981.

Hart, Jack. *Wordcraft: The Complete Guide to Clear, Powerful Writing*. Chicago: University of Chicago Press, 2021.

Hart, Jack, and Amanda Bennett. "A Tale of Two Tales: A Pulitzer Prize–Winning Play in Six Acts." *Columbia Journalism Review*, September/October 2001.

Harvey, Chris, "Tom Wolfe's Revenge." *American Journalism Review*, October 1994.

Hillenbrand, Laura. *Seabiscuit*. New York: Ballantine, 2001.

Hogan, Dave. "A Boy Seeks Help after Watching His Father Overdose on Heroin." *Oregonian*, May 3, 1990.

Hsu, Jeremy. "We Love a Good Yarn." *Scientific American*, August 2008.

Irizarry, Adrienne. "Why Is Storytelling So Compelling?" *Leviosia Communication: Storytelling* (blog). August 16, 2018. https://leviosacomm.com/2018/08/16/why-is -storytelling-so-compelling/.

Johnson, Rheta Grimsley. "A Good and Peaceful Reputation." *Memphis Commercial Appeal*, November 1, 1982. Reprinted in American Society of Newspaper Editors, *Best Newspaper Writing 1982*. St. Petersburg, FL: Modern Media Institute, 1983.

Junger, Sebastian. *The Perfect Storm*. New York: W. W. Norton, 1997.

Kaufman, Naomi. "Learning Not to Go to School." *Oregonian*, June 30, 1990.

Kessler, Lauren. *Dancing with Rose: Finding Life in the Land of Alzheimer's*. New York: Viking, 2007.

Kidder, Tracy. "Facts and the Nonfiction Writer." *Writer*, February 1994.

Kidder, Tracy. *Mountains beyond Mountains: The Quest of Dr. Paul Farmer*. New York: Random House, 2003.

Kidder, Tracy. "Small-Town Cop." *Atlantic Monthly*, April 1999.

Kidder, Tracy. *The Soul of a New Machine*. New York: Little Brown and Company, 1981.

Kidder, Tracy, and Richard Todd. *Good Prose: The Art of Nonfiction*. New York: Random House, 2013.

Kluger, Jeffrey. "How Telling Stories Makes Us Human." *Time*, December 5, 2017.

Krakauer, Jon. *Into the Wild*. New York: Anchor Books, 1996.

Kramer, Mark. "Narrative Journalism Comes of Age." *Nieman Reports*, Spring 2000.

Kramer, Mark, and Wendy Call. *Telling True Stories: A Nonfiction Writers' Guide from the Nieman Foundation at Harvard University*. New York: Plume, 2007.

Kurtz, Howard. "Rick Bragg Quits at New York Times." *Washington Post*, May 29, 2003.

Larabee, Mark. "Clinging to Life—and Whatever Floats." *Oregonian*, December 12, 2007.

LaRocque, Paula. *The Book on Writing: The Ultimate Guide to Writing Well*. Oak Park, IL: Marion Street Press, 2003.

Larson, Eric. *The Devil in the White City*. New York: Vintage Books, 2003.

Larson, Eric. *Isaac's Storm*. New York: Random House, 2000.

Leonard, Elmore. *Ten Rules of Writing*. New York: William Morrow, 2001.

Levine, Mark. "Killing Libby." *Men's Journal*, August 2001.

Levy, Shawn. "Give It to Me Straight, Doc." *Oregonian*, February 4, 2007.

Lopate, Phillip, ed. *The Art of the Personal Essay*. New York: Anchor Books, 1995.

Lukas, J. Anthony. *Common Ground*. New York: Vintage Books, 1986.

Lyall, Sarah. "What You Read Is What He Is, Sort Of." *New York Times*, June 8, 2008.

Macauley, Robie, and George Lanning. *Technique in Fiction: Second Edition*. New York: St. Martin's Press, 1987.

Maclean, Norman. *Young Men and Fire*. Chicago: University of Chicago Press, 1992.

Malcolm, Janet. *The Journalist and the Murderer*. New York: Vintage Books, 1990.

Margolis, Michael. "Humans Are Hard-Wired for Story." *Storied* (blog). May 8, 2013. https://www.getstoried.com/hard-wired-for-storytelling/.

Margulis, Elizabeth Hellmuth, et al. "What the Music Said: Narrative Listening across Cultures." *Nature Communications*, November 26, 2019. http://www.nature.com/articles/s41599-019-0363-1.

Martinez-Conde, Susana, et al. "The Storytelling Brain: How Neuroscience Stories Help Bridge the Gap between Research and Society." *Journal of Neuroscience* 39, no. 42 (October 16, 2019): 8285–90. https://doi.org/10.1523/JNEUROSCI.1180-19.2019.

McGinniss, Joe. *Fatal Vision*. New York: Penguin Putnam, 1983.

McHugh, Siobhan. "Subjectivity, Hugs and Craft: Podcasting as Extreme Narrative Journalism." *Nieman Storyboard*, October 8, 2019. https://niemanstoryboard.org/story board-category/digital-storytelling/.

McKee, Robert. *Story*. New York: ReganBooks, 1997.

McMaster University. "The Art of Storytelling: Researchers Explore Why We Relate to Characters." *ScienceDaily*, September 13, 2018.

McPhee, John. *Coming into the Country*. New York: Farrar, Straus, and Giroux, 1976.

McPhee, John. *Control of Nature*. New York: Farrar, Straus, and Giroux, 1982.

McPhee, John. *Draft No. 4: On the Writing Process*. New York: Farrar, Straus and Giroux, 2017.

McPhee, John. "A Fleet of One." *New Yorker*, February 17, 2003.

McPhee, John. *The Pine Barrens*. New York: Farrar, Straus, and Giroux, 1968.

McPhee, John. "Travels in Georgia." *New Yorker*, April 28, 1973. Reprinted in *The Literary Journalists*, ed. Norman Sims. New York: Ballantine, 1984.

Meinzer, Kristen. *So You Want to Start a Podcast: 7 Steps That Will Take You from Idea to Hit Show*. New York: HarperCollins, 2019.

Miller, G. Wayne. *King of Hearts*. New York: Times Books, 2000.

Monroe, Bill. "A Night on the River." *Oregonian*, September 14, 1994.

Morrison, Blake. "Ex–USA Today Reporter Faked Major Stories." usatoday.com, March 19, 2004.

Muldoon, Katy. "Guitar Guy, Harmonica Man Liven Up a Dreary Wait at Gate 66." *Oregonian*, July 16, 2006.

Murali, Geetha. "Books Can Rewire Our Brains and Connect Us All." Hill, September 1, 2018.

Murray, Don. *A Writer Teaches Writing*. Boston: Heinle, 2003.

Murray, Don. *Writing for Your Readers: Notes on the Writer's Craft from the Boston Globe*. Boston: Globe-Pequot, 1992.

Newman, Barry. "Fisherman." *Wall Street Journal*, June 1, 1983.

Nigam, Sanjay K. "The Storytelling Brain." *Science and Engineering Ethics* 18, no. 3 (September 2012): 567–71.

Oatley, Keith. "A Feeling for Fiction." *Greater Good Magazine*, September 1, 2005.

Orlean, Susan. *The Orchid Thief*. New York: Random House, 1998.

Pancrazio, Angela. "His Rolling Cross to Bear." *Oregonian*, March 5, 1997.

Pancrazio, Angela. "His Work in Time." *Oregonian*, October 28, 1996.

Parker, Ian. "The Real McKee." *New Yorker*, October 20, 2003.

Paterniti, Michael. "The Long Fall of One-Eleven Heavy." *Esquire*, July 2000.

Perl, Sondra, and Mimi Schwartz. *Writing True: The Art and Craft of Creative Nonfiction*. New York: Houghton Mifflin, 2006.

Pinker, Steven. *How the Mind Works*. New York: W. W. Norton, 2009.

Pinker, Steven. *The Language Instinct: How the Mind Creates Language*. New York: Morrow, 1994.

Pinker, Steven. "Toward a Consilient Study of Literature." *Philosophy and Literature* 31 (April 2007): 161–77.

Plimpton, George. *Paper Lion*. Guilford, CT: Lyons Press, 1965.

Plimpton, George. "The Story behind a Nonfiction Novel." *New York Times*, January 16, 1966.

Pollan, Michael. "An Animal's Place." *New York Times Magazine*, November 10, 2002.

Pollan, Michael. *The Omnivore's Dilemma: A Natural History of Four Meals*. New York: Penguin, 2006.

Preston, Richard. *The Hot Zone*. New York: Random House, 1994.

Price, Michael. "World's Oldest Hunting Scene Shows Half-Human, Half-Animal Figures—and a Sophisticated Imagination." *ScienceMag.org*, December 12, 2019. https://www.sciencemag.org/news/2019/12/world-s-oldest-hunting-scene-shows -half-human-half-animal-figures-and-sophisticated.

Radostitz, Rita. "On Being a Tour Guide." *Etude: New Voices in Literary Nonfiction* (online magazine), Autumn 2003.

Raver-Lampman, Greg. "Adrift." *Virginian-Pilot*, October 22–24, 1991.

Raver-Lampman, Greg. "Charlotte's Millions." *Virginian-Pilot*, August 11–17, 1997.

Rayfield, Donald. *Anton Chekhov: A Life*. New York: Henry Holt and Company, 1997.

Read, Rich. "The French Fry Connection." *Oregonian*, October 18–21, 1998.

Read, Rich. "Racing the World." *Oregonian*, March 7–9, 2004.

Roach, Mary. *Grunt: The Curious Science of Humans at War*. New York: W. W. Norton, 2016.

Roach, Mary. *Gulp: Adventures on the Alimentary Canal*. New York: W. W. Norton, 2013.

Roach, Mary. "Just Sharp Enough." *Sports Illustrated Women*, October 2001.

Roach, Mary. *Spook: Science Tackles the Afterlife*. New York: W. W. Norton, 2005.

Roach, Mary. *Stiff: The Curious Lives of Human Cadavers*. New York: W. W. Norton, 2003.

Roach, Mary. "White Dreams." A Wanderlust column for *Salon*, December 1, 1997.

Roberts, Michelle. "Law Man Races Time and Elements." *Oregonian*, December 10, 2006.

Rose, Joseph. "Thief Learns Lessons in Do's and Doughnuts." *Oregonian*, January 19, 2005.

Ruark, Robert. *The Honey Badger*. New York: McGraw-Hill, 1965.

Rubie, Peter. *The Elements of Storytelling*. Hoboken, NJ: John Wiley and Sons, 1996.

Rubie, Peter. *Telling the Story: How to Write and Sell Narrative Nonfiction*. New York: HarperCollins, 2003.

Rule, Ann. *Small Sacrifices*. New York: E. P. Dutton, 1987.

Savchuk, Katia. "5(ish) Questions: Ted Conover and *Immersion: A Writer's Guide to Going Deep*." *Nieman Storyboard*, February 7, 2017. https://niemanstoryboard.org/stories /5ish-questions-ted-conover-and-immersion-a-writers-guide-to-going-deep/.

Savchuk, Katia. "Singular Moments, Timeless Questions: Two-Time Pulitzer Winner Gene Weingarten Finds the Beating Heart at the Center of His New Book about One Ordinary, Extraordinary Day." *Nieman Storyboard*, October 22, 2019. https://nieman storyboard.org/stories/singular-moments-timeless-questions/.

Schroeder, Peter. "The Neuroscience of Storytelling Will Make You Rethink the Way You

Create." *The Startup* (blog). January 3, 2018. https://medium.com/swlh/the-neuro
science-of-storytelling-will-make-you-rethink-the-way-you-create-215fca43fc67.

"The Science of Storytelling: A Conversation with Jonathan Gottschall." PBS *Newshour's Science Thursday*. June 14, 2012.

Shadid, Anthony. "In a Moment, Lives Get Blown Apart." *New York Times*, March 27, 2003. Reprinted in American Society of Newspaper Editors, *Best Newspaper Writing*, 2004. St. Petersburg, FL: Poynter Institute, 2004.

Shontz, Lori. "From Basketball Stardom to Rosary Beads: Twenty-Five Years after a College Athlete Keeps a Promise to God, ESPN Follows Up with a Rare Story from Inside a Cloistered Convent." *Nieman Storyboard*, December 10, 2019. https://niemanstoryboard.org/stories/from-basketball-stardom-to-rosary-beads/.

Simon, David. *Homicide: A Year on the Killing Streets*. New York: Houghton Mifflin, 1992.

Simon, David. "Making the Story More than Just the Facts." *NewsInc*, July/August 1992.

Simon, David, and Edward Burns. *The Corner: A Year in the Life of an Inner-City Neighborhood*. New York: Broadway Books, 1997.

Sims, Norman, ed. *The Literary Journalists*. New York: Ballantine Books, 1984.

Sims, Patsy. *Literary Nonfiction: Learning by Example*. New York and Oxford: Oxford University Press, 2002.

Singer, Mark. "The Castaways." *New Yorker*, February 19 and 26, 2007.

Smith, Daniel, et al. "Cooperation and the Evolution of Hunter-Gatherer Storytelling." *Nature Communications*, December 5, 2017.

Stabler, David. "Lost in the Music." *Oregonian*, June 23–25, 2002.

Stein, Michelle. "Branded by Love." *Oregonian*, January 19, 1990.

Stepp, Carl Sessions. "I'll Be Brief." *American Journalism Review*, August/September 2005.

Strauss, Darin. "Notes on Narrative." Blog entry at Powellsbooks.com. July 11, 2008.

Swift, Earl. "The Dark Side of Valentine's Day." *Virginian-Pilot*, February 15, 2000.

Talese, Gay. *Fame and Obscurity*. New York: Laurel, 1981.

Talese, Gay. *Honor Thy Father*. New York: Ballantine Books, 1971.

Thompson, Hunter. *Hell's Angels*. New York: Random House, 1966.

Thompson, Hunter. "The Kentucky Derby Is Decadent and Depraved." *Scanlan's Monthly*, June 1970.

Tomlinson, Stuart. "John Lee Hooker." *Oregonian*, January 19, 1990.

Tomlinson, Stuart. "An Officer Reacts." *Oregonian*, October 13, 2004.

Tomlinson, Tommy. "A Beautiful Find." *Charlotte Observer*, November 16, 2003.

Volz, Jan. "Of Time and Tashina." *Redmond Spokesman*, October 1, 1997.

Voutilainen, Liisa, Pentti Henttonena, Mikko Kahria, Maari Kiviojab, Niklas Ravajacd, Mikko Samse, and Anssi Peräkyläa. "Affective Stance, Ambivalence, and Psychophysiological Responses during Conversational Storytelling." *Journal of Pragmatics* 68 (2014): 1–24.

Walker, Spike. "Tragedy in the Gulf of Alaska." *Northwest Magazine*, December 26, 1982.

Weinberg, Steve. "Tell It Long, Take Your Time, Go in Depth." *Columbia Journalism Review*, January/February 1998.

Weingarten, Gene. "The Beating Heart: A Tragic Crime. A Medical Breakthrough. A Last Chance at Life." *Washington Post Magazine*, September 30, 2019.

Weingarten, Gene. *One Day: The Extraordinary Story of an Ordinary 24 Hours in America*. New York: Blue Rider Press, 2019.

Weingarten, Gene. "The Peekaboo Paradox." *Washington Post Magazine*, January 22, 2006.

Weller, Debra. "Storytelling, the Cornerstone of Literacy." *California Kindergarten Association*, 2016. http://www.californiakindergartenassociation.org/wp-content/uploads/2009/01/Weller-Article1.pdf.

White, E. B. "Once More to the Lake." *Harper's*, August 1941.

Wilkerson, Isabel. *The Warmth of Other Suns: The Epic Story of America's Great Migration*. New York: Random House, 2010.

Wolfe, Tom, and E. W. Johnson, eds. *The New Journalism*. New York: Harper and Row, 1973.

Woods, Keith, ed. *Best Newspaper Writing 2004*. Chicago and St. Petersburg, FL: Bonus Books and Poynter Institute, 2004.

Wyatt, Edward. "Frey Says Falsehoods Improved His Tale." *New York Times*, February 2, 2006.

Zak, Paul J. "Why Your Brain Loves Good Storytelling." *Harvard Business Review*, October 28, 2014.

Index

Devil in the White City, The (Larson), 30–31, 47–49, 63, 69, 87–89, 120, 148, 198, 229; footnotes in, 227–28; quotation marks, 237

Devor, Robinson, 225

dialogue, 123; action line, 126; character, 125–26; direct quotations, 121–22; exposition, 124; internal monologue, 127–29; paraphrased, 124; quotation marks, 236–37; reconstructed, 128–29, 239; scene, 125; story, 56

Dickens, Charles, 27

Didion, Joan, 27, 121

digression, explanatory narrative, 180–83, 185, 187, 191; exposition, as pause, 119

Dillard, Annie, 66

Dirty John (serial), 218

distance: summary narrative, 52; scenic narrative, 52

Doctor Zhivago (film), 89

documentary films, 213–14, 236

Dodge, Wag, 66

Door to Door (TV movie), 2

D'Orso, Michael, 42

Downs, Diane, 10

Draft No. 4 (McPhee), 21

drafts, 72; first, 22, 71; rough, 71

Drake, Don, 109

Durant, Will, 136

Eagle Blue (D'Orso), 42

Eastwood, Clint, 35

editing, 237; prosecutorial, 238–39

"Education of Richard Miller, The" (Hallman), 11–12

Egri, Lajos, 7, 11, 24, 73, 77, 107, 134, 137

Eiffel, Alexandre Gustave, 48

Ellis, Barnes, 2, 128

"Encounters with Chinese Writers" (Dillard), 66

Ephron, Nora, 19, 134, 146

Ermert, Karen, 81

Escobar (film), 225

ethics, 219–20, 238–40; casting, 237; deception, 237; fiction and nonfiction, mixing of, 235–36; of immersion, 230–31; quotation marks, 236–37; reconstruction, 237, 240; sources, 232–33

explanatory narrative, 178–79, 194, 196, 199; action line, 180, 192; core purpose of, 192; curiosity, 185; digressions, use of, 180–83, 185, 187, 191; drop cap, 180; layer cake structure of, 183, 188, 193; outline of, 188–89; reporting tactics, 185; revealing detail, 185; scenes, 192–93; star line, 180; typographical devices, 180

exposition: action, 116–19; backstory, 26, 28, 116, 118; characters, defining of, 24; dialogue, 124; digression, as pause, 119; explanation, minimization of, 117, 119; narrative, as enemy of, 25–26, 116; narrative arc, 174; structure, 24–28; teasing of, 27

falling action, 176; kicker, 37–38; structure, 37–38. *See also* denouement, dragging on; unknotting

Fallows, James, 211–12

Farmer, Paul, 44, 75–76, 85–86, 94, 99, 125–26, 153, 191

Fatal Vision (McGinniss), 232

Fear and Loathing in Las Vegas (Thompson), 44

"Feature Game, The" (Wolfe), 121

fiction, 33, 73, 136–37, 241; character, 77–78, 80–81; nonfiction, mixing of, 235–36; plot, 132; voice in, 61–62

Field, Syd, 214

"Fifty-First State" (Fallows), 211

Final Frontiersman, The (Campbell), 42

Finch, Rob, 167, 172, 176

Finkel, David, 65–66

Finkel, Michael, 222

first-person narrative issue essays, 211–13